"Take this journey into the dense jungle of clients' experience of GAD. This wonderful book on how to work therapeutically with the painful emotions of these clients provides a virtual feast of theory, practice, bottom-up research, and case examples. If you want to deepen your practice with GAD clients, you must not miss reading this book. Good for beginners and experienced clinicians alike."

Leslie S. Greenberg, PhD, Distinguished Research Professor Emeritus, Dept. of Psychology, York University, Toronto, Canada

"Building on Timulak's previous book, *Transforming Emotional Pain in Psychotherapy*, this book illuminates the extension of emotion-focused therapy to generalized anxiety with a high level of clarity and precision, while also staying true to humanistic therapy values and the clinical complexities of a challenging client population. Timulak and McElvaney manage to encompass the different main threads that have emerged in EFT over the past 25 years, while also providing an up-to-date presentation of the latest developments. It is a very impressive achievement."

Robert Elliott, PhD, Professor of Counselling, University of Strathclyde, Scotland

"This volume is the innovative development of emotion-focused therapy and may ignite a paradigm shift in the understanding and treatment of GAD that has long been dominated by cognitive behavioral therapy. What is unique about this book and Timulak and McElvaney's approach is that every aspect of their treatment model is supported by research findings, which validate its effectiveness and delineate a conceptual framework for tracking client progress to determine when and how to intervene in order to best facilitate emotional transformation…"

Shigeru Iwakabe, PhD, Associate Professor, Human Science Division, Ochanomizu University, Tokyo, Japan

Transforming Generalized Anxiety

Transforming Generalized Anxiety: An Emotion-Focused Approach examines an approach to treating generalized anxiety disorder (GAD) which attempts to uncover the deeper, underlying emotional experiences that clients fear. It also demonstrates how these painful experiences can be transformed in therapy into a form of emotional resilience by generating experiences of self-compassion and healthy, boundary-setting, protective anger.

Though most of the literature on treating GAD is dominated by cognitive behavioral therapy, this book presents emotion-focused therapy as an alternative treatment of this condition. The emotional resilience this particular approach instills serves as a resource when encountering triggers of emotional vulnerability, but also decreases the client's need to avoid hitherto feared triggers and the emotional experiences they bring. Developed through a series of research studies and illustrated with reference to case examples, this book offers a practical, theoretically informed, evidence-based guide to conducting therapy with clients.

Using clinical material, and applying the outcome of a series of research studies, *Transforming Generalized Anxiety* will equip psychotherapists and counselors with the means to help GAD clients transform core painful experiences into a sense of empowerment and inner confidence.

Ladislav Timulak is Course Director of the Doctorate in Counselling Psychology at Trinity College Dublin. He has authored a number of publications, and is currently involved in the training of psychologists and psychotherapists.

James McElvaney is Adjunct Teaching Fellow at Trinity College Dublin, as well as a Counselling Psychologist at the Central Remedial Clinic Dublin.

Transforming Generalized Anxiety

An Emotion-Focused Approach

Ladislav Timulak and James McElvaney

Routledge
Taylor & Francis Group

LONDON AND NEW YORK

First published 2018
by Routledge
2 Park Square, Milton Park, Abingdon, Oxon OX14 4RN

and by Routledge
711 Third Avenue, New York, NY 10017

Routledge is an imprint of the Taylor & Francis Group, an informa business

British Library Cataloguing in Publication Data
A catalogue record for this book is available from the British Library

Library of Congress Cataloging in Publication Data
Names: Timulak, Ladislav, author. | McElvaney, James, author.
Title: Transforming generalized anxiety: an emotion-focused approach / authored by Ladislav Timulak and James McElvaney.
Description: Abingdon, Oxon; New York, NY: Routledge, 2018. | Includes bibliographical references.
Identifiers: LCCN 2017027269| ISBN 9781138681507 (hardback) | ISBN 9781138681538 (pbk.) | ISBN 9781315527253 (Master) | ISBN 9781315527246 (Adobe) | ISBN 9781315527239 (epub) | ISBN 9781315527222 (Mobipocket)
Subjects: | MESH: Anxiety Disorders–therapy | Emotion-Focused Therapy–methods
Classification: LCC RC531 | NLM WM 172 | DDC 616.85/22–dc23
LC record available at https://lccn.loc.gov/2017027269

ISBN: 978-1-138-68150-7 (hbk)
ISBN: 978-1-138-68153-8 (pbk)
ISBN: 978-1-315-52725-3 (ebk)

Typeset in Times New Roman
by Deanta Global Publishing Services, Chennai, India

Dedicated to my parents, Katka, Adam,
Dominika, and Natalia.
(LT)

Dedicated to my parents, Helen and Jim, my wife,
Micheli, and daughter, Gabriela-Flor.
(JM)

Contents

PART IV
Practicalities of delivering EFT for GAD   **161**

Acknowledgments

This book would not be possible without the generous contribution of many people around us. We would like to thank all the clients and research collaborators who contributed to our learning and to the ideas presented in this book. The book is also based on the project of developing emotion-focused therapy for generalized anxiety, sponsored by the Irish Health Research Board (H01388-HRA POR/2010/7). The project involved a lot of collaboration with our colleagues, Daragh Keogh and Elaine Martin, and a special collaboration with Les Greenberg.

A large number of research projects investigating the process of emotion transformation has directly contributed to the ideas outlined in this book. Many of Ladislav Timulak's students (now colleagues) contributed to them (thanks to Katie O'Brien, Niall Crowley, Sam Hughes, Jen Murphy, Lucy Rowell, Anne McQuaid, Richard Meacham, Peter Clare, Nora O'Keeffe, Rosie O'Flynn, Aoife Durcan, Hannah Cullen, and Rochelle Toolan). I (LT) would like to thank those students and colleagues with whom I continue to collaborate on other, related, EFT research projects. It is hoped that these studies will lead to new publications in the near future. I would also like to thank my colleagues on the counselling psychology program in Trinity College Dublin for their continuing support, and for creating an excellent working environment.

We would like to thank Joanne Forshaw and Kristin Susser at Routledge for their work on this book.

Finally, I (LT) would like to thank my family, my parents, my sister, and especially my wife, Katka, for all the support they have given me over the years.

In addition to the foregoing, I (JM) would also like to thank the cohort of colleagues/collaborators who emerged from the doctoral program in counselling psychology at Trinity College Dublin who have made such an invaluable contribution to the formation of this EFT research laboratory. I would like to thank my co-author (LT) for his patience, drive, and inspirational thinking in terms of EFT. Finally, I wish to thank my family for all their support over the years.

Chapter 1

Introduction

Emotion-focused therapy (EFT; Greenberg *et al.*, 1993; Greenberg, 2002; Greenberg & Johnson, 1988) is a research-informed, psychological therapy, which derives from a tradition of humanistic therapies such as person-centered and Gestalt therapy. To date, EFT has mainly been studied in the context of depression, trauma, and couples distress (Elliott, Greenberg, Watson, Timulak, & Freire, 2013). This form of therapy is supported by a solid body of research evidence (cf. Angus, Watson, Elliott, Schneider, & Timulak, 2015; Elliott *et al.*, 2013). The approach is also very popular among clinicians and many EFT-related books have been published (e.g., Elliott, Watson, Goldman, & Greenberg, 2004; Goldman & Greenberg, 2015; Greenberg, 2002; 2011; 2015; 2016; Greenberg & Johnson, 1988; Greenberg & Paivio, 1997; Greenberg, Rice, & Elliott, 1993; Greenberg & Watson, 2006; Johnson, 2004; Paivio & Pascual-Leone, 2010; Timulak, 2015; Watson, Goldman, & Greenberg, 2007; Watson & Greenberg, 2017). More recently, this approach has been applied to anxiety difficulties, such as social anxiety (Elliott, 2013; Shahar, 2014; Shahar, Bar-Kalifa, & Alon, 2017) and generalized anxiety (Timulak & McElvaney, 2016; Watson & Greenberg, 2017).

Generalized Anxiety Disorder (GAD), as currently conceptualized (see the next chapter, where we discuss diagnostic issues), is a debilitating condition characterized by excessive anxiety and worry, and other symptoms such as restlessness, being easily fatigued, difficulty concentrating, irritability, muscle tension, and sleep disturbance (American Psychiatric Association, 2013). Cognitivebehavioral therapy (CBT) is the most widely recognized psychological treatment of GAD, but not all clients benefit from it (Hanrahan *et al.*, 2013). Some authors have recommended that more psychological therapies be developed to offer a broader range of treatment options (Hunot, Churchill, Teixeira, & Silva de Lima, 2007). This book reports on learnings from a project which aimed to develop emotion-focused therapy for generalized anxiety disorder (GAD) difficulties, carried out by a research group based in Dublin under the lead of the first author, Ladislav (Laco) Timulak (LT). The project was conceived in 2006 (Timulak, 2006a; 2006b) and further developed in subsequent years (e.g., Timulak, 2008), driven by the first author's interest in contributing to the development of EFT and a particular personal interest in anxiety as an area requiring further development in experiential psychotherapies (cf. Elliott, Greenberg, & Lietaer, 2004).

Funding for the project was sought in 2009. The second author, James McElvaney (JMcE), became the project manager in 2010 (the project was finalized under the management of our colleague Daragh Keogh to whom we are indebted for all the support he provided). The project was sponsored by the Irish Health Research Board, and its first phase focused on the development of EFT for GAD on the basis of a series of case studies, reported in the form of an open trial (Timulak, McElvaney, Keogh, Martin, Clare, Chepukova, & Greenberg, 2017). The project also involved several doctoral dissertations. Several publications have already been published, focusing on different aspects of the project (e.g., Murphy et al., 2017; O'Brien et al., 2017; Timulak, 2015; Timulak & McElvaney, 2016; Timulak & Pascual-Leone, 2015). The project has now entered a new phase, in which the developed approach is being tested against an established treatment in an RCT (again the project is sponsored by the Irish Health Research Board).

This book presents an EFT model, which we refer to as an emotion-transformation model of conceptualizing GAD, as well as practical guidelines for conducting EFT with clients meeting criteria for GAD, based on our learning and experience from the project as clinicians, as well as researchers and theoreticians. To date, we have presented the model and interventions in a published paper (Timulak & McElvaney, 2016). Concurrently, Watson and Greenberg (2017) have made a distinct contribution to the development of EFT for GAD, and this is also described below.

Our approach

Most current psychotherapeutic treatments of GAD (see Chapter 2) focus on working with the experience of anxiety and pervasive worry. This book, on the contrary, describes an approach which focuses primarily on the underlying emotional experiences and their triggers, which clients worry about, are afraid of, and want to avoid. While the approach highlighted in this book also focuses on working with worry (through increasing clients' awareness of their own agency, and by highlighting the cost of worry) and apprehensive anxiety, and the avoidance that worry feeds into, its primary focus is on working with the underlying feared experiences. These experiences appear to center on felt loneliness/sadness, shame and primary terror/fear and respective unmet needs for closeness (love), acknowledgment, and safety (Timulak, 2015). These core painful experiences are transformed in therapy by the generation of experiences of (self-) compassion and healthy, boundary-setting, protective anger. These experiences of compassion and protective anger lead to natural grieving (as a natural follow on from compassionate experience) and the building of a sense of empowerment and inner confidence (see Pascual-Leone & Greenberg, 2007; Pascual-Leone, 2009; Timulak, 2015; Timulak & Pascual-Leone, 2015). Transformation of underlying vulnerabilities, and the corresponding self–self and self–other relating processes that contributed to those vulnerabilities, increases clients' sense of emotional resilience and their confidence in being able to bear painful emotional experiences and handle the (interpersonal and intrapersonal) processes that trigger them. The client's emotional resilience can then serve as a resource when encountering triggers of emotional vulnerability. Furthermore, the gradual building of emotional resilience decreases clients' need to avoid the feared triggers and the emotional experiences they bring (Timulak & McElvaney, 2016).

Watson and Greenberg's EFT for GAD model

As we were finishing our work on the book, a new book by Jeanne Watson and Les Greenberg (2017) was published that described their conceptualization of generalized anxiety and an emotion-focused treatment of it. Given that our book was practically finished by that time, we decided not to comment on Watson and Greenberg's work throughout our book, as it would delay our contractual deadline. Instead, we decided to read through it and see whether we might offer a more global statement on the similarities and potential differences. In general, we do not see any major differences between the contents of their book and what we are outlining in the pages that follow. One of us (LT), had an opportunity to work on a chapter with Jeanne and Les (Watson, Timulak, & Greenberg, in press) a few months before their book was published, and it was apparent that there were no major theoretical or clinical differences in their thinking about EFT for GAD to ours. Indeed, we suspect that if the readers saw EFT for GAD in practice, based on either of the two books, they would not be certain on which of the writings the observed treatment was based. It is more likely that there may be individual differences due to the idiosyncratic styles of the therapists, rather than because of adherence to any particular, written account of working with clients with GAD from an EFT perspective.

If we were to comment on some of the differences, they would mainly concern the language used, and various differences in emphasis regarding certain conceptualizations and descriptions. This, however, is not surprising in a process where thoughts and observations have developed independently between two groups (although we would have been in professional contact with Jeanne and Les during the period when we were working on our project). We see our book as building on previous work described in Timulak (2015), that was influenced by the research on sequential emotional processing by Pascual-Leone and Greenberg (Pascual-Leone & Greenberg, 2007; Pascual-Leone, 2009) and of course on other classical EFT writings (the works of Greenberg, Elliott, Watson, Goldman, Paivio, etc.). Furthermore, almost all examples of the actual work in Timulak's (2015) book were based on work with clients who met criteria for GAD.

In comparison, we see Watson and Greenberg's book (2017) as being more in line with the conceptualizations presented in their previous book on working with depression (Greenberg & Watson, 2006) and other traditional EFT writing. For instance, if we were to pick some examples of difference, we do not use the language of "resolution", as we do not see the goal of therapy as necessarily *resolving* worry, negative self-treatment, or emotional injuries. We rather emphasize the importance of increased emotional flexibility and resilience (cf. Pascual-Leone, 2009) without postulating that there is a particular end point, at which painful emotions or problematic self–self or self–other processes are *resolved*. Another point of difference arises in our discussion of our difficulties with the GAD diagnosis, which is not such a prominent issue with Watson and Greenberg. Furthermore, we do not think in terms of the *vulnerable self*, when conceptualizing core chronic painful feelings and corresponding self-organizations, although we see that term as useful. We simply refer to chronic painful feelings (and corresponding self-organizations), perhaps capturing the fluidity of the process. We can, of course, clearly recognize that fluidity in Watson and Greenberg's account.

On a more clinical level, we can see that at times there may be some different emphases or variations. These could be attributed to different creative ways of using emotion-focused strategies and tasks, while following the same goals. At times, however, we had a sense that a self-soothing (self-compassion) process could be seen as somewhat more central than protective anger, in Watson and Greenberg's account. In line with our previous writing (e.g., Timulak, 2015) we see both processes as equally important, although for a particular client one or other of these processes may be more important at a certain point in time. For example, if the client has difficulty accessing self-compassion, this may become a more central focus of therapy. Conversely, if the client has difficulty accessing anger, this may become targeted more in therapy. If we see any shared feature with regard to compassion and anger, when working with clients with anxiety difficulties, we see the importance of being able to access protective anger as particularly important, as it supports the person in feeling confident, expansive, and powerful, in other words, the opposite of scared and avoidant.

While we have attempted to point out some potential differences, we have not had an opportunity to discuss them with our esteemed colleagues. It may well be that they mainly represent language-influenced differences, which may become very small differences in actual EFT practice. We warmly recommend the expertly presented conceptualization of generalized anxiety and its emotion-focused treatment by Watson and Greenberg (2017). We found their account inspiring. It offered a great deal of opportunity for fruitful and stimulating reflection.

The book outline

After this introduction, the book will consist of four parts. The first part will outline the theoretical background, comprising three chapters. Chapter 2 will cover essential information on GAD such as definitions (including historical conceptualizations), prevalence, course, comorbidity, and the overall burden it imposes. The chapter will also present current psychological conceptualizations of GAD, particularly those stemming from a CBT theoretical framework. An outline of treatments based on these theoretical models will also be provided, together with information on their effectiveness.

Chapter 3 will present a brief overview of EFT theory. It will briefly summarize research evidence supporting the approach and will present the main theoretical concepts. It will also present the basic principles of clinical practice such as case conceptualization, use of the therapeutic relationship, and the use of a variety of treatment tasks.

Chapter 4 will present our Emotion Transformation model of GAD, based on the research projects run in the first author's lab. The model assumes that there are particular, painful triggers in the client's life that are difficult for the client to process emotionally. The client is afraid of these triggers and of the emotional experiences they bring, and attempts either to avoid the triggers, or manage them, by toughening up or by preparing him or herself for them through worry. This leads to an undifferentiated state of distress combined with anxiety and avoidance. The underlying feared core emotional pain characterized by feelings of loneliness, shame, and primary fear is then obscured, and unmet needs linked with those core experiences are unarticulated. A brief outline of therapy will also be offered here.

The second part of the book will focus on the initial building blocks of working with clients who suffer with generalized anxiety disorder in an emotion-focused way. Chapter 5 will present research-informed propositions about the qualities of the therapeutic relationship offered by the therapist that contribute to the client's sense of safety, emotion regulation, and corrective emotional experiences. Attention will be paid to interpersonal sensitivities, which clients may bring to therapy and how they may impact on the development of safe, corrective relationships. Space will be devoted to showing how the therapist strives to build an authentic, compassionate, and validating relationship with the client.

Chapter 6 will follow on from Chapter 4 and will introduce our case conceptualization model in therapy. The model presents a conceptual framework consisting of: *triggers of emotional pain; problematic self-treatment* in the context of the triggers; *apprehensive anxiety* of the triggers, leading to *emotional avoidance* of the painful feelings and *behavioral avoidance* of painful triggers; *global distress;* the underlying feared *core emotional pain;* and related *unmet needs.* The model also refers to a strategy for therapy, which aims towards bringing in therapeutic experiences that respond to the underlying pain and unmet needs (e.g., compassion and healthy anger). The cost of avoidance is also highlighted, as is the way it can be used to contribute to the mobilization of determination to overcome anxiety. The chapter will also discuss how the therapist uses case conceptualization in therapy.

Chapter 7 will introduce some EFT tasks and strategies that can be used in therapy to help clients overcome their avoidance of the core emotional pain that needs to be transformed in therapy. The chapter will particularly focus on working with self-interruption and self-worry tasks. There will be an original description of working with worry, which was developed in our lab. The model assumes that worry is enacted in the two-chair task. The anxiety that the worry produces is amplified, the need and vulnerability (exhaustion) in the anxiety is articulated, and protective anger and self-compassion are generated.

The third part of the book presents Chapter 8, which focuses on accessing and transforming core, feared painful feelings. This chapter will focus on the strategies employed to access and differentiate the core emotional pain in the context of working with clients with GAD difficulties. The parts of the experiential tasks that allow access to the underlying painful emotions will be presented, with a specific focus on how the primary maladaptive emotions are accessed. The chapter will also focus on how the unmet needs present in the core painful feelings can be articulated in therapy. It also examines ways of generating experiences of self-compassion and healthy protective anger that serve as antidotes to the core painful feelings and as responses to the unmet needs.

The final part of the book presents a chapter which discusses adaptions of therapeutic strategy to various stages in therapy, and a chapter focusing on learning EFT for GAD. Chapter 9 will discuss the stages of therapy (beginning, middle, and end). It will also focus on issues of timing and the strategic use of therapy in specific circumstances such as time-limited therapy, work with comorbid conditions, personality characteristics of clients, problems in therapy, et cetera. It will also discuss the use of homework and various psychoeducational formats that can be applied, based on the formulations presented in the book. Chapter 10 will provide information on how to incorporate the therapeutic strategies highlighted in the book into one's existing therapeutic repertoire (e.g., other therapeutic orientations such as CBT). Information on training in EFT as well as other resources that the reader may use in their learning will be provided here as well.

Part I

Theoretical underpinnings

Chapter 2

Generalized anxiety disorder

Robert,[1] a 41-year-old single male, was referred to therapy by his GP for treatment of his chronic high anxiety and low mood. When he first attended therapy, Robert was so agitated, upset, and stressed in-session that he could barely sit still or maintain eye-contact. He reported feeling physically sick and constantly on edge.

A variety of factors, both historic and current, had brought Robert into therapy. Most devastating of all was the sudden and unexpected death of his father, when Robert was fourteen, in an automobile accident. Robert idealized his father and described feeling as though he had lost his best friend. Shortly after, Robert's close aunt passed away. This complicated Robert's grieving process and he became massively anxious in case further tragedy might befall the family. Robert now felt the need to protect his mother and siblings, yet struggled with his own sense of loss and uncertainty regarding the future.

Robert had an 11-year-old son, Joe, but was estranged from Joe's mother, Mary. Their marriage had been complicated and unhappy. Robert had an excellent relationship with his son, but feared that he may be refused permission to see him because of his poor relationship with his ex-wife. This had happened in the past. Additionally, Robert's business had been hit by the recession, and now faced considerable uncertainty about its future. The pain, sadness, and loss attached to the death of Robert's father was curiously mirrored in the sadness and loss attached to his own experience of fatherhood. These experiences fueled Robert's sense of loneliness and isolation: "I lost my best friend, I have no one"; while his inability to live up to the standards set by his idealized father and his acute awareness of the mistakes he made, intensified his sense of shame: "I am a failure, I've made such a mess of everything". He struggled with a sense of not being good enough, linked historically to his mother's emotional unavailability and criticism (she herself was quite vulnerable and did not have the energy to look after Robert) and his father's high standards. The loss of his father, the most significant attachment relationship in his life, left him feeling abandoned and uncertain, with a heightened need for a sense of security and safety in a cruel and unpredictable world.

Robert's anxiety was characterized by the awful, nagging fear that something terrible might happen to a member of his family. He constantly worried about *things that he was afraid would turn into disasters and he or his close ones would be endangered, abandoned, or humiliated. He worried constantly: "the worst is not knowing what it's going to be", and described living in "constant fear", referring to "weeks that I didn't sleep … losing days by simply staring into space while my mind was running riot". Robert described several intensely experienced somatic symptoms, including breathlessness, palpitations, and nausea; he described how "you would be feeling claustrophobic in yourself, you just kind of feel boxed in … you're struggling for air". Indeed, Robert's physical presentation in therapy was characterized by uneasiness, constant fidgeting, almost writhing in his seat, and continuous shaking of one or other leg, which varied in intensity with his emotional state. His description of his current lifestyle painted a picture of hopelessness and helplessness as he chronicled his gradual withdrawal from society. He expressed the high levels of shame he experienced from a sense of having let his father down due to his current, complicated life situation. Faced with the complexity of this situation, Robert often experienced a profound sense of hopelessness and helplessness which found expression in a defeatist, resigned attitude in the face of the many losses and challenges that he faced. He described himself as a failure. Although he had previously been a very socially active young man, he now spent most evenings at home, wracked with emotional pain.*

Furthermore, over time, Robert had evolved patterns of behavior which helped him avoid his emotional experience. Robert described engaging in numerous avoidance strategies, both emotional (e.g., shutting down) and behavioral (e.g., avoiding contact with people). Robert's concern for the well-being of others (i.e., family) distracted him from some of his own issues but left him vulnerable to feelings of shame if, for example, he felt he had failed in his responsibilities. Robert internalized the belief that he must suffer alone, for if he were to share his worries with others, they might become burdened. This reinforced his sense of loneliness and further complicated the possibility of his sharing his pain with another person, such that it might be resolved. He was stuck with the belief that he deserved all the painful experiences in his life.

Robert's emotional pain represents one of the many forms of suffering that meet criteria for generalized anxiety disorder as conceptualized by the current version of the Diagnostic and Statistical Manual of Mental Disorders (DSM-5; American Psychiatric Association, 2013) and the International Classification of Diseases (ICD-10; the World Health Organization, 1992). As we explain below, we are aware of difficulties in the diagnosing of emotional suffering, similar to that which is described in Robert's case, as generalized anxiety *disorder* (and comorbid *disorders* that are visible in the description of his suffering). Nevertheless, we will be referencing the description of a condition that is shared by people who scan their environment for potential threat and engage in worrying, for more time than not, about a variety of potential threats and experience corresponding with anxiety and accompanying physiological symptoms. The same people often suffer with other difficulties, many of which are similar to those experienced by

Robert, such as low mood (depression), helplessness, hopelessness, interpersonal difficulties, et cetera (traditionally classified as comorbid disorders).

Generalized anxiety disorder

As we highlighted in the introduction, humanistic psychotherapies maintain a somewhat ambivalent position regarding labeling human psychological suffering, or emotional pain, as disorder. We share this ambivalence. We see the suffering of people who meet diagnostic criteria for these disorders as being much broader then the specific criteria suggest, and as not necessarily disordered. We believe that the experienced difficulties can, in many cases, be understood as serving some adaptive function, either in the past or in the present. Nevertheless, for pragmatic purposes in this book, we will be referring to generalized anxiety disorder (GAD), as currently conceptualized by the Diagnostic Statistical Manual of Mental Disorders (DSM-5; American Psychiatric Association, 2013) and the International Classification of Diseases (ICD-10; World Health Organization, 1992) as GAD difficulties.

Furthermore, we are not persuaded that people with GAD difficulties represent a homogenous group. In our clinical and research experience, we could see that even beyond the problems of multiple comorbidities and the difficulty with reliability in assessing diagnostic criteria, the reported experiences of people who meet criteria for GAD (see below) vary. We also believe that worry and anxiety, in people with this type of difficulty, serve varied functions and it may not be helpful to cluster them under the one GAD umbrella. Indeed, the classification of GAD that can be found in DSM and ICD is not derived from broad, population-based studies, examining clustered psychological symptoms, indicative of human suffering. This classification is rather based on the perspectives of scholars and practitioners functioning in a particular societal and cultural context (cf. Stein, 2014). Although they have reviewed existing research evidence relevant to the psychopathology of a particular condition, relative to other conditions, they embed their work in pre-existing classifications, which may not be the most useful way of classifying psychological suffering. Consequently, any classification of psychopathology is embedded in the history of clinical experience and scientific thinking about human suffering (for psychological perspectives on DSM see, for instance, an edited volume of Beutler and Malik, 2002). Furthermore, the classification of suffering as being disordered as per DSM is based on value judgments (cf. Sadler, 2005). Furthermore, anxiety "disorders", in common with many other psychiatric conditions, have few distinct biological markers (American Psychiatric Association, 2013). The existing diagnoses, therefore, should be seen as attempts to pragmatically and informatively capture clinical presentations, so that they might inform prognosis, treatment, and research (cf. Blashfield, Keeley, Flanagan, & Miles, 2014).

Existing classification systems such as the DSM are therefore based on consensus, taking into account conceptual and ontological issues, levels of impairment, diagnostic validity, and clinical utility (Stein, 2014). This implied consensus does not mean that there is unanimous agreement, as is clear from the extensive changes made with each revision of the classification system. For instance, there is considerable debate regarding whether mental health "disorders" are dimensional or categorical, that is, on the continuum (including a normative part) or distinct entities (Blashfield *et al.*, 2014). Each revision of a classification system such as DSM reviews the most current research evidence (e.g., psychological, physiological, neuroscientific, genetic). However, this investigation is based on the way in which various "disorders" were classified in the previous system (Craske *et al.*, 2009) in so far as the reviewed research simply uses a pre-existing classification system.

Diagnostic criteria for generalized anxiety disorder

Despite our reservations, for the remainder of the book we will refer to work with clients that currently meets diagnostic criteria for GAD, as conceptualized by the DSM-5 (American Psychiatric Association, 2013). These criteria have evolved over time. What is currently conceptualized by the DSM-5 as GAD initially belonged to the category of anxiety reaction (DSM-I), and subsequently anxiety neurosis (DSM-II). It formally appeared as GAD in DSM-III (without the emphasis on worry and the six-month duration criteria, and was often regarded as a residual diagnosis, i.e., if other diagnoses were excluded) and was included in its more or less current form in the DSM-III revision (DSM-III-R) in 1987 (cf. Hazlett-Stevens, 2009; Mennin, Heimberg, & Turk, 2004; Rickels & Rynn, 2001). Interestingly, as Rickels and Rynn (2001) point out, the origins of worry, currently a defining feature of GAD, can be traced back to Freud's notion of anxious expectation, which is present in what he describes as anxiety neurosis. It is therefore apparent that in comparison to the other diagnostic categories which comprise the DSM suite of disorders, the currently recognized GAD diagnosis is both a relative newcomer and has undergone several revisions in recent, consecutive editions of the DSM from its original, formal inception in DSM-III to its current incarnation in DSM-5. This has obvious implications regarding the relative novelty of manualized therapeutic approaches for the range of difficulties that are currently conceptualized as GAD.

The Diagnostic and Statistical Manual of Mental Disorders, published by the American Psychiatric Association (DSM-5; American Psychiatric Association, 2013, p. 222) defines GAD per the following criteria. GAD is characterized by excessive anxiety and worry (apprehensive expectation), which the sufferer describes as difficult to control, occurring more days than not for a period of at least six months. For a diagnosis of GAD to be made (see also Box 2.1) the anxiety and worry must be associated with at least three of the following six symptoms: (i) restlessness or feeling keyed up or on edge, (ii) being easily fatigued, (iii) difficulty concentrating or mind going blank, (iv) irritability, (v) muscle tension, (vi) sleep disturbance (difficulty falling or staying asleep, or restless, unsatisfying sleep). The focus of the anxiety ought not to be better explained as related to features of another disorder (i.e., worry about having a panic attack, worry about being embarrassed in public, etc.). The anxiety, worry, or physical symptoms must cause distress or impairment in social, occupational, or other important areas of functioning. The condition must not be due to the direct physiological effect of a substance (i.e., drugs or medication), or a general medical condition, and must not occur exclusively during a mood disorder, a psychotic disorder, or a pervasive developmental disorder. Differential diagnosis includes other anxiety disorders (e.g., social anxiety) or anxiety-related disorders (e.g., obsessive-compulsive disorder, post-traumatic stress disorder and adjustment disorder) that are diagnosed if they better explain the client's presentation then GAD (this does not preclude them being seen as comorbid, i.e., present alongside the GAD).

The International Classification of Diseases (ICD-10; World Health Organization, 1993; ICD-11 is expected this year) and its section focusing on classification of mental and behavioral disorders also recognizes GAD. The description of difficulties is comparable to the DSM-5, insofar as it characterizes GAD as being defined by anxious tension and worry, experienced over a six-month period and related to everyday issues. There is some variation over symptoms, with the ICD-10 requiring four out of a possible twenty-two symptoms, of which at least one must come from the following list of four autonomic symptoms: (i) palpitations or pounding heart, or accelerated heart rate, (ii) sweating, (iii) trembling or shaking, and (iv) dry mouth (not due to medication or dehydration). Although the DSM-5 and ICD-10 criteria for GAD appear to be very similar, Slade and Andrews (2001) who analyzed Australian National Mental Health Survey Data based on more than 10,000 adult people representing an Australian population, found that while prevalence rates for both classification systems were largely the same (around 3%, see also below), only about 40% of the sample was diagnosed as meeting the criteria for GAD in both classification systems. Again, this raises questions about the reliability of these widely used classification systems.

Box 2.1 *Diagnostic criteria for generalized anxiety disorder according to the DSM-5* (American Psychiatric Association, 2013, p. 222).

A.

Excessive anxiety and worry (apprehensive expectation), occurring more days than not for at least six months, about a number of events or activities (such as work or school performance).

B.

The individual finds it difficult to control the worry.

C.

The anxiety and worry are associated with three (or more) of the following six symptoms (with at least some symptoms having been present for more days than not for the past six months):

Note:
Only one item required in children.

1   Restlessness, feeling keyed up or on edge.
2   Being easily fatigued.
3   Difficulty concentrating or mind going blank.
4   Irritability.
5   Muscle tension.
6   Sleep disturbance (difficulty falling or staying asleep, or restless, unsatisfying sleep).

D.

The anxiety, worry, or physical symptoms cause clinically significant distress or impairment in social, occupational, or other important areas of functioning.

E.

The disturbance is not attributable to the physiological effects of a substance (e.g., a drug of abuse or a medication) or another medical condition (e.g., hyperthyroidism).

F.

The disturbance is not better explained by another medical disorder (e.g., anxiety or worry about having panic attacks in panic disorder, negative evaluation in social anxiety disorder [social phobia], contamination or other obsessions in obsessive-compulsive disorder, separation from attachment figures in separation anxiety disorder, reminders of traumatic events in post-traumatic stress disorder, losing weight in anorexia nervosa, physical complaints in somatic symptom disorder, perceived appearance of flaws in body dysmorphic disorder, having a serious illness in illness anxiety disorder, or the content of delusional beliefs in schizophrenia or delusional disorder).

Anxiety

The main feature of GAD is anxiety. *Anxiety* is often conceptualized as representing an emotional response to future threat, while the related concept of *fear* is understood as an emotional reaction to imminent threat (cf. DSM-5; American Psychiatric Association, 2013). LeDoux (2015) stresses that fear is a response to current experience of danger, whereas anxiety is not only about the future, but also about uncertainty, that is, whether there will be any harm caused to the person. Like Barlow (2002), we see fear as an emotional response to current danger and anxiety as related to *potential* future danger. As will be seen in later chapters, we also share Barlow's (2002) recognition of anxious *apprehension* as an important feature of the experience of anxiety. We also see fear as something acute. Obviously, these overlap as what constitutes current and potential future danger is a fleeting concept. Physiologically, there is also a distinction (although DSM-5 and others also see a good deal of overlap). DSM-5 represents fear as surges of autonomic arousal, necessary in the flight or fight response, with corresponding thoughts and behavior: while anxiety is characterized more as hyper-vigilance, muscle tension, and behavioral avoidance (American Psychiatric Association, 2013; p. 189). Another concept that is important here is *panic (attack)*, which DSM-5 sees as a particular form of fear, while others such as Barlow (2002) see it more as an expression of fear. Nevertheless, there appears to be a lot of debate about defining and then distinguishing fear/panic from anxiety and seeing them as either overlapping on a continuum, or as qualitatively different (see Barlow, 2002).

The DSM, and others (cf. Barlow, 2002), conceptualize fear/panic as an 'abrupt surge' that may come from a calm or an anxious state, and is characterized by symptoms such as pounding heart, sweating, shaking, choking, chest pain, abdominal distress, feeling dizzy, chills, heat, numbness, tingling, derealization, depersonalization, fear of losing control/dying, et cetera, with potential, specific, cultural expression (American Psychiatric Association, 2013, p. 214). We also recognize an acute fear, present in therapy sessions, in the form of dissociations, sudden attempts to avoid experience, et cetera. Anxiety is not particularly well-defined in the DSM apart from being characterized by vigilance, muscle tension, and behavioral avoidance (see above), although in the description of GAD, the following accompanying symptoms are mentioned: restlessness, fatigue, difficulty concentrating, irritability, muscle tension, and sleep disturbance (American Psychiatric Association, 2013). GAD is linked to worry (apprehensive expectation), however, the concepts are not well distinguished (i.e., where one finishes and the other begins). Barlow (2002, p. 65) provides a comprehensive conceptualization of what he calls anxious apprehension, in which he also includes cognitive and affective components such as: a sense of uncontrollability and unpredictability, preparatory coping with a supportive physiology, hypervigilance, cognitive biases, increased arousal, attentional biases, and attempts to cope through avoidance and worry. Barlow stresses that the process of anxious apprehension does not have to entail a conscious or rational appraisal of anxiety-provoking cues and propositions (p. 64). Again, worry, like avoidance, is somewhat subsumed into anxiety.

Many (e.g., Barlow, 2002) acknowledge that anxiety may serve an adaptive function. Anxiety leads to preparation, which in many instances is highly adaptive; it prepares us for significant dangers or for things that are simply important for living. Although it may be an unpleasant experience, it is still very valuable to us. This suggests that problematic, non-adaptive anxiety is on the opposite end of a continuum from adaptive anxiety. The DSM (American Psychiatric Association, 2013) defines problematic anxiety as chronic (e.g., in the case of GAD, lasting more than six months), causing significant distress, and causing impairment in social, occupational, or other aspects of functioning. Thus, "pathological" anxiety ceases to fulfill its adaptive function and becomes the enemy rather than a protector; an enemy that places a significant burden on us (for the burden of anxiety see below).

Worry

According to the DSM, worry is a defining feature of GAD. Worry was first studied in the context of test anxiety (cf. Mennin, Heimberg, & Turk, 2004), but in the context of GAD, it was Borkovec's group that paid the most attention to worry in their development of psychological treatment for GAD (Borkovec, Alcaine, & Behar, 2004). Borkovec and colleagues see worry as a cognitive activity which attempts to solve the problem of possible future danger and sees its function as facilitating avoidance of distant bad events (Borkovec et al., 2004). Like anxiety, worry appears to be a dimensional phenomenon, which suggests that it may have an adaptive function. However, some dispute this, and see it rather as interfering with problem solving (cf. Borkovec et al., 2004). In people with GAD difficulties worry is present in an excessive and chronic form causing significant distress and impairment (American Psychiatric Association, 2013). In any case, worry is present in both clinical and non-clinical populations, although in the case of the former, it is present in a much more extensive way and causes much more distress (Hazlett-Stevens, Pruitt, & Collins, 2009).

When constructing their worry questionnaire (Penn State Worry Questionnaire), Borkovec and colleagues asked both clinical and non-clinical groups what benefits they saw in worry. Both groups indicated that they saw worry as motivational, helping them to avoid or prevent bad events, prepare for the worst, problem-solve, superstitiously lessen the likelihood of bad events occurring, and distract themselves from more upsetting emotional topics (Borkovec et al., 2004, p. 88). Borkovec and colleagues' last point refers to distraction from topics in the area of past trauma, early childhood relationships, and current problematic relationships. Thus, worry may provide an illusion of control over such potential threatening future events (cf. Roemer, Orsillo, & Barlow, 2002). Roemer and colleagues (2002), reviewing the research evidence, also suggest that people with GAD difficulties do not believe in their problem-solving skills (although those skills may, in fact, be adequate). The effect of worry on physiology appears to manifest in terms of autonomic inflexibility rather than autonomic hyperactivity (Hazlett-Stevens et al., 2009) and causes a negative impact on the body (Llera &

Newman, 2010). Worry appears to sustain negative affect and prevents a further drop in it (Newman, Llera, Erickson, Przeworski, & Castonguay, 2013).

Worry should be distinguished from other psychological phenomena such as ruminations or obsessions. Depressive rumination (cf. Hazlett-Stevens *et al.*, 2009; Mennin *et al.*, 2004) refers to repetitive cognitive activity in which the person repeatedly goes over distressing situations/experiences and, in its problematic form, is typically seen as a feature of depression. Both worry and rumination are present in people with GAD. Rumination can be found among people with GAD, although it is higher if comorbid depression is also diagnosed (Yang, Kim, Lee *et al.*, 2014). Obsessions are "recurrent and persistent thoughts, urges, or images that are experienced as intrusive and unwanted" (American Psychiatric Association, 2013, p. 235) that cause anxiety and distress (Mennin *et al.*, 2004). While it appears that there is some overlap between worry and obsessions, they can be reliably discriminated, even though both are found in clients with principal diagnoses of GAD and OCD; with obsessions being particularly distinctive in the OCD group (cf. Brown, Moras, Zinbarg, & Barlow, 1993).

Etiology

What is known about the etiology of GAD is multifaceted. The study of genetic influences is still in its early days, although there appears to be a relevant genetic influence (Gelernter & Stein, 2009), most likely non-specific, shared with a vulnerability to other anxiety and depressive disorders (Smoller, Cerrato, & Weatherall, 2015; Stevens, Jendrusina, Sarapas, & Behar, 2014). The relationship between genotype and phenotype is complex, with the same genes being potentially responsible for different phenotype presentations as well as different genes being responsible for similar phenotype presentations, all of which is further complicated by interaction (epigenetic relationships) between genes, and genes and environment (Sadler, 2005). Neuroscientific studies (although relatively underrepresented for GAD – Britton & Rauch, 2009) suggest that individuals with GAD appear to be vulnerable to emotional and neural hyperactivity, which may be difficult to regulate (Newman *et al.*, 2013; Stevens *et al.*, 2014).

Developmental studies suggest that there are early predictors of later GAD, such as early irritability, attachment difficulties, parenting issues, early adversity in the form of uncontrollable events, et cetera, all of which have an impact on early, physiological functioning (cf. reviews in Hudson & Rapee, 2004 and Newman *et al.*, 2013; for a prospective study see Moffitt, Caspi, Harrington *et al.*, 2007; for a retrospective study see Newman, Shin, Zuellig, 2016). In a study of retrospectively viewed childhood attachment and current attachment to parents, Cassidy, Lichtenstein-Phelps, Sibrava, Thomas, and Borkovec (2009) reported that clients with GAD difficulties, on average, experienced less maternal love or more maternal rejection in childhood, and a potential role-reversal/enmeshment, than did participants without GAD difficulties. The clients with GAD difficulties were also more likely to feel vulnerable in their current relationship with their mother.

Burden

Historically, the burden of GAD difficulties has been underestimated (cf. DSM-III), however, the truth is quite the opposite. GAD sufferers have a high prevalence of disability, decreased work productivity, and increased use of health care services (Wittchen, 2002). People with GAD experience significant impairment in quality of life (Loebach Wetherell *et al.*, 2004), in well-being, and occupational and family satisfaction, to a degree which is comparable to depression (Stein & Heimberg, 2004; cf. also Grant *et al.*, 2005 or Kessler, Walters, & Wittchen, 2004). GAD and other anxiety difficulties also impact on general health (e.g., cardiovascular diseases, gastrointestinal diseases; cf. Härter, Conway, & Merikangas, 2003; Kessler, Alonso, Chatterji, & He, 2014).

Prevalence, course and comorbidity

One-year prevalence of GAD in community samples in the US is around 3% and its lifetime prevalence is around 5% (Kessler, Berglund, *et al.*, 2005; Kessler, Chiu, *et al.*, 2005; Wittchen, 2002). International studies suggest a similar prevalence (although see the issues above with different criteria leading to diagnosing different groups of people; e.g., Carter, Wittchen, Pfister, & Kessler, 2001; Jenkins *et al.*, 1997). GAD is twice as common in women than in men (Wittchen, Zhao, Kessler, & Eaton, 1994). A quarter of people who meet criteria for GAD have diagnosable difficulties by the age of 20 and 50% of people with GAD by the age of 31 (Kessler, Berglund, *et al.*, 2005). 10% of people meeting criteria for GAD report onset of GAD difficulties by age 13 (Kessler, Berglund, *et al.*, 2005). GAD is chronic and full remission is rare, with symptoms ebbing and increasing again (cf. American Psychiatric Association, 2013).

GAD has high comorbidity with other psychiatric/psychological disorders. A study conducted by Brown and colleagues (Brown, Campbell, Lehman, Grisham, & Mancill, 2001), suggests 65% of people meeting criteria for GAD meet criteria for other anxiety or mood disorders concurrently, with 33% meeting criteria for social anxiety and 26% for major depression. If we consider a lifetime prevalence of other diagnoses, 88% meet criteria for other mood or anxiety disorders with 64% meeting criteria for major depressive disorder (Brown *et al.*, 2001). A study by Carter *et al.* (2001) in Germany found 12-month comorbid prevalence of 59% for major depression, and 56% for other anxiety disorders, with over 93% of people meeting criteria for at least one additional disorder in addition to GAD. Between 34% and 49% of people who meet criteria for GAD also meet criteria for at least one personality disorder, most commonly avoidant and dependent (Lenzenweger, Lane, Loranger, & Kessler, 2007; Sanderson, Wetzler, Beck, & Betz, 1994). All of this suggests that GAD is highly comorbid.

Box 2.2 Some facts about GAD difficulties.

Large-scale community studies place one-year prevalence rates for GAD around 3% with a lifetime prevalence around 5%.

GAD research suggests that GAD is a chronic and enduring condition which most sufferers describe as unremitting in nature. GAD difficulties are also found to be twice as high among women as men in clinical samples.

GAD difficulties have high levels of comorbidity with other mood and anxiety disorders. It also frequently co-occurs with personality disorders.

The burden of GAD difficulties may be comparable to that of depression.

Treatment of GAD

Various approaches are recommended in the treatment of GAD. For instance, the National Institute for Health and Clinical Excellence in the United Kingdom, which prepares recommendations for the National Health Service, recommends a stepped-care approach, starting with guided self-help and psychoeducation in a group format based on the principles of cognitive behavioral therapy (CBT) and, at a higher step, antidepressant medication and/or CBT as manualized for clinical trials (see below) or applied relaxation. The recommended and most studied pharmacological treatment (cf. Mathew & Hoffman, 2009) typically involves antidepressants (particularly Selective Serotonin Reuptake Inhibitors [SSRI], Serotonin-Norepinephrine Reuptake Inhibitors [SNRI]) and more recently anticonvulsants (e.g., pregabalin). Medication use is typically recommended for at least six months (cf. Baldwin & Brandish, 2014; Mathew & Hoffman, 2009). There are a limited number of comparisons of the effectiveness of various medications (Baldwin, Woods, Lawson, & Taylor, 2011).

It is well recognized that psychological therapies play an important role in addressing GAD difficulties. Several approaches have been developed (see below), each with its own conceptualization of GAD and strategies for addressing GAD difficulties. These approaches differ, but also share some common perspectives on understanding GAD, as well as on therapeutic procedures. The largest evidence base exists for the various forms of cognitive behavioral therapies (Cuijpers, Sijbrandij, Koole, Huibers, Berking, & Andersson, 2014; Hanrahan, Field, Jones, & Davey, 2013; Hunot, Churchill, Teixeira, & Silva de Lima, 2007). There are not many comparative trials comparing CBT approaches with non-CBT approaches (Cuijpers *et al.*, 2014). However, there are recommendations in the literature to investigate non-CBT models of working therapeutically with GAD difficulties (Hunot *et al.*, 2007). This is important, as clients appreciate having a choice of treatments (cf. Williams *et al.*, 2016). The importance of choice is also emphasized in many of the recommendations for mental health treatments. Some studies (not on GAD specifically) also suggest that clients may opt for therapies other than CBT (cf. King *et al.*, 2000). All of this was an important encouragement in our endeavor to adapt emotion-focused therapy (EFT) to address GAD difficulties.

Existing psychological models and therapies of GAD

Descriptions of GAD difficulties presented in the DSM-5 and ICD-10 classifications are relatively atheoretical and therefore do not offer a coherent psychological rationale that could be used to inform a psychological therapy. This may be a reason why there are several psychological conceptualizations of GAD embedded in existing psychotherapeutic theories (predominantly CBT) that try to explain the dynamic present in GAD difficulties in a theoretically coherent manner, with implications for subsequent therapeutic strategies. Psychological understanding of GAD therefore, primarily stems from established psychotherapeutic approaches, which have been developed to treat GAD. The theories underlying those treatments utilize a corresponding understanding of GAD that can further inform treatment strategy. We will now briefly discuss existing psychological (psychotherapeutic) conceptualizations of GAD difficulties and corresponding therapeutic approaches that have been, so far, the most comprehensively researched.

The avoidance theory of worry

Some of the most important early research into GAD and the role of worry has been carried out by Borkovec and colleagues, who, since the 1980s have worked on the development of what was later named as an *avoidance theory of worry* (Borkovec, Alcaine, & Behar, 2004). Apart from understanding worry as an attempt to avoid future threats and potential aversive emotional experiences, Borkovec and colleagues also see worry as cognitive avoidance of more upsetting emotional experiencing. It conceptualizes worry as a linguistic, cognitive activity, which facilitates the inhibition, or avoidance, of upsetting imaginal experience. According to Borkovec and colleagues worry decreases the experiencing of somatic or emotional arousal. It can also help in avoiding more emotionally difficult issues. Worry, according to Borkovec, prevents proper emotional processing of underlying fears, past traumas, or past or current problematic relationships. Furthermore, according to Borkovec worry is negatively reinforced, as the majority of feared threats never materialize.

Borkovec and colleagues conducted many studies on the GAD dynamic that have contributed to firming up aspects of this theory (see the review in Borkovec *et al.*, 2004 and Behar *et al.*, 2009). He and his group also developed the first cognitive behavioral treatment of GAD that was initially tested, alongside Applied Relaxation, in several trials (Borkovec & Costello, 1993; Borkovec *et al.*, 1987; Borkovec, Newman, Pincus, & Lytle, 2002). The treatment involves various cognitive behavioral interventions such as; self-monitoring, relaxation techniques, self-control desensitization (a form of exposure), gradual stimulus control (planned worrying), cognitive restructuring, worry outcome monitoring, present-moment focus and expectancy-free living (cf. Behar *et al.*, 2009; Borkovec *et al.*, 2004). The treatment protocol was later supplemented by interventions from interpersonal and emotion-focused therapies that were aimed to target core (interpersonal) fears (Borkovec *et al.*, 2004). This was later tested in a randomized controlled trial (RCT) (Newman *et al.*, 2011). The work of Borkovec and his group remains the bedrock of interventions for GAD. Their later shift towards targeting the underlying fears is a direction that will be presented later in this book. We can also see similarities in their explicit reference to emotion-focused techniques. However, their thinking focuses primarily on symptoms of anxiety and worry, while our conceptualization focuses primarily on chronic painful emotions and the unmet needs embedded in them. Therapeutic strategies presented later in this book also differ markedly from Borkovec's model as they focus on chronic painful feelings of sadness/loneliness, shame, and primary fear in the context of salient emotional relationships.

The intolerance of uncertainty model

This model proposes that intolerance of uncertainty (IU) is the principal underlying agent at the core of GAD, in so far as GAD sufferers find ambiguous situations with uncertain outcomes difficult to tolerate and consequently experience intense and chronic worry (Dugas, Buhr, & Ladouceur, 2004; Dugas & Robichaud, 2007). Dugas and colleagues distinguish intolerance of uncertainty from worry. They see IU as a cognitive schema or filter through which individuals assess their environment, while worry is conceptualized as a cognitive reaction to threat (Dugas *et al.*, 2004, p. 146). Dugas and colleagues conducted a series of studies (see review in Behar *et al.*, 2009 and Dugas *et al.*, 2004), which showed that increased IU is present in people with GAD difficulties, although it may not be entirely specific to them (people with OCD difficulties showed a similar elevation). The intolerance of uncertainty model proposes that intolerance of uncertainty may be linked to cognitive biases such as holding *positive beliefs* regarding the utility of worry, enduring *negative problem orientation* (negative appraisal of the problem and own abilities) and *cognitive avoidance* as proposed by Borkovec, and more broadly.

Treatment in the IUM focuses primarily on developing an increased tolerance for uncertainty (Dugas & Robichaud, 2007), and includes psychoeducation alongside worry awareness training (classification and monitoring of worrying), uncertainty recognition and behavioral exposure, reevaluation of worry (a variation of cognitive restructuring), problem solving training (incorporating a focus on uncertainty), imaginal exposure (to situations that sufferers are worried about), and relapse prevention (focusing on the review of therapy and preparation for future). Several experimental trials have been conducted that examined the efficacy of IUM-based CBT in individual (e.g., Dugas, Brillon, Savard *et al.*, 2010) as well as group formats (e.g., Dugas *et al.*, 2003). IUM and the treatment based on it, as conceptualized by its developers, has only some elements that correspond to our thinking, which will be laid out in later chapters. Imaginal exposure to feared outcomes is somewhat close to our thinking, as is Borkovec and colleagues' thinking about the underlying vulnerabilities that need to be addressed in therapy, the activation of which, clients want to avoid.

A cognitive model of GAD

A cognitive (also referred to as metacognitive) model was developed by Wells (1999, 2004, 2005). The model distinguishes between *Type 1 worry* which refers to worry about external or internal threatening events that may recede, if the goal of worrying is achieved, and *Type 2 worry* or *metaworry*, which comprises of troubling and negative thoughts regarding worry as uncontrollable and harmful (Wells, 2004). Type 1 worry is led by positive beliefs (metacognition) that worrying helps the person to cope, while Type 2 worry is informed by negative beliefs that worry is uncontrollable and harmful. Type 1 worry can bring either relief or further upset and continuation of the worry. Type 2 worry is always experienced as upsetting and leads to avoidance of events that could bring worry and are trying to stop it, which is unsuccessful and leaves people feeling that they have no control over their worry. The beliefs about worry develop through various means, but also evolve through the experience of worry and its effects.

Metacognitive therapy treatment (Wells, 2004) starts with an idiosyncratic case formulation and then with modification of negative and positive beliefs about the worry. Modification of beliefs about uncontrollability of worry starts early in therapy (using behavior experiments and worry controlling exercises). Similarly, beliefs about the harmfulness of worrying are challenged through behavioral experiments. Positive beliefs about worry are challenged subsequently in therapy (again using behavioral experiments) and finally, alternative thinking strategies are introduced (such as positive ending of the worry process). Relapse prevention is focused on at the end of treatment (for more, see Wells, 2004).

Metacognitive therapy (MCT) of GAD has been studied in several trials. Wells and colleagues (Wells *et al.*, 2010) piloted MCT in comparison with applied relaxation, yielding promising results. Van der Heiden and colleagues (Van der Heiden, Muris, & van der Molen, 2012) successfully tested an MCT in comparison to an intolerance of uncertainty treatment, and delayed treatment. The cognitive model of GAD, and therapy stemming from it, differs markedly from the propositions that we will be making later in the book. However, one feature that we see as equally important (although we use different language for it) is recognition of the person's agency in the worry process; like MCT, we facilitate the recognition of this agency.

The emotion dysregulation model of GAD

The emotion dysregulation model of GAD (e.g., Mennin, 2004, 2006; Mennin, Heimberg, & Turk, 2004) builds on Borkovec and colleagues' work examining why people with GAD difficulties want to avoid emotion. Mennin and colleagues postulate that people with GAD difficulties struggle with experiencing and expressing emotions, as they are highly emotionally sensitive (e.g., Mennin, 2004). People with these types of difficulties, according to Mennin, struggle to understand their emotions, have problems modulating them, and experience them as highly aversive.

Emotion regulation therapy (ERT) relies on a combination of CBT treatment principles, such as self-monitoring, relaxation exercises, and other principles, which address emotion regulation, such as increasing emotional awareness and exposure (Mennin, 2004). Mennin (2004, 2006) further presents four phases of therapy. The first focuses on psychoeducation about GAD and worry, the second on identification of avoidance strategies and development of somatic awareness skills, the third on utilizing experiential exposure exercises that focus on core issues (fear of loss, inadequacy, and failure), and the final phase focuses on relapse prevention. ERT explicitly refers to the use of some emotion-focused techniques such as focusing and, in particular, experiential chair work in the third phase of treatment (Mennin, 2004). ERT was successfully tested in an open trial (Mennin, Fresco, Ritter, & Heimberg, 2015). ERT shares some similarities with EFT and uses some EFT techniques. However, the application of ERT interventions appears to be anchored in a CBT formulation and grouped with other CBT techniques. While in CBT treatments, exposure aspects of experiential interventions are stressed, in EFT these interventions are used above and beyond exposure, with the goal of emotion transformation. This would, for instance, mean that the fear is not only overcome through habituation (via exposure), but is transformed by other emotionally laden experiences such as adaptive anger.

The acceptance based behavioral model of GAD (ABM)

Roemer and Orsillo's acceptance-based behavioral model of generalized anxiety disorder (2014) sees worry as a habit that is strengthened by repetition and reinforced by non-occurrence of the feared outcomes. The model proposes that the GAD dynamic in some people is fueled by: distressing responses to internal experience (particularly anxiety), rigid experiential avoidance of this distress, and ensuing behavioral avoidance (they also use the term constriction) of activities that may bring the distress. Acceptance-based behavioral therapy (ABBT) comprises: a thorough assessment (of symptoms, reactions to internal experiences, experiential, and behavioral avoidance), psychoeducation regarding the ABM model, self-monitoring, mindfulness practice (formal and informal, that also includes progressive muscle relaxation), engagement in activities that are otherwise avoided due to anxiety, and finally relapse prevention (Roemer & Orsillo, 2014). ABBT was successfully tested in a trial comparing ABBT to a delayed treatment (Roemer, Orsillo, & Salters-Pedneault, 2008) and in comparison to applied relaxation (Hayes-Skelton, Roemer, & Orsillo, 2013).

In comparison to the EFT model that we are going to present later (see also Timulak & McElvaney, 2016), we can see an overlap in observing experiential as well as behavioral avoidance in people with GAD difficulties. Our model is more specific about what this avoidance refers to (we do not see it as entirely "general", but rather as idiosyncratic, tied to the individual's personal history). Our focus in therapy is not so much on training clients to be able to stay with the experience, although we do emphasize the importance of this process for therapy, but rather in accessing chronic emotional vulnerabilities, currently avoided, that we want to transform. We see the overcoming of behavioral and experiential avoidance as a natural step that follows. We also conceptualize that clients overcome avoidance as they become increasingly aware of its personal cost.

The contrast avoidance model

The contrast avoidance model was developed by Newman and colleagues (Newman & Llera, 2011; Newman, Llera, Erickson, & Przeworski, 2014; Newman, Llera, Erickson, Przeworski, & Castonguay, 2013), is based on a review of the research evidence on the function of worry, and aims at amending Borkovec's conceptualization of worry as cognitive avoidance. The model assumes that people with GAD trade off a sustained state of distress caused by worry against the unexpected negative experience of the potential outcome of the worry. Newman and colleagues therefore stress that worry does not prevent distress, but rather utilizes continuous "known" distress to offset a potential, significant, "unexpected" distress ("a sharp increase in negative emotion" Newman *et al.*, 2013). They are thus trying to avoid emotional "contrast" by preferring chronic, but familiar distress. The cost of the worry, however, is that it prolongs negative emotionality and corresponding physiological distress. This theory has not yet lead to the development of a comprehensive treatment, but Newman *et al.* (2014) have offered some clinical suggestions, among them, that the focus of exposure in CBT ought not be on the feared outcomes, but rather on the experiences of emotional contrast.

Again, we see aspects of this model as relevant to our conceptualization (Timulak & McElvaney, 2016; see Chapter 4). We also see worry as a way of preparing for the unexpected threatening trigger. However, we see worry as only one of the strategies for not experiencing chronic, idiosyncratically developed emotional vulnerability, which can potentially be (or is) activated by particular triggers. Our therapeutic strategy focuses on transformation of this vulnerability and on developing the person's sense of being more emotionally resilient.

Supportive expressive psychotherapy (core conflictual relationship themes model)

Crits-Christoph and colleagues (Crits-Christoph, Connolly Gibbons, Crits-Christoph, 2004) present a variation of Luborsky's (1984) supportive-expressive psychoanalytic therapy for the treatment of GAD difficulties. Crits-Christoph and colleagues see worry as a defence mechanism, activated to keep an arguably greater threat out of awareness, thereby protecting the individual from more troubling concerns. The psychodynamic view point also considers the impact of interpersonal relationships on early development and the way in which internalized representations in childhood may become activated in adulthood with consequences for adult relationships. The supportive-expressive model of GAD emphasizes how difficult, interpersonal experience may contribute to the formation of expectations and beliefs regarding self and other, and how anxiety is seen as an indicator that fulfilment of interpersonal wishes and needs is under threat. The supportive-expressive model conceptualizes client distress in terms of core conflictual relationship themes (CCRTs), which have three main elements, (1) the wish or desire, (2) the perceived or expected response from the other person, and (3) the response of self (see Luborsky, 1984; Luborsky & Crits-Christoph, 1998); with anxiety being a response of self to an interpersonal wish under threat (Crits-Christoph *et al.*, 2004). Crits-Christoph *et al.* recognize that CCRTs of people with GAD vary and are particularly idiosyncratic, and based on personal history.

Supportive-expressive therapy for GAD follows its general features as with other presentations (cf. Crits-Christoph *et al.*, 2004). It relies on a good therapeutic alliance and interpretative work aimed at bringing an understanding to CCRTs and lowering of defences. From that understanding a new adaptive behavior is then encouraged. Crits-Christoph and colleagues (Crits-Christoph, Connolly, Azarian, Crits-Christoph, & Shappell, 1996) examined a brief supportive expressive psychodynamic psychotherapy for GAD in an open trial with promising results. Again, the supportive expressive model shares some aspects of our thinking about GAD difficulties. We are also looking at unmet needs in real or psychological interaction with emotionally salient others. Our perspective focuses not on interpersonal patterns, but chronic emotional experiences signaling unfulfilled needs. Our therapeutic strategies focus on accessing and then transforming those painful chronic emotions, and not so much on understanding of an interpersonal functioning that is seen as more superficial, although playing a role in consolidating new experiences and creating a meaningful narrative and identity.

We have presented the main, current psychological (particularly CBT) models of understanding GAD difficulties along with the main therapeutic approaches stemming from those models. We summarize those models in terms of some aspects of Robert's (whom we presented in the beginning of this chapter) presentation or a potential presentation (Box 2.3). Our ambition in the rest of the book is to contribute with an alternative (although at times overlapping) conceptualization of the difficulties, and then offer a very different therapeutic approach. Before we proceed with presenting our model and our (emotion-focused) therapeutic approach to working with GAD difficulties, we will present general tenets of emotion-focused therapy in the next chapter.

Box 2.3 A brief presentation of some of Robert's difficulties (or potential difficulties) per current models of GAD difficulties.

The avoidance theory of worry

By continually worrying about things, which may befall his family, Robert manages to avoid thinking about other issues, which might cause him greater pain, such as the feeling that he is a failure and has made a mess of his life. He holds multiple positive beliefs about worry: for example, it helps him protect his family and enables him to prepare for a precarious future. Robert's emotional processing is so highly avoidant that many issues go unresolved as he cannot bear to be in psychological contact with them. Robert has problematic interpersonal relations (e.g., with his ex-wife). He is above all greatly impacted by the emotional sequelae of several traumatic losses, abandonments, and betrayals.

The intolerance of uncertainty model

Here, the main drive behind Robert's anxiety are the feelings of discomfort produced by his inability to tolerate the uncertainty in his life, in relation to his business, his family's safety and so on. He holds multiple positive beliefs about worry: for example, it helps him protect his family and enables him to prepare for a precarious future. He has a negative problem orientation, underestimating his own problem-solving skills, which incapacitates him and undermines his sense of agency. This is coupled with cognitive avoidance that makes potential threats even more threatening.

The (meta)cognitive model

According to this model Robert's positive beliefs about worry (i.e., its protective function) feed into his type 1 worry profile while his negative beliefs about worry (i.e., "sometimes I can't sleep for days – I think I'm going crazy!") supports his Type 2 meta-worries (worry about worrying). He engages in behavior that avoids potentially distressing situations (e.g., social events) and tries to (ineffectively) stop his distress including worrying (reinforcing Type 2 worry). When a catastrophe does not occur he attributes it to worry (which reinforces his worry 1).

The emotion dysregulation model

Here we can see how Robert's discomfort with his emotional world (which is perceived as dangerous, a source of fear, and something to be avoided) does not help him to understand his emotional experience and also leaves him feeling very distressed if any emotions seep through. Worrying (he believes) helps him prepare for potential emotionally upsetting events.

The acceptance based behavioral model

Here again we can see how Robert's discomfort with his emotional world (which is perceived as dangerous, a source of fear, and something to be avoided) leads him to avoid experience (e.g., emotional suppression, thought suppression) as well as behaviors that could lead him to situations that could be distressing (e.g., social situations), none of which actually prevent the internal upset that he still carries with himself. Worrying (he believes) helps him prepare for potential emotionally upsetting events. This is reinforced if the negative consequences of events do not occur.

The contrast avoidance model

From the perspective of this model Robert may be engaging in continuous worry in an implicit transaction which ensures that he will be spared the horror of negative emotional contrast, if any of the feared outcomes (e.g., something would happen to his family) occur, in exchange for a semi-permanent dysphoric state characterized by worry. The possibility of his being in a relatively good mood, only to be plunged into despair or fear (i.e., by recalling how he let down his father, or fears about his lack of control over his life) is offset by embracing constant, medium level worry which maintains him in a state of such negatively laden affect that he should not have too far to fall if he were to encounter a negative stressor.

The core conflictual relationship themes model

From this perspective, Robert's take on the world may have been colored by some early relationship issues, his idealized, but hard to please father, his constantly critical, but also vulnerable mother. In his adult life, he also experienced considerable interpersonal difficulties. Robert's wish or desire to be loved and respected as a capable person have been continuously denied by the significant others in his life. The lens through which Robert now sees life is one which shows the world as a hostile and unwelcoming place, which brings experiences of anxiety of what other responses he will get from important people in his life. Worry is a defence against the uncertainties of the world and the unpredictability and hurt caused by interpersonal relationships.

Conclusion

In this Chapter we presented an example of a client who met the criteria for a diagnosis of GAD. We discussed diagnostic issues pertinent to GAD, and to the DSM and ICD in general. We provided some information on anxiety and worry and distinguished them from similar processes. We discussed the issues of etiology, burden, prevalence, course, and comorbidity of GAD. We then presented the main psychological models of GAD and associated treatments of GAD. Finally, we discussed the case example in terms of the main characteristics of the existing psychological models of GAD.

Note

1 All examples we use throughout the book are either composite examples based on our experience with many clients or examples of clients that consented to be included in the form of examples. In any case examples we use have many potentially identifying characteristics changed.

Chapter 3

Emotion-focused therapy

Emotion-focused therapy (EFT) is an empirically supported, humanistic-experiential treatment with roots in person-centered, Gestalt, experiential and existential therapies (Greenberg, Rice, & Elliott, 1993; Greenberg, 2002). It has evolved gradually, over time, through a systematic program of psychotherapy research. It also incorporates elements of contemporary cognitive and emotion theory (Greenberg, 2015). EFT is mainly identified with the work of Les Greenberg and his colleagues. Emotion-focused therapy was first presented under the name *process-experiential therapy* in Greenberg, Rice, and Elliott's 1993 book and later renamed *emotion-focused therapy* (Greenberg & Paivio, 1997; Greenberg, 2002). A number of years prior to this, Les Greenberg, in collaboration with Sue Johnson, published a book on couples therapy describing their approach as *emotionally focused couple therapy* (Greenberg & Johnson, 1988). In his later work, however, he used the term *emotion-focused couples therapy* (Greenberg & Goldman, 2008) when referring to the couples version of this therapy.

Strongly influenced by the psychotherapy process research tradition, EFT developed out of a research-based investigation of therapeutic change processes (see for instance the early studies in Rice & Greenberg, 1984), with a particular focus on the role of emotion (Greenberg & Safran, 1987) in psychotherapy. This program of research illustrated how a combination of experiential tasks in therapy, occurring within a facilitative relationship characterized by Rogerian (1957, 1959) relational conditions, led to different types of change and change processes. Awareness of this specificity allowed for the development of EFT as a marker-based and task-oriented form of psychotherapy, in which therapists facilitate clients' attempts to resolve emotional difficulties by addressing identifiable markers with specific tasks. EFT is also distinctive for its focus on the adaptive role of emotion in human functioning and the way in which it deals with chronic painful emotions by accessing the underlying emotion schemes which produced them, and transforming them with healthy adaptive emotions (Greenberg, 2015; 2016).

EFT has been empirically demonstrated to be an effective psychological therapy for individuals with depression and complex trauma (see summaries in Elliott, Greenberg, Watson, Timulak, & Freire, 2013) and distressed couples (see summaries in Wiebe & Johnson, 2016) in several randomized controlled trials (RCTs).

EFT has also generated a large number of process studies (cf. Angus, Watson, Elliott, Schneider, & Timulak, 2015; Elliott *et al.*, 2013; Wiebe & Johnson, 2016). Further developments in EFT have taken place in the area of social anxiety (Elliott, 2013; Shahar, 2014), eating disorders (Dolhanty & Greenberg, 2009) and, as this book illustrates, in the area of generalized anxiety (see also the brand new book by Watson & Greenberg, 2017). A practitioners' approach to EFT is presented in *Learning Emotion-Focused Therapy* (Elliott, Watson, Goldman, & Greenberg, 2004). Several other books have presented various applications of this therapy to different populations, for example, depression (Greenberg & Watson, 2006) and complex trauma (Paivio & Pascual-Leone, 2010). A more "transdiagnostic" approach is presented in the original books (e.g., Greenberg *et al.*, 1993; Greenberg & Paivio, 1997) and in more recent updates (Greenberg, 2015). Our book is particularly informed by an approach outlined in Timulak (2015).

Box 3.1 Some of the key points about emotion-focused therapy.

- EFT is a research-informed humanistic-experiential therapy.
- EFT focuses on the transformation of chronic painful emotions by accessing underlying emotion schemes and transforming them with adaptive emotions.
- EFT values the therapeutic relationship, which it views as pivotal in bringing about lasting therapeutic change in clients.
- EFT is recognized as an empirically supported treatment for depression, complex trauma, and couple distress; with new developments in the areas of eating disorders and anxiety disorders.

Basic assumptions

Contrary to many traditional conceptualizations of emotion that regard it with suspicion, as a source of disruption, and as something to be controlled, EFT recognizes emotion as a central component in the formation of the self and a vital agent in the process of self-organization (Greenberg, 2011, 2015, 2016). Considered at the most fundamental level, emotion is construed as an evolutionarily adaptive source of information which allows the human organism to orient to, and engage successfully with, its environment (Greenberg, 2011, 2016; Greenberg & Safran, 1987). Emotions tell us whether our interaction with the environment is adaptive, promoting optimal and fulfilling living; they tell us whether our needs are being met (cf. Greenberg, 2011, 2015; Timulak, 2015). From an EFT perspective, people are seen as synthesizing experience from several levels of processing, including sensorimotor, emotion schematic, and conceptual processing (Greenberg, 2011, p. 32). People are seen as "dynamic self-organizing systems in constant interaction with the environment" and "affect regulation is seen as a core aspect of motivation" (Greenberg, 2011, p. 35).

Emotion schemes and self-organizations

An important concept in EFT is that of emotion schemes, which are seen as "the base of [our] emotional response system" (Greenberg, 2011, p. 38). Greenberg (2011, p. 38) describes them as "[...] internal emotion memory structures that synthesise affective, motivational, cognitive and behavioural elements into internal organisations that are activated rapidly, out of awareness, by relevant cues." Significantly, according to Greenberg, these emotionally motivated processes occur out of awareness (being only indirectly accessible through the experiences they generate) and impact upon subsequent conscious processing. Thus, despite its essentially flexible and adaptive nature, this form of emotional schematic learning-informed functioning opens the possibility of generating maladaptive emotional responses. For example, whilst one might experience an adaptive protective anger in the face of a boundary violation, one may also experience maladaptive fear or shame when criticized by a significant other (cf. Greenberg, 2011). Emotion schemes provide a scaffolding for processing and experiencing our interactions with the environment. They are the building blocks of our *self-organizations*, the way we understand how we are, and how we experience ourselves in our relationships and in the world (cf. Greenberg, 2011). These self-organizations give rise to a sense of self that is optimally characterized by a sense of coherence (cf. Greenberg, 2011). The self emerges as a synthesis of internal and external influences (Greenberg, 2011, p. 51). The self is fluid and in a continuous process of construction. A "self" composed of multiple self-organizations allows for experiencing current problematic experience as a temporary event involving part of the person's totality rather than the person's whole being (i.e., "part of me feels worthless" rather than "I am worthless"), which has implications for therapy (cf. Greenberg, 2011).

Types of emotions

Emotion-focused theory distinguishes various facets of emotional experiencing. For instance, it recognizes a variety of emotional experiences such as primary (adaptive and maladaptive), secondary, and instrumental emotions (Greenberg & Safran, 1987; see also Box 3.3). *Primary adaptive emotions* are the very first reactions we feel in response to a situation, in a clear and appropriate manner. It is natural, for example, that one might experience sadness in the face of loss. These uncomplicated responses enable us to react appropriately to given situations, are evolutionarily adaptive and feel "fit for purpose". For example, a primary adaptive emotional response such as assertive anger is a core response to a situation, and provides not only adaptive information but activates an action tendency which might, in this instance, be a defence of a threatened boundary (i.e., *I won't let you speak to me that way*). Therapeutically it is important to work with primary adaptive emotions because they represent the individual's initial and immediate response to a given situation and contain adaptive information.

Primary maladaptive emotions are direct responses to situations, but they do not help the individual cope with current circumstances and frequently interfere with functioning (Greenberg, 2011; Greenberg & Safran, 1987). They are based on emotion schemes, formed in past traumatic experiences of neglect, abuse, or humiliation, et cetera. While they might originally have been adaptive, for example, learning to fear emotional warmth as it might, in the past, have been followed by abuse or humiliation; continuing to respond this way to warmth in adult life may become harmful or self-defeating. Greenberg (2011) describes them as old, familiar feelings that we experience repeatedly and have a sense of being stuck in. They usually point to a chronic sense of sadness/loneliness, shame, and/or fear (cf. Greenberg, 2011, 2015; Timulak, 2015). Whereas primary adaptive emotions are accessed in therapy and utilized for their adaptive information, and for the action tendencies contained in them, primary maladaptive emotions require accessing in order that they be regulated and transformed (Greenberg, 2011).

Secondary emotions are generally responses to primary, internal, emotional, or cognitive processes (Greenberg, 2011; Greenberg & Safran, 1987). From an emotional perspective, a female client might experience a strong primary adaptive emotion, such as anger, for being disrespected. However, for any number of reasons (perhaps a sense that anger is somehow unacceptable in a woman), she may become hopeless instead and thus the secondary reactive emotion comes to the fore. Secondary emotions are normally acknowledged in therapy, but the therapist shifts his or her focus from them to the underlying primary emotions.

Instrumental emotions generally occur when an individual's emotional response to a situation is intended to influence or in some other way exert control over others (Greenberg & Safran, 1987; Greenberg, 2011). They may be consciously, or out of awareness, intended to either control the behavior of others or to present oneself in a certain light. For example, one may express anger to dominate others or alternatively, sadness to gain their sympathy; consequently, these emotions are sometimes referred to as "manipulative or racket feelings" (Greenberg, 2011, p. 44). These emotions are often considered to be "shown" or displayed, rather than truly experienced or felt. In therapy, the focus is on what needs they fulfil for the client and what primary emotions around them are at play.

Box 3.2 Types of emotions in emotion-focused theory (cf. Greenberg & Safran, 1987; Greenberg, 2011).

Primary adaptive emotions

Primary adaptive emotions are the very first reactions we feel in response to a situation in a manner that is clear, appropriate, informative, bearable, and informs adaptive action.

Primary maladaptive emotions

Primary maladaptive emotions are direct responses to situations involving emotion schemes formed in past traumatic experiences that are difficult to bear and do not inform adaptive action.

Secondary emotions

Secondary emotions are generally responses to primary, internal processes (emotions, thoughts).

Instrumental emotions

Instrumental emotions are emotional responses intended to influence or control others.

Emotional arousal and emotional productivity

Another two concepts in EFT theory, *emotional arousal* and *emotional productivity*, are important for understanding EFT emotion-processing theory. From an EFT perspective, not all emotional processes are equal, or indeed useful. To facilitate effective emotional processing, an optimal level of productive emotional experiencing and arousal is required. Warwar and Greenberg (1999) developed the Client Emotional Arousal Scale (CEAS; see Box 3.3) that can be used to assess the in-session level of arousal for research purposes. If the client is either over- or under-regulated in terms of emotional arousal, it will be difficult for them to fully engage with their experience. The over-regulated client may tend to intellectualize their experience, while the under-regulated client may repeatedly collapse into maladaptive secondary emotion when distressed.

For a client's emotion to be productive in terms of therapeutic work, (a) it must be activated in the session, (b) it must be a primary emotion, and (c) the client must be contact-fully aware of it (Auszra & Greenberg, 2007; Greenberg, Auszra, & Herman, 2007). Contact-fully aware means that the client is attending to the emotion, symbolizes it in awareness, there is a congruence between verbal and non-verbal aspects of the experience, the client is not emotionally overwhelmed and is accepting of emotion, the client owns the emotion and is able to differentiate his or her own experiencing of it and subsequent experiences (cf. Auszra & Greenberg, 2007). Greenberg and colleagues (Greenberg, Auszra, & Herrmann, 2007) developed the Emotional Productivity Scale, the main tenets of which are in an abbreviated form presented in Box 3.4.

Box 3.3 An abbreviated description of Client Emotional Arousal Scale-III (Warwar & Greenberg, 1999).

This is a 7-level scale beginning at level 1, in which voice or gestures do not disclose any arousal. The mid-point (level 4) is characterized by moderate arousal in voice and body (e.g., ordinary speech patterns are disrupted, there is freedom from control and restraints, but somewhat restricted). Level 7 is characterized by extremely intense arousal in voice and body (e.g., usual speech patterns are completely disrupted; expression is completely spontaneous and unrestricted).

Box 3.4 A brief description of Productivity Scale (Auszra & Greenberg, 2007; Greenberg, Auszra, & Herman, 2007).

This is a scale that distinguishes productive and unproductive emotions. Emotions are scored as productive when they are experienced in the present, are primary and (a) are primary adaptive or (b) are primary maladaptive, but the client does not have a stance of a victim, is not blocking them and is not overwhelmed by them.

EFT theory of dysfunction: Origin and maintenance of problems

In EFT, psychological problems were originally viewed as a result of several factors, principally lack of awareness of the richness of emotional experiencing and chronic problematic emotion schemes (cf. Greenberg et al., 1993). Later EFT literature also recognized problems in emotion regulation and problems in narrative construction and meaning-making (Greenberg, 2011; Greenberg & Watson, 2006). These processing difficulties often originate early in the individual's developmental history and may derive from circumstances where the level of available support offered to an individual has failed to meet their emotional or practical needs; or the individual encountered traumatic emotional experiences (occasionally later in life) that impacted upon their ability to develop patterns of healthy interaction with their environment.

Lack of emotional awareness occurs when the individual's conceptual processing cannot integrate the totality of information contained in their emotional processing. Lack of emotional awareness refers to the inability to symbolize bodily-felt experience in awareness (Greenberg, 2011; Greenberg et al., 1993; Greenberg & Watson, 2006). In this state, the individual is cut off from emotions. Thus, deprived of valuable, adaptive emotional information, the individual is unable to identify needs and have them met, or to activate appropriate action tendencies. This can result in difficulties in interpersonal functioning and a diminished sense of mastery over their environment. For example, someone who is unaware, or cannot accept that they feel anger, cannot activate assertive/protective anger to set appropriate boundaries and consequently, may become confused and upset over repeated intrusions or violations perpetrated upon them by others in their environment. In GAD difficulties, for example, worry may be experienced as a dysfunctional attempt to protect the individual from primary emotions such as sadness/loneliness, shame or fear/terror that are not fully in awareness.

At times, clients are able to attend to their emotions, however, their self-organizations may center around problematic *maladaptive emotion schemes*. Maladaptive emotion schemes form in a variety of ways, but are most frequently the result of historical interpersonal situations that produce strong primary emotional reactions to particular circumstances or sets of circumstances (cf. Greenberg, 2011). If important needs were continually unmet during development it is likely that the individual would develop several core, maladaptive emotion schemes. When activated, these emotion schemes may lead to experiences (self-organizations) dominated by core chronic painful maladaptive feelings, such as shame or loneliness, that may be experienced as defining the person at that moment.

Problems in emotion regulation reflect the notion that many difficulties in human functioning are, put simply, the result of having too much or too little emotion (cf. Greenberg, 2011). It is frequently the regulating process governing emotion (in terms of, say, duration or intensity) that is the source of difficulty rather than the specific emotion itself. Greenberg recognizes that capacity for emotion regulation is influenced by the quality of early attachment relationships and caregivers' capacity to help the child to symbolize emotion and corresponding needs, and sooth upsetting experiences by offering a relational presence. Many psychological problems that manifest themselves in the therapist's office can be seen as failed attempts at emotion regulation (e.g., substance abuse, problematic eating, chronic anxiety, etc., cf. Greenberg, 2011). Appropriate emotion regulation is an important part of a healthy emotional processing. Finally (cf. Greenberg, 2011, 2015; Greenberg & Watson, 2006), a person's healthy psychological functioning is also affected by the capability of *coherent meaning making* of the totality of their experiences in the world.

Theory of change

Therapeutic change in EFT is achieved via two basic processes. Firstly, the client's awareness of the richness of information contained in their emotional schematic processing is increased and made available for use at a conceptual level, and secondly, problematic emotional schemes are reworked or transformed. Additionally, Greenberg (2004, 2006, 2011, 2015) differentiates several other principles of change: increased emotion awareness, experience and expression of emotions, emotion regulation, constructive reflecting on emotion, emotion transformation, and corrective emotional experience. The vehicle of change in the change process is the therapeutic relationship, which either facilitates optimal client intrapersonal emotional processes or directly contributes interpersonally to new transformative experiences (cf. Greenberg & Elliott, 2012).

Emotion transformation is, in particular, one of the concepts most central to EFT in so far as it introduces the novel concept of transforming one emotion into another. This process refers to the transformation of primary maladaptive emotions such as fear or shame into more adaptive emotions (Greenberg, 2002, 2004, 2006, 2011, 2015, 2016). Rather than attempting to reason with emotion, or think one's way out of distress, EFT proposes that clients access maladaptive emotions, not as a source of adaptive information or action tendencies, as would be the case in primary adaptive emotion, but to transform and balance them with a more adaptive alternative. Maladaptive emotions are open to transformation by the introduction of dialectically opposite adaptive emotions (i.e., maladaptive shame can be transformed by accessing adaptive pride).

More recently the process of change (emotion transformation), as conceptualized by EFT, was enriched by studying productive sequences of emotional experiencing in a particular session in therapy (cf. Pascual-Leone & Greenberg, 2007; Pascual-Leone, 2009), or in the course of the whole therapy (Dillon, Timulak, & Greenberg, 2016; McNally, Timulak, & Greenberg, 2015). In an analysis of how emotional transformation occurs in therapy, Pascual-Leone and Greenberg (2007) developed a sequential model of the optimal therapeutic processing of core emotional pain, through the task analysis of observable, moment-to-moment steps in emotional processing as they occurred in therapy. The emotional processing model, which emerged from this analysis, suggested that clients in good therapy sessions moved from an initial position of undifferentiated *global distress* and secondary emotions to maladaptive primary emotions such as *fear* or *shame*. The model then proposed that by the identification and expression of previously unmet *needs* that were juxtaposed to *negative self-evaluations*, the client may then, through a process of accessing adaptive *grieving*, *assertive anger* and a hitherto unavailable capacity for *self-soothing*, achieve a position of *acceptance and agency* (Pascual-Leone & Greenberg, 2007). The authors also presented an alternative pathway in which the client progressed from global distress through a more reactive, less differentiated *rejecting anger* to higher stages of processing, bypassing core vulnerability in the fear/shame stage. Pascual-Leone (2009) later showed that the progression across the stages of sequential emotional processing is complicated by setbacks, but that in successful sessions collapses were shortened, and the experienced span of more advanced stages broadened.

The studies spearheaded by Antonio Pascual-Leone then served as a basis for a therapeutic model and strategies which were formulated in the first author's previous book (Timulak, 2015). The model (cf. also Timulak, 2017) articulates an emotional change sequence that starts with (1) problematic, secondary, global undifferentiated distress (e.g., *I feel hopeless, helpless, down, distressed*, etc.) and emotional (e.g., *I cannot stay with the pain*) and behavioral avoidance (e.g., *I want to avoid situations that may cause the pain*); followed by (2) the accessing of core painful (maladaptive) feelings, emotions schemes (e.g., *I feel alone, worthless, scared*), which are triggered by the client's interaction with the environment (e.g., rejection by others) and problematic self-treatment (e.g., *The problem must be in me*); and (3) the identification of unmet needs (e.g., *I want to feel loved, secure, and accepted*); that are responded to in therapy by (4) experiences of adaptive emotions such as compassion (e.g., *I am loved*) and healthy protective anger (e.g., *I deserve to be accepted*), which is typically followed by grieving (e.g., *it is sad that I had to experience that pain*) but also a sense of empowerment (e.g., *I am proud of myself*).

The theory of human functioning, psychological dysfunction and human transformation is excellently described in revisions of Les Greenberg's landmark books on emotion-focused therapy (Greenberg, 2015, 2016). EFT theory is distinct from other psychological and psychotherapeutic theories of human functioning and suffering, and other theories postulating healing processes. The focus is on emotional vulnerabilities, which signal that the basic needs for human safety, love, and recognition are not currently being met in the person's interaction with their primarily (interpersonal) environment. We will elaborate on this theory from our perspective, and in the context of GAD difficulties, in the next chapter (Chapter 4).

Theory of therapeutic work in emotion-focused therapy

The fundamental basis of emotion-focused therapy is the provision of an authentic caring relationship by the therapist. The therapist provides a relationship that is characterized by the therapist's non-judgmental and empathic, authentic presence (cf. Rogers, 1961). The therapist's default in-session behavior is empathic responding. Empathic presence in EFT is, however, somewhat broader than in person-centered therapy as the therapist not only wants to encourage exploration of the client's experiencing and communicate understanding of it, but also wants to help the client to access core painful feelings (primary maladaptive feelings), evoke them, and differentiate various felt and symbolized aspects of them. To achieve this, the therapist uses a variety of empathic responses (cf. Elliott *et al.*, 2004; see Box 3.5).

Box 3.5 Varieties of empathic responding (based on Elliott *et al.*, 2004, p. 81–88).

Empathic understanding responses

Empathic reflections – communicate therapist understanding of the client's message, thereby communicating that the therapist "gets" the client.

Following responses – demonstrate the therapist is tracking and understanding the client's narrative (e.g., uh-huh, yeah), which propel the conversation along.

Empathic affirmations – are supportive statements used by the therapist to validate the client in particular moments of distress, acknowledging the depth of the client's suffering.

Empathic exploration responses

Exploratory reflections – facilitate client experiential self-exploration, and commonly appear as tentative, hesitant formulations, designed to assist clients in exploring unclear aspects of the narrative or focusing on a desire for personal growth.

Evocative reflections – communicate empathy while simultaneously heightening emotional experiencing using evocative language and imagery.

Exploratory questions – are open-ended questions, used to facilitate deepening of client experiencing.

Fit questions – are used to check the accuracy of the therapist's conjectured account of the client's experiencing with the client.

Process observations – draw the client's attention to verbal and non-verbal indicators of emotion in session, to heighten awareness of experiencing, and are generally followed by an exploratory question.

Empathic conjectures – tentatively attempt to capture unexpressed aspects of client experiencing, and gently offer them to the client (often as fit questions).

Empathic refocusing – helps to redirect the client's attention back to painful experience, which may be difficult to stay with; the avoidance of which, however, may interfere with effective processing.

The therapist thus provides a soothing presence, characterized by gentleness, and warmth, but also unfolds the painful aspects of the client's experiencing, the layers of, often chronic, vulnerability. This not only helps to unfold the painful experiences, but also helps to regulate them through the therapist's presence (cf. Watson, 2002; Watson, Goldman, & Vanaerschot, 1998). The therapist's caring and validating presence, during moments of increased vulnerability, as the most painful aspects of experience are accessed, also provides an interpersonal, corrective emotional experience (cf. Greenberg & Elliott, 2012). We will present our take on the relational, empathic, caring, and validating presence of the therapist in Chapter 5.

Another pillar of the work in EFT is the therapist's case conceptualization. Although initially in line with the humanistic tradition, which is skeptical of the "expert" role of the therapist and prefers a fresh encounter with the client's evolving experiencing (Rogers, 1951), EFT theorists have been reluctant to formulate their therapeutic strategy explicitly. However, over the years there have been several contributions to case conceptualization by EFT writers (Goldman & Greenberg, 2015; Greenberg & Goldman, 2007; Timulak & Pascual-Leone, 2015; Watson, 2010). The EFT case conceptualization framework scaffolds the therapist's perspective on his or her interaction with the client at any given moment of therapy. Phenomenological features, such as client identity and attachment related presenting issues, client's emotional processing style (i.e., emotional arousal [see Box 3.3], emotional productivity [see Box 3.4], the depth of experiencing and client vocal quality [see Boxes 3.6 and 3.7]), underlying painful emotions, central emotion schemes, et cetera, are focused on the therapist's conceptualization. The therapist is also focused on microprocesses such as the client's process in therapy tasks (see below). The therapist thus empathically follows the client's unfolding painful experiencing (pain compass; Greenberg & Goldman, 2007) and conceptualizes a strategy to transform chronic painful experiences. We will present our detailed thinking in this area in the context of GAD difficulties in Chapter 6.

Box 3.6 An abbreviated description of the Experiencing Scale (Klein, Mathieu, Gendlin, & Kiesler, 1969).

This is an observer-based 7-level rating scale, assessing the content and treatment of what is being disclosed. Level 1 is impersonal and the client here refers to external events, while at the mid-point the client discloses feelings and is self-descriptive. The highest level is expansive with easy presentation.

Box 3.7 A brief description of Client Vocal Quality Scale (Rice, Koke, Greenberg, & Wagstaff, 1979).

This is a nominal observer-based rating scale that distinguishes four vocal qualities in the client's in-session expression: externalizing, limited, emotional, and focused. Each of the qualities is defined independent of the content communicated.

Another important pillar of EFT is the use of therapeutic tasks, prompted by particular markers. Indeed, EFT originally developed as an approach focused on responding to in-session markers, with the application of specifically developed experiential tasks to achieve therapeutic aims (Greenberg, Rice, & Elliott, 1993). Markers represent specific clients' in-session presentations characterized by a problematic processing. Typical markers that EFT recognizes are unfinished business, that is, lingering emotional injury(ies) in relation to a significant other, self-criticism (problematic self-treatment), unclear felt sense, puzzling emotional reaction, interrupted (blocked) emotional experiencing, intense emotional vulnerability, et cetera. The varied markers are then an opportunity to employ particular therapeutic tasks (specific therapeutic processes such as imaginary dialogues using chairs) that lead to optimal emotional processing of the difficulty and/or transformation of maladaptive emotional experience with a more adaptive experience. The experiential tasks include (see Elliott *et al.*, 2004; see Box 3.8 for a short description): *systematic evocative unfolding* for the marker of puzzling emotional reaction; *clearing a space* for the marker of being emotionally overwhelmed; *experiential focusing* for the marker of unclear felt sense; *two-chair dialogue* for the marker of self-criticism; *two-chair enactment dialogue* for the marker of self-interruption; *empty chair dialogue* for the marker of unfinished business (emotional injury), et cetera. Many of these tasks were developed through a programmatic process research that is a landmark of emotion-focused therapy (see for instance, Rice & Greenberg, 1984).

Each task represents a specific therapeutic microstrategy, informed by micromarkers, which are specific in-task presentations. These inform the therapist's guidance of the client towards enacting certain aspects of their experience and feeling the responses they bring, so that more adaptive responses might be eventually generated. An excellent example of micromarkers for various tasks involving chair dialogues is presented in Goldman and Greenberg (2015, p. 120–122). The therapist's interventions in the tasks represent a mixture of empathic responses together with process guidance. More than 50% of therapy time in short-term (16 to 20 sessions) is spent in those tasks, with some tasks, mainly the ones focused on emotion transformation, such as imagined self–self or self–other chair dialogues, being dominant.

Several EFT books have described major therapeutic tasks (Greenberg *et al.*, 1993; Elliott *et al.*, 2004). The most comprehensive detail can be found in Elliott and colleagues' (2004) book devoted to training EFT therapists, which explicitly conceptualizes EFT from the perspective of markers and tasks. In total, 13 distinct tasks are described in the text. Each is present in the form of a model (consisting of six steps) that the therapist holds as a conceptual map. Some of those tasks refer to general therapeutic processes such as empathic exploration or alliance formation, whereas others are more specific experiential enactments such as imaginary dialogues in chairs (e.g., two-chair dialogue). Box 3.8 provides a short outline of the tasks described in Elliott *et al.* (2004).

Chapters 7 and 8 will present a detailed account of the experiential tasks we recommend using when working with clients with GAD difficulties. These tasks supplement the empathic exploration and processing of painful experience offered by the therapist's relational caring, validating presence, and use of skillful interventions which facilitate emotional processing. These tasks include the worry dialogue for problematic worrying, self-interruption dialogue for interrupting of internal emotional experience, clearing a space for being emotionally overwhelmed, systematic evocative unfolding for puzzling emotional reaction, self–self dialogue for problematic self-treatment and self–other (empty chair) dialogue for emotional injury (unfinished business) involving a significant other. We also use aspects of self-soothing dialogue (cf. Greenberg, 2015) that are typically integrated in the other, particularly transformative tasks such as self–self and self–other dialogues. In Chapter 7 and 8, we present adapted models of working within the tasks drawing on our conceptualization, which is presented in Chapters 4 and 6.

Box 3.8   A brief description of emotion-focused therapeutic tasks based on the models presented in Elliott et *al.*'s (2004) book focused on learning EFT.

Empathic exploration

In this task, which continues throughout therapy, the client's problem-relevant emotional experience is unfolded by the therapist using a variety of empathic responses (focus on internal experiencing, searching edges, elaborating, re-experiencing, differentiating). While the therapist empathically attends to all the client's experiencing, the focus is on the client's most salient, painful experience and the eliciting of primary emotions. The task focuses also on eliciting other potential markers for therapeutic work or differentiating the experiencing, and gaining a broader awareness, understanding, and owning of the experience.

Empathic affirmation

Here, the therapist responds to the client's vulnerability, expressed by painful self-related feeling (shame, fragility, etc.), by compassionate non-intrusive responding and affirmation, which allows the client to stay with and further explore their painful experience without interruption. The therapist ultimately trusts that the client's growth potential will respond to empathic validation. The client experiences hope, relief, and connection to the therapist and may become more self-accepting.

Alliance formation

Central to the early stages of therapy, focus on the working alliance in therapy ensures the provision of a therapeutic relationship, which is healing, but also creates the level of trust between client and therapist necessary for frequently painful, emotionally focused self-exploration. Together, collaboratively, client and therapist establish a focus for therapy, and then agree on goals and the ways in which they will work together. Optimally, this leads to the development of a trusting and collaborative relationship.

Alliance dialogue

In response to alliance difficulties, the therapist may initiate a relationship dialogue aimed at repairing the rupture, which may show in the client's confrontation or withdrawal. A dialectical exploration of the difficulty is conducted in a genuine and open manner, allowing for meaningful exploration of practical solutions based on a shared understanding of the situation. Optimally, the client's concerns are acknowledged and seen as a resource for understanding the client's experience of therapy, and experiencing in general.

Clearing a space (for attentional focus difficulties)

This task is used to assist clients who struggle with establishing and maintaining in-session therapeutic focus; particularly clients that are overwhelmed. The client is invited to turn to a bodily felt-sense of his/her concerns and these are then put aside in imagination. The process is repeated until the client is relieved and has a sense of being freer. This allows clients to achieve a productive relationship with difficult experiences, which might otherwise be obscured or overwhelming.

Experiential focusing

Focusing is used when clients present with unclear feelings, which are troubling, but are vague or poorly symbolized. The client is invited to focus inwards. Clients are encouraged to attend to the unclear feeling in its entirety and to symbolize aspects of it in language or images. The process is repeated until there is a felt shift and greater clarity is experienced.

Allowing and expressing emotion

This is a more general task, which informs the therapist's interventions, when clients have trouble expressing feelings. This may be due to blocked awareness of emotional responses, or limited awareness of emotional experience, limited knowledge or experience of emotion, negative attitudes towards emotion, and problems with disclosure of emotion to others. Each of the difficulties requires patient exploration of blocks and facilitation of emotional experience and its expression on the part of the therapist as client fears around emotion require sensitive treatment before productive work can take place.

Trauma retelling

Commonly used in treating post-traumatic stress issues, this can be used when working with intense emotional reactions when the client experiences a need to relate to a difficult life experience. The process facilitated by the therapist's empathic attunement allows the client to "dwell" in the trauma, that is, re-experience key elements of trauma from the relative safety of therapy, so that alternative views of trauma may be generated and new elements of the story may be integrated.

Meaning creation work

This refers to a task, which is indicated when a client's "cherished belief" is threatened by a life event – leading them to present as upset and confused. When the belief is challenged, a *meaning protest* occurs, commonly in situations of loss, bereavement, trauma, or chronic illness. Clients first specify the challenged belief and then are encouraged to explore the tenability of the cherished belief and emotional reactions to the life event (especially considering their new situation), and are facilitated in revising the belief.

Systematic evocative unfolding

This task is used when clients are confused or perplexed by a strong, idiosyncratic, emotional response to a particular situation. The client is guided to recall in a slow-process, experiential mode, the situation that puzzled him or her. Aspects of the situation and emotional responses to them are explored, in order to get a sense of what it was within that situation that sparked an unexpected or problematic reaction. This leads to experientially making a connection between a specific aspect of the situation and the client's emotional and behavioral response to it, allowing for the emergence of a meaning bridge that links an aspect of the situation to the emotional reaction and a broader self-functioning.

Two-chair dialogue (for self-evaluation conflict splits)

This is generally prompted by the therapist's identification of a self-evaluative split, that is, a marker in which the client criticizes, attacks, puts down, denigrates, et cetera, him or herself. In the task, the client enacts problematic self-treatments such as self-criticism, accessing core painful feelings, articulates the needs embedded in those feelings and is facilitated towards softening towards own pain or standing up for the self in the face of self-mistreatment.

Two-chair enactment (for self-interruption splits)

This task is implemented when a self-interruption split is identified by the therapist. This can occur on its own or may be contained within another task. Often clients find themselves blocked when it comes to expressing strong emotion to another, in empty-chair work, which may be attributable to guilt, shame, or internalized principles which guide expression of emotions. In this task, the client enacts the interrupter, becomes aware of his/her own role in the self-interruption, experiences the cost of the interruption (e.g., resignation), and ultimately is facilitated by the therapist to access and express the hitherto avoided unexpressed emotion.

Empty chair work

Empty chair work is prompted by the marker of unfinished business; a lingering, unresolved emotional hurt (injury) related to an emotionally significant other. The signs of restriction in the experience are also present. The original injury stems particularly from rejection, criticism, neglect or abandonment, and abuse or trauma. The client is invited to express their hurt to the identified other in imaginary dialogue. The client is facilitated in accessing the primary emotions, which have been obscured. The client is also facilitated to express their unmet needs. In the resolution stage, clients can let go of their unresolved feelings, either through forgiveness, or by assertively attributing appropriate responsibility for past injury to the other. The perception of other may also change.

Conclusion

Emotion-focused therapy (EFT) is an empirically supported, humanistic-experiential treatment which has evolved gradually, over time, through a systematic program of psychotherapy research, and has been demonstrated to be an effective psychological therapy for individuals with depression and complex trauma, as well as distressed couples. EFT has been more recently investigated as a treatment of social anxiety, eating disorders, and, in this book, generalized anxiety. EFT focuses on the transformation of chronic painful emotion by accessing underlying emotion schemes and transforming them with adaptive emotions. EFT recognizes a variety of emotional experiences such as primary (adaptive and maladaptive), secondary, and instrumental emotions. In EFT, psychological problems are attributed to several factors, such as lack of awareness of the richness of emotional experiencing, as well as chronic problematic emotion schemes. Therapeutic change in EFT is achieved via the client's awareness of the richness of information contained in their emotional processing and through transformation of problematic emotion schemes. Emotion transformation is central to EFT in so far as it introduces the novel concept of transforming one emotion with another. This process refers to the transformation of primary maladaptive emotions, such as fear or shame, with more adaptive emotions. To achieve this, EFT uses therapeutic tasks, prompted by particular markers, to achieve therapeutic aims.

Chapter 4

Emotion-focused conceptualization of GAD – transformation model

In Chapter 2, we outlined the most established, current psychological models (predominantly cognitive behavioral) conceptualizing GAD. Some of these models see worry (the defining feature of GAD) as an unproductive avoidance mechanism that prevents adaptive functioning, and some of them see it as an unproductive form of problem solving. In any case, it is recognized that despite efforts to use worry to alleviate distress or prepare for threat, a certain level of anxiety remains (cf. Newman & Llera, 2011). There is a recognition that worry is intended to stifle difficult emotions (e.g., Borkovec *et al.*, 2004; Mennin, 2004; Newman & Llera, 2011) and thus, represents an attempt to lower potential emotional discomfort. In the long-term, worry prevents more effective coping and frustrates the development of skills, or engaging in fulfilling activities (e.g., Roemer and Orsillo, 2014). Some models (Borkovec *et al.*, 2004; Crits-Christoph *et al.*, 2004; Newman & Llera, 2011) also emphasize a common interpersonal dimension to the situations that clients with GAD worry about.

Our understanding of GAD, presented in this chapter, was primarily shaped by clinical experience derived from our treatment-development project of EFT for GAD (Timulak *et al.*, 2017). It was also informed by a thorough analysis of the presentations of clients with GAD in our initial project (cf. O'Brien *et al.*, 2017). The interpretative framework we brought to analyzing the clients' presentations was embedded in EFT theory (cf. Greenberg, 2011). We also considered theoretical developments in EFT for anxiety disorders in general (Elliott, 2013) or for other specific anxiety disorders, such as social anxiety (Shahar, 2014). However, our awareness of other psychological models (mainly CBT), meant we were constantly comparing our conceptualization to theirs. Another influence on our thinking came from general research on the nature of the problems currently clustered under the GAD diagnosis (again see the overview in Chapter 2).

Our conceptualization of GAD was further informed by a generic EFT case conceptualization framework that was recently developed by our lab (cf. Timulak & Pascual-Leone, 2015), which was, in turn, inspired by original work on transformative emotional-sequences by Pascual-Leone and Greenberg (2007), then further developed by Pascual-Leone and colleagues (Berthoud, Kramer, Caspar, & Pascual-Leone, 2015; Kramer, *et al.*, 2015; Kramer, Pascual-Leone, Despland,

& De Roten, 2014, 2015; Pascual-Leone, 2009). The model (see Figure 4.1) can be used as a basis for case conceptualization, which guides the therapist's overall treatment strategy (we will present the work with case conceptualization in Chapter 6). When we started to develop the model, we were unaware of other EFT conceptualizations (Watson & Greenberg, 2017). For the sake of clarity, we refer to our model as an emotion transformation model (of GAD). We presented the basics of it in the *Journal of Contemporary Psychotherapy* (Timulak & McElvaney, 2016), and what follows is an expanded version of that paper.

The model (see Figure 4.1) uses an EFT case conceptualization framework, first articulated by Timulak and Pascual-Leone (2015). Although GAD is sometimes characterized as a disorder that does not have distinct triggers of the clients' distress (i.e., the clients worry about non-existent, diffuse, potential, and not necessarily clear, threats), our research suggests that there are, in fact, clear, idiosyncratic (case specific) triggers of anxiety that can be traced back to emotion schemes developed in the client's personal history (O'Brien *et al.*, 2017). These potential *triggers* (situations or perceptions contained in them) are client specific, resembling or matching real threats that brought unbearable painful feelings in the past (*core feared painful feelings*) that the client was unable to process in an adaptive manner. Clients are apprehensive (*apprehensive anxiety*) of these triggers and are involved in various strategies to cope with them, often involving avoidance (see below).

Our research and clinical experience suggests that in the context of these triggers, clients attempt to manage their experience through various forms of non-adaptive *problematic self-treatment*. They can be, for instance, self-critical, self-judgmental, self-doubting, push themselves, or try to pre-empt problematic situations by over-preparing for them, or worrying about them. They may also try to manage their own experience through various forms of *emotional avoidance,* or attempt to avoid potential threats through *behavioral avoidance*. A common feature, however, is that the clients have difficulty in staying with chronic, feared emotions and, if at all possible, avoid primary maladaptive (Greenberg, 2011) feelings that they are unable to process (we refer to those feelings as *core [emotional] pain* or *core painful feelings* or *core feared painful feelings* in this book). Rather than being able to feel and process those chronically painful feelings, clients present with undifferentiated *global distress* (cf. Pascual-Leone & Greenberg, 2007; see also work from basic research on emotion differentiation – Kashdan, Barrett, & McKnight, 2015) characterized by what are traditionally recognized in EFT as secondary emotions (see Chapter 3). These feelings typically include hopelessness, helplessness, tiredness, anxiety, tension, et cetera. (see below).

The model that we are going to present in greater detail below does not address how GAD difficulties might have developed across the client's personal history. Rather, it characterizes the client's presentation as currently seen, with some reference to potential historical developments. We do not recognize the model as specific to current conceptualizations of GAD. As we stated in the previous chapter, we do not believe that the group of people currently meeting current

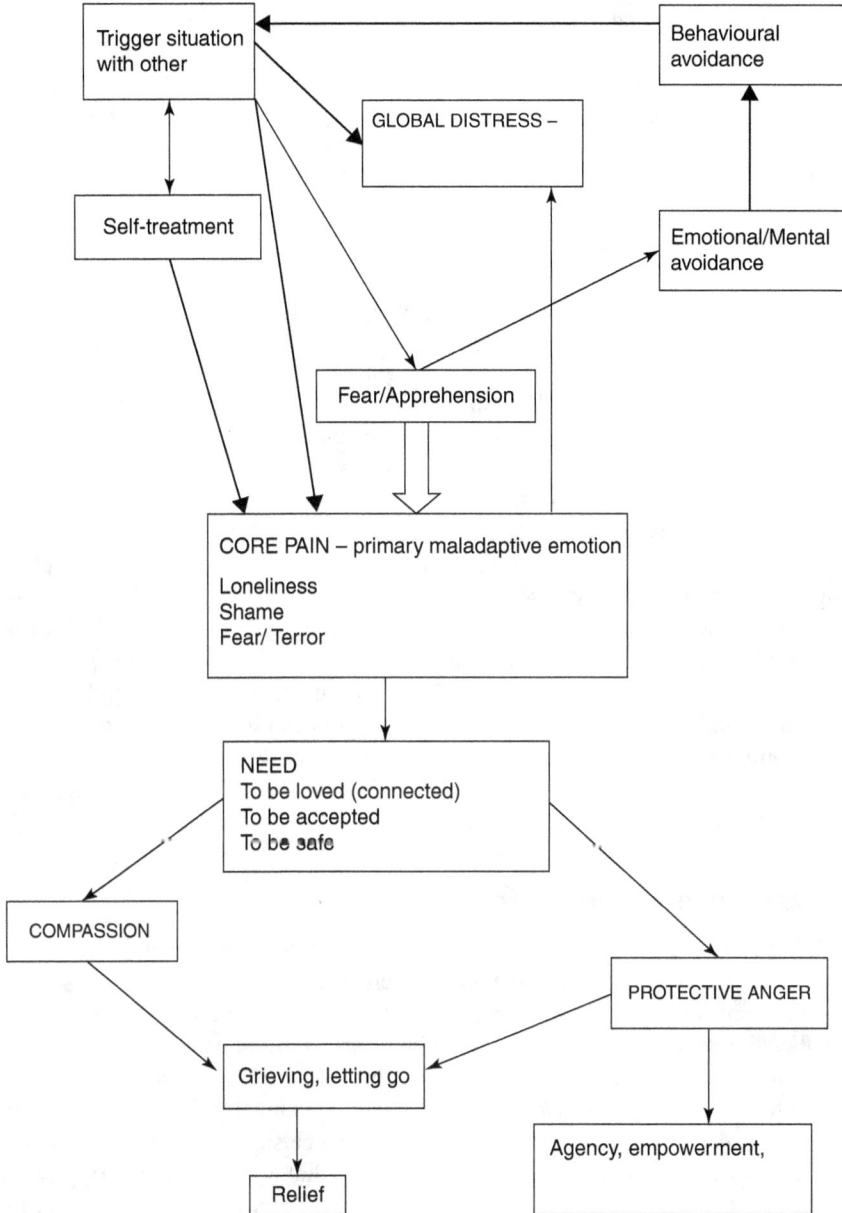

Figure 4.1 Case conceptualization framework of transformation model

Note. Based on emotion transformation model (adapted from Transforming Emotion Schemes in Emotion-Focused Therapy: A Case Study Investigation. McNally, S., Timulak, L., & Greenberg, L. S. *Person-Centered & Experiential Psychotherapies*, 13, 128–149. © 2014 reprinted by permission of the publisher Taylor & Francis, doi 10.1080/14779757.2013.871573).

diagnostic criteria for GAD is necessarily a homogenous group. On the contrary, we rather think that this is not the case. There are probably alternative, and more useful, ways of establishing a taxonomy of human distress than the current practice of clustering people with similar presentations together, and identifying them as GAD clients. The model is a generic framework, which can be applied idiosyncratically to a particular client presentation in the context of common psychological difficulties.

We also assume that there may well be different developmental pathways and etiological influences that evolve into the difficulties currently classified as GAD. In the brief introduction to GAD in the previous chapter we highlighted some of the potential factors, and the importance of their interplay. It may well be that for some people, particularly painful experiences of adversity or trauma brought unbearable feelings, which led to further avoidance of them or over-preparing for them through worrying or self-management. It could be that for others, a particular intolerance and generally upsetting emotionality causes them to focus on the avoidance of potential threats and the feelings they bring, leading to over-preparation for threat (Newman *et al.*, 2013; Stevens *et al.*, 2014). Additionally, there may be a mixture of both types of overwhelming experience (i.e., overwhelming triggers paired with hypersensitive and upsetting emotionality). Again, at this stage of knowledge and, given how the psychiatric/psychopathological classification of disorders developed, we cannot be sure whether the current grouping of presentations/symptoms in the GAD category is the most meaningful way of clustering and conceptualizing the distress experienced by this population. With these limitations in mind, we will now look at a more detailed description of the phenomenology of GAD using Timulak and Pascual-Leone's EFT conceptualization framework (2015; see also Timulak, 2015).

Triggers of emotional pain

GAD is commonly seen as a disorder defined by pervasive and generalized worrying about virtually everything (see previous chapter). However, we have observed (cf. O'Brien *et al.*, 2017) that there are identifiable, situational triggers, explained by the client's personal history, which clients are afraid of as they bring chronic difficult feelings that clients have not been able, and are still not able, to process. We refer to these triggers as *historical triggers* (cf. Timulak & McElvaney, 2016; see Figure 4.1). Our research and clinical experience suggests that these historical triggers are clearly linked to *current triggers*; that is, the situations (typically of an interpersonal/social nature) that clients may worry about, or may want to avoid. An example may be the experience of trauma such as sudden death (e.g., of a caregiver or other close person), particularly at a developmentally sensitive period (historical trigger) that is linked to current worry and the fearful expectation that a similar, sudden trauma/loss may happen (current trigger). This in turn leads to overprotection around any circumstances that may increase the likelihood of such a trauma occurring (e.g., overprotection around the client's own children).

Sometimes the historical trigger may be more diffuse. For instance, a worrying and anxious caregiver, communicating that there is an imminent threat, may impart that there is a threat (which may be named by the caregiver, e.g., social ridicule, sudden death, financial disaster, etc., perhaps even based on personal or relatives' history). In such a case the client may internalize the possibility of a threat ("potential" historical trigger) and be sensitive to similar threats currently (current trigger).

A study from our lab (O'Brien *et al.*, 2017) suggested that several types of adversity are present in clients' in-session retrospective presentations that appear to be linked to their current triggers. These include sudden death and a loss of a close one (typically caregiver), chronic lack of support by caregivers, neglect by caregivers, rejection or invalidation by significant others or peers, bullying, exposure to overanxious and vulnerable caregiver, witnessing physical trauma or death, early hospitalization, shame linked to the behavior of caregivers (such as alcoholism), unwanted early responsibility (teen pregnancy, loss of parent, and assumption of responsibility), experience of being targeted by physical violence by a caregiver or powerful other, experience of being a victim of sexual abuse, et cetera. Many of these experiences led to the experience of being intruded upon, overpowered, saddled with unwanted responsibility, feeling ashamed, alone, unprotected, et cetera. The feelings that form the basis of the chronic, unprocessed, and unbearable emotions that we (following Greenberg & Goldman, 2007) classify as core pain (see below).

These historical triggers appear to be logically linked to the current stressors described by clients with GAD in their therapy sessions (again, see O'Brien *et al.*, 2017). Current stressors of clients with GAD may include their experiences (and fear of experiences) of being criticized (by children, partner, employer, peers, colleagues, friends, etc.), invalidated, rejected, verbally or physically attacked, excluded, et cetera. They may be subtler, such as exposure to the behavior of a significant other that damages trust (e.g., betrayal). There appears to be an understanding that these current triggers are happening, and that they, or their past-trigger predecessors, may happen again. Some of the current/past triggers thus become *potential* triggers. The past and current painful triggers thus inform fearful perception of future *potential triggers*. The current/past triggers can become "potential" triggers, such as sudden traumas, for example, physical harm or death of a close one. Many clients with GAD are also afraid of failure (at work, in the care they provide, etc.) for which they would feel responsible and could be blamed.

Global distress

While the above-mentioned triggers appear to be perceived or potential threats to clients currently clustered under GAD criteria, what brings clients to therapy is a sense of unmanageable distress that is referred to in EFT as *global distress* (Pascual-Leone & Greenberg, 2007; see Figure 4.1). Global distress in clients with GAD difficulties resembles the global distress of other clients with mood and anxiety disorders. Obviously, a high level of anxiety is present (linked to apprehending the activation of feared triggers) with corresponding hyper-vigilance, tiredness, (muscular) tension, various body aches linked to tension or constriction (headache, stomach ache, chest pain), or sleeplessness (cf. O'Brien *et al.*, 2017). Many clients have other comorbid anxiety disorders and so panic attacks may be present as well, along with the various symptoms that go with them, such as blushing, breathlessness, chest pain, shaking or trembling, palpitations, nausea, feelings of choking, or suffocation and dizziness.

Global distress in clients with GAD difficulties also reflects symptoms found in clients with low mood. While the anxious response in global distress is typically expressed as fear of the painful triggers or the emotional pain (impact they may bring), in the low-mood response we rather see a sense of resignation, in that due to chronic, unbearable pain, clients feel that they will not have their needs met. The most prevalent characteristic is a feeling of hopelessness and helplessness, a fear that the distress and the underlying feared emotions will neither resolve, nor become more bearable. The hopelessness and helplessness appears as resignation, an undifferentiated emotional pain, or a profound unintelligible sadness that cannot be not linked to any specific trigger, as the link with the triggers has been buried in an undifferentiated distress accumulated over weeks, months, or even years. Specifically, in the case of GAD, exhaustion and tiredness can be present as the overall GAD dynamic focuses on a sense of continuous danger, requiring constant readiness that physiologically wears the person down over time (see other sections below). O'Brien *et al.* (2017) also observed that many clients evinced an overall loss of interest and motivation in engaging in once-cherished activities. Some clients reported tearfulness. Suicidal ideation may also be present. Indeed, the risk of suicide attempts in people with GAD difficulties is not uncommon (Sareen *et al.*, 2005; Weisberg, 2009).

While some clients present with profound sadness, others present with irritability and anger. EFT theory typically sees this type of anger as secondary or rejecting anger (Pascual-Leone & Greenberg, 2007), to distinguish it from a healthier, protective, or assertive anger (Timulak & Pascual-Leone, 2015) that would be seen as adaptive. Secondary anger and irritability are understood as defensive positions against the underlying vulnerability and hurt. For instance, a client may be unable to tolerate and bear feelings of shame and may lash out at any direct or indirect insinuation of being shamed, criticized, et cetera. Irritability and rejecting anger are often repeated without any resolution; a sense of being wronged remains, and thus they may have a ruminative quality (e.g., constant complaining). They often go hand in hand with low mood and depression. They do not lead to the sense of empowerment, inner confidence, and healthy personal strength, that are a sign of a healthy, boundary-setting, protective anger (see below and Chapter 8).

Interestingly for some clients with GAD, global distress may be subtler and, alongside the anxiety and low mood, one can detect a sense of flatness and indifference. This may be a sign of low mood, hopelessness, helplessness, and eventual resignation, but may also signify emotional avoidance (see below). A defining characteristic of global distress is its undifferentiatedness. Clients are anxious, stressed, tense, and unhappy, but may not know quite why. They may not be fully aware of what is most painful in their life or what they are most missing. The experience remains unarticulated and undifferentiated, because the underlying pain is simply too strong.

Problematic self-treatment

In our previous work (cf. Timulak, 2015; Timulak & Pascual-Leone, 2015) we pointed out that one of the strategies that people evoke when they encounter distressing triggers is management of self (self-treatment; see Figure 4.1). We observed it was likely that self-treatment strategies were developmentally important when the individual's autonomy was limited (i.e., in childhood). For instance, the child with an unresponsive caregiver may seek to elicit a better response by changing the self. Of course, the child first must attribute the caregiver's unresponsiveness to some characteristic of self in order to see changing the self as a solution. In adult life, self-treatment strategies may be learned strategies concerned with how to deal with distressing triggers, or potentially distressing triggers.

One of the central, self-treatment strategies that has potential value, but typically goes wrong in people with GAD difficulties, is *self-worry* (although some researchers, such as Borkovec *et al.* [2004], doubt whether worry has any adaptive function). Worry is a mental process by which the person engages cognitively (thinking can be complemented by images; however, thoughts dominate; Borkovec & Inz, 1990) with a potential situation that can bring undesirable consequences (and particular chronically feared emotions – see below). The cognitive process (thinking) can be intentional or automatic (or a mixture of both). It is driven by an anticipatory anxiety of the feared triggers and the emotional consequences they may bring. The aim of the worry may be to prepare for the undesirable consequence and corresponding emotions. Many clients with GAD difficulties see worry as serving a protective function in so far as it keeps them vigilant, apprehensive, and ready to face the feared situation (see Borkovec *et al.*, 2004; O'Brien *et al.*, 2017; Wells, 2004). An unwanted consequence of constant worry however, is tiredness. Clients either do not know how, or do not want, to switch off the worry and consequently, experience constant anxiety as engaging the potentially threatening situation in thoughts/images makes it more present and therefore also more real and frightening. Worry also contributes to avoidance, both behavioral (e.g., over-controlling behavior) and emotional (e.g., displaced anxiety).

Many CBT authors (e.g., Wells, 2005) pay attention to clients' beliefs about worry. While we share the observation that worry may be thought of by clients as a useful protection strategy, we do not see the focus on worrying about worrying (Wells's meta-worry) as especially relevant (although we observed this phenomenon in some clients) for treatment (see later parts of the book). We postulate that worry about worrying just becomes another one of the more superficial worries, similar to worries about other symptoms (e.g., some people worry about being depressed or are unaccepting of their distress in general), associated with GAD.

Like worrying, but less frequently mentioned in the context of GAD difficulties, other than to make the distinction, is another form of self-treatment, rumination. Ruminations are more commonly associated with depression, although they have been found to be present to an equal degree in people with GAD difficulties (Ruscio *et al.*, 2015). It is perhaps not surprising, as people with GAD difficulties share significant comorbidity with depression (some studies suggest robust similarities, speculating that it may refer to the same population; Curtiss & Klemanski, 2016). Our research (cf. O'Brien *et al.*, 2017) also observed rumination in clients with GAD difficulties.

Ruminations are sometimes difficult to distinguish from worries (see Chapter 2 for the discussion of this) as they may often be interspersed throughout worries. Ruminations, in contrast to worry, do not focus on the anticipated event, but are rather retrospective replays and/or perhaps re-analyses of difficult, emotional-distress-bringing situations. It appears that clients are attempting to master their distress by re-engaging with triggers and their emotional consequences, in the hope of getting some relief (Papageorgiou & Wells, 2004). There also appears to be a biological substrate corresponding to this activity (Hamilton, Farmer, Fogelman, & Gotlib, 2015). Unfortunately, relief seldom comes, as the triggers or the emotional impact they bring, remain upsetting. It may well be that ruminations follow a similar pattern to compulsion in obsessive-compulsive disorder (OCD; cf. also Veale & Roberts, 2014), where engaging in rumination may bring brief and subtle emotional relief that is not long-lasting (as the actual act of ruminating, by re-engaging with triggers and their emotional consequences, brings further upset and thus perpetuates the cycle).

The most typical self-treatment strategy is self-criticism or, in its adaptive form, self-coaching. Self-criticism, in its maladaptive forms, has been captured by theoreticians from various psychotherapeutic approaches (in psychodynamic psychotherapy, see Blatt, 1995; in CBT see Gilbert & Procter, 2006). Self-criticism, as a concept, was pivotal in the development of EFT (e.g., Whelton & Greenberg, 2005). Early on it was recognized that it was an extremely common, problematic process that needed to be addressed in therapy (see Greenberg, 1979; Greenberg & Dompierre, 1981; Greenberg & Higgins, 1980). Indeed, it was regarded as one of the two central processes in depression (Greenberg & Watson, 2006), linked to issues of identity (*I am flawed, I am a failure*, etc.), which, alongside attachment issues, were seen as central in depression (and overall human psychopathology) as conceptualized by EFT (cf. Goldman & Greenberg, 2015).

As we hypothesized earlier (cf. Timulak, 2015, and in the beginning of this section), we see self-criticism as developmentally relevant and, initially, as an adaptive effort to cope with adversity. It is, however, possible that some of the sources of self-criticism may be an internalization of criticism and rejection from significant others (e.g., a message from a caregiver: *You are a bad girl*). Occasionally, it is possible to clearly see the self-protective function of the critic (*I criticize myself, so I am not that hurt when others reject me – I am preparing myself*). Sometimes self-criticism is an expression of "harsh" caring (similar to adaptive self-coaching) such as, *You should work harder, you should study more*, et cetera, which becomes maladaptive if it is accompanied with an emotional treatment of the self that is punitive, cold, contemptuous, et cetera. As Les Greenberg often points out in his trainings, it is the *quality of self-treatment* such as self-contempt and self-disgust that is particularly hurtful and leads to the experience of core painful chronic feelings (typically shame). As such, self-criticism often directly contributes to the core-painful, chronic, primary feelings that we refer to here as the core pain. In comparison, self-worrying (or ruminations or self-interruption, mentioned below) are more accurately regarded as secondary processes that try to avoid or manage core painful feelings rather than initiating them. More recently (Toolan, 2017), we started to investigate the link between self-worrying and self-criticism, for example, *I worry that I may be rejected* (worry), *because I am unworthy* (criticism). We comment on this more in Chapter 7.

O'Brien and colleagues (2017) reported several forms of self-criticism in clients with GAD. These included, for instance, expressions of self-judgment, of being fundamentally flawed, inadequate, or weak; having no worth, no rights; being undeserving of love; or failing in the role of a worker, parent, child, et cetera. This was typically represented by an omnipresent judgment of being responsible for all possible (potential) errors or failures. It also incorporated a sense of criticizing the self for letting others down or causing their distress or even harm. A process we refer to as secondary self-criticism (as it is more superficial and undifferentiated) was also highly typical, and was generally expressed as anger at the self for being anxious and depressed.

In concluding the section on problematic self-treatment it is important to refer once more to the self-interruption process. Like worry or rumination, this process focuses on managing or avoiding the emotional experience. Specifically, it is a matter of stopping, suppressing, or interrupting emotion as it is arises (also a component of emotional avoidance). The significance of this avoidance process for therapy has already been highlighted in the early works on EFT (cf. Greenberg *et al.*, 1993). The self-interruption process is typically noticed by therapists in session (as opposed to worry or rumination, which may be self-reported) as clients are generally unaware of it. It may reveal itself as tension, gritted teeth, headaches, self-distraction, dismissal of emotional experience, changing emotionally charged topics, deflection (e.g., through joking), et cetera (O'Brien *et al.*, 2017) or, interestingly, by expressing an emotion other than the one that is dreaded (e.g., anger instead of shame). Again, self-interruption may have adaptive forms, but the one that we consider problematic is enduring, defines the person's functioning, and ultimately, prevents the processing of chronic painful emotions, thereby contributing to the GAD dynamic.

Anticipatory anxiety

Early work on emotion-focused therapy (cf. Greenberg & Safran, 1987; 1989; see Chapter 3) distinguished between primary and secondary emotions. Many theories of anxiety disorders do not make a distinction between secondary anxiety and primary fear. For instance, a CBT theory of social anxiety (cf. Clark, 2001) focuses primarily on targeting anxiety symptoms triggered by the threat of negative evaluation without fully articulating that socially anxious people dread potential, future experiences of shame in social situations. Therefore, we believe, it is shame that should be primarily targeted in the treatment (e.g., *I am anxious* [secondary emotion] *that I will come across as inept* [primary shame] *in a social situation such as public speaking*). In contrast to CBT, EFT theory of social anxiety sees shame as the primary treatment focus (cf. Shahar, 2014).

As with EFT formulations concerning social anxiety, we regard the omnipresent anxiety found in clients diagnosed with GAD as a secondary emotion. It is experienced as having an apprehensive quality rather than as an acute experience of terror and panic (a similar distinction is offered by Barlow, 2002; in Timulak, 2015 we offer a more detailed distinction of secondary anxiety and primary fear). People with GAD symptoms are apprehensive of triggers of emotional pain (situational clues) and of the (primary) chronically painful emotions those triggers bring. Clients with GAD symptoms thus experience chronic *apprehensive anxiety* (see Figure 4.1), which leads to scanning their (typically social and interpersonal) environment for potential threats (e.g., rejection, judgment, accusation, abandonment, loss, trauma, illness, etc.; see O'Brien *et al.*, 2017). GAD sufferers perform this scanning to manage their emotional experience in a way that facilitates avoidance of unbearable painful experiences (chronically known) that would be emotionally overwhelming (cf. O'Brien *et al.*'s work).

Apprehensive anxiety is, therefore, a source of emotional and behavioral avoidance (see below) as well as a driving force behind protective self-treatment (such as worry, self-interruption, and some forms of self-criticism). These anxiety-driven varieties of problematic self-treatment (e.g., worry, self-interruption) can be also conceptualized as emotional avoidance; which often leads to behavioral avoidance. To conclude this vicious cycle, this secondary anxiety may also include fear of symptoms of anxiety (again see the work of O'Brien *et al.*, 2017), for example, being anxious about one's own anxiety. The toll of this anxiety and all the processes that stem from it is exhaustion and tiredness (the danger is omnipresent, and so is the bodily, physiological, reaction to it).

Emotional avoidance

As has already been stated, apprehensive anxiety fuels avoidance. A portion of this avoidance is an internal process. We refer to it as *emotional avoidance* (see Figure 4.1). Worrying and self-interruption processes, described in the section on problematic self-treatment, can be also conceptualized as emotional avoidance, as their purpose is to manage/avoid/prepare for emotional pain. In the case of worrying, this is also recognized by the majority of CBT theories (cf. Behar *et al.*, 2009), with some seeing it as a substitute for engaging with the underlying emotions (Borkovec *et al.*, 2004) and some seeing it as a way of managing emotional shifts (Newman & Llera, 2011).

Our qualitative analysis (cf. O'Brien *et al.*, 2017) of in-session presentations or narratives, as well as clinical experience, encountered further forms of reported emotional avoidance such as comfort eating, using of anxiolytic medications or alcohol (self-medication), engagement in distracting activities, somatic experiences of tension (interruption of emotion), et cetera. Within therapy sessions, clients might attempt to change the topic, avoid engagement in experiential tasks that they found evocative, laugh-off the subject under exploration, minimize their emotional experience, et cetera. (Note. Some of these may be seen as self-interruptions.) Some clients wanted to stay with a particular emotional experience, such as anger, rather than go to a more vulnerable experience such as shame. A form of numbing may be also self-harming that can be a combination of anger directed at the self, but also the instilling of the pain that overshadows and distracts from the more specific core emotional pain (this is a complex topic and any self-harming behavior needs to be understood in the context of an idiosyncratic client presentation, cf. Sutton, 2007).

Behavioral avoidance

Apprehensive anxiety not only fuels mental processes (e.g., worrying), preparing the client for feared situations (potential threats) and management of feared emotions, but can also lead to behavior that attempts to minimize the likelihood of encountering the feared triggers/situations, *behavioral avoidance* (see Figure 4.1). People with GAD symptoms can be fearful of rejection and judgment and thus may present as very appeasing, perfectionistic (cf. O'Brien *et al.*, 2017). Fearful of escalating conflict, they may be reluctant to assert their perspective. On the other hand, they may attack to avoid admitting vulnerability (such as shame). They may be avoidant to the extent that they would try to avoid assuming responsibility for projects in the event that they might be blamed for the outcomes. They may procrastinate to avoid engaging in activities that might be evaluated by others. A very typical example would be that of controlling behavior, that is, trying to prevent disaster from happening to loved ones (overprotective behavior directed at children or a partner). The actual avoidant behavior can be understood in the context of idiosyncratic personal history and tailored case conceptualization (see Chapter 6). Although avoidant behavior is not as commonly stressed in the context of GAD difficulties as it is with some other anxiety problems, several authors highlighted the role of avoidant behavior in GAD (Mahoney *et al.*, 2016; Roemer, Orsillo, & Barlow, 2002; Roemer & Orsillo, 2014). Both emotional and behavioral avoidance lower the person's tolerance threshold for difficult situations and emotional experiences and thus, in the long-term, may contribute to the feeling of upset when those situations occur or when emotional experiences seep through.

Core (feared) emotional pain

Most CBT theories of GAD (cf. Behar *et al.*, 2009) assume that clients with GAD symptoms are avoidant of emotional experience. Some of those theories (e.g., Mennin *et al.*, 2004; Newman & Llera, 2011) assume that the clients are emotionally sensitive, have a problem with emotion regulation and with tolerance of emotional contrast (sudden changes in emotion experience). These theories, however, assume that it is an issue of the individual's global emotionality. Our studies (e.g., O'Brien *et al.*, 2017), inspecting the GAD dynamic in clients' in-session presentations and narrative disclosures during sessions, suggest that the feared emotions are specific, idiosyncratic, chronically unbearable emotions that are at the center of problematic emotion-schemes. We observed that these dreaded emotions were the emotions activated by specific triggers, best understood through individual clients' personal histories. We refer to those emotions as *core emotional pain*. Indeed, EFT theory assumes that any current experience is informed by memory structures that are involved in processing our perceptual field, and provide a template for experiencing and acting (Greenberg, 2011; 2015; cf. also Lane, Ryan, Nadel, & Greenberg, 2015). This is referred to as emotional schematic (emotion-schemes) processing (see Chapter 3).

A series of studies (not exclusively on clients with GAD symptoms, but also with clients experiencing trauma or depression) suggests that these chronic, feared, unbearable experiences can be clustered into three groupings (cf. Timulak, 2015; Timulak & Pascual-Leone, 2015; see Figure 4.1): (1) loneliness/sadness-based emotional experiences, (2) shame-based emotional experiences, and (3) primary fear-based emotional experiences. *Loneliness/sadness-based* emotional experiences are experiences of chronic isolation or loss (e.g., *I feel profoundly alone, abandoned*). Clients may be touching on the sadness linked to a particular trigger (e.g., *I was left out* or *I lost you*). This can be a current trigger that the client may encounter or potentially encounter in their everyday life, but typically (and here is the root of chronicity), this trigger maps well onto historical triggers of pain such as omission, neglect, abandonment, missing of the deceased or otherwise absent loved one, et cetera. The experienced sadness/loneliness is all consuming and self-defining and thus, clients collapse into global distress characterized by hopelessness, helplessness, resignation, and depression; a sort of undifferentiated secondary sadness (cf. Pascual-Leone & Greenberg, 2007; Pascual-Leone, 2009; Timulak, 2015; Timulak & Pascual-Leone, 2015).

Loneliness/sadness that we see as a part of the core emotional pain is a primary maladaptive sadness (cf. Greenberg, 2011; 2015) as it does not inform an adaptive action (e.g., seeking support, comfort, connection). Rather, it is dreaded and, when touched on, leads to collapse into an undifferentiated global distress characterized by hopelessness, and helplessness that may contain undifferentiated sadness. Hopelessness, helplessness, and undifferentiated sadness are conceptualized as secondary – that is, they do not have a clear connection to specific triggers; it is not possible to clearly establish the link between the trigger and the reaction from the narrative of the client, et cetera.

Primary maladaptive loneliness/sadness/loss informs us that we are missing connection and that our needs for connection are not fulfilled (see the part below on unmet needs), which may often be a painful and, for some, an unbearable realization. Phenomenologically, it appears in the form of situation (trigger) specific sadness, or mourning, that is accompanied by crying, vulnerability, and closing down; indicating an unfilled need for connection, sharing, or comfort. Sometimes experiences of emptiness may be articulated by clients. Historical predecessors (triggers) that appear to be contributing to the development of loneliness/sadness-based chronic emotions (emotion schemes) seem to be experiences of early loss (e.g., the death of a significant other), unbearable losses (such as the death of a child), profound experiences of neglect, when nobody was present for the person (particularly in their childhood), experiences of being ostracized, left out (e.g., by peers), et cetera.

The second cluster of feared core emotional experiences (again not necessarily limited to clients with GAD symptoms) are *shame-based emotions* (cf. Timulak, 2015; Pascual-Leone & Greenberg, 2007). These experiences appear in the form of felt shame, embarrassment, humiliation, the situation-not-matching guilt, et cetera. The typical verbal expressions are: *I am worthless, I am flawed, I am inadequate, I am a failure, it is my fault, I let him (her) down,* et cetera. The experience is chronic, self-defining, unshakable, et cetera. Usually, there are current triggers or, particularly in the GAD dynamic, potential triggers of being rejected, judged, condemned, et cetera, by others, but also by the self through self-critical processes. For instance, the person may see the pain of their child and they will start to blame themselves for causing it. Again, as in the other forms of core emotional pain (core chronic maladaptive emotions), current triggers (e.g., rejection) normally map onto the historical, original triggers (hence the chronicity) of being rejected, ridiculed, or humiliated on a consistent basis by significant others (e.g., parents or peers). The experience of shame feels as though it matches the reality and is defining of the self. The action tendency in shame is to hide and disappear, thereby avoiding further shaming; consequently this experience often goes hand in hand with the experience of loneliness. As in primary sadness/loneliness, the unbearable pain leads to resignation, avoidance, hopelessness, helplessness, further isolation, and other secondary maladaptive emotions that we conceptualize as global distress (cf. Pascual-Leone & Greenberg, 2007). The unmet needs in shame-based experiences are those of acknowledgment, acceptance, and validation (see below), which, if not fulfilled, lead to the resignation and secondary distress when not fulfilled.

The experience of shame may be experientially subtle, but profoundly painful due to its defining features. From an evolutionary perspective, condemned and rejected people became outcasts, expelled from a community and therefore unable to survive in the long-run. Thus, despite being subtle, the shame has a very profound impact and appears to be significant for a whole range of psychopathological symptoms. As it is closely linked to various forms of problematic self-treatment (self-criticism, self-contempt, self-harshness, etc.), it may go together with various self-attacks including suicide attempts and self-harming behavior; physically harming the self through direct and indirect means.

The final cluster of chronic painful emotions that clients with GAD appear to be attempting to avoid (cf. for instance, O'Brien *et al.*, 2017) are *primary fear-based experiences (panic)*. Here we talk about acute fear that should be viewed as distinct from secondary apprehension and anxiety (cf. Timulak, 2015). Primary experiences of fear are so dreaded that they often do not show in therapy sessions. Clients may touch on acute fear in some of the experiential tasks, in which they imagine the threatening trigger (e.g., a violent other), or in the experiences of acute panic that sometimes occur in the session, in the context of a terrifying trigger (e.g., *I am terrified, scared*). Historically, the chronic inability to tolerate an acute fear seems to be linked with sudden traumatic experiences, particularly in the formative years (e.g., beatings from significant others or peers, seeing accidents or unnatural experiences of death or illness of significant people, seeing scared significant others, etc.). In later adult-life, various traumatic experiences (violence, war, etc.) may have a similar impact. These experiences bring a sense of current, acute danger. When triggered, they bring acute fear, dissociations, somatic symptoms of fear such as palpitations, dizziness, sense of fainting, shallow breathing, a sense of getting a heart attack (or dying) – chest pain, shaking, trembling, nausea, sweating, bowel movement, et cetera.

The distress can be so uncomfortable that the person may be further scared by the intensity of their reaction. Attempts to avoid this unpleasant fear reaction may become so ingrained that they override any other life priorities. The need, implicit in the fear reaction, is the need for control, protection, and comfort. Any possibility of ending this intense form of distress is seized; usually taking the form of avoidance (see the section on emotional avoidance above). To many sufferers, experiences of acute fear lead not only to behavioral and emotional avoidance, but to overall tiredness, exhaustion, resignation, and a sense of hopelessness/helplessness that one might never gain mastery over such experiences (i.e., global distress). Acute fear (panic) is a complex physiological event that has physiological consequences, especially when chronic (Barlow, 2002).

As we highlighted earlier (Timulak, 2015; Timulak & Pascual-Leone, 2015), the three clusters of core painful emotion that are feared by clients with GAD are not simply idiosyncratic for individual clients, but also have a high level of overlap. For instance, being rejected may not only bring feelings of shame, but also experiences of abandonment, sadness, and loneliness. They may also signal that one is unprotected and thus point to the presence of danger through fear. Therapeutic work focuses on increasing the client's understanding of his/her core chronic vulnerability, increasing the capacity to tolerate those feared chronic painful feelings and transforming emotion schemes involving these chronic painful feelings.

Unmet needs

The pain contained in the core emotions that clients with GAD symptoms want to avoid, signals that the needs embedded in those emotions are not met (Greenberg, 2011). Indeed, the fact that these needs (see Figure 4.1) are chronically unmet, hinders the processing of these painful emotions and leads to a collapse into secondary distress, characterized by hopelessness/helplessness and resignation, or leads to avoidance of activation of those chronic emotions through various psychological or behavioral strategies. Our studies, which looked at the articulation of those unmet needs in the context of a successfully unfolding therapeutic process (in GAD see, for instance, Crowley, Timulak, & McElvaney, 2013; Keogh, Timulak, & McElvaney, 2014; in depression see for instance Dillon, Timulak, & Greenberg, 2016; McNally, Timulak, & Greenberg, 2014), found that chronic unmet emotional needs correspond with the above-highlighted clusters of emotions, classified as core emotional pain.

Thus, we identified unmet needs that corresponded (1) with chronic experiences of loneliness/sadness. These included (cf. O'Brien *et al.*, 2017) the need to be loved (e.g., *Every girl needs a mom and I needed you too*), connected to, cared for, shown affection to, shared with, belong, et cetera. The typically unmet needs linked to the cluster of (2) shame-based emotions include (O'Brien *et al.*, 2017) to be accepted (e.g., *I need you to like me for who I am*), validated, acknowledged (e.g., *I need you to see me*), respected (for instance in the need for autonomy), et cetera. The unmet needs linked to (3) the fear experiences include, the need for protection, safety, control, comfort (e.g., *I needed you to hug me and tell me that it will all be all right*), basic care, et cetera (for more see O'Brien *et al.*, 2017). Again, as in the case of chronic painful emotions, the unmet needs are idiosyncratic and frequently overlapping (e.g., *I need you to understand me and comfort me; I just needed a hug, etc.*) and the therapist works with the client in therapy in articulating them freshly in the context of aroused experience of chronic painful and feared emotions. After identifying their needs, clients can then organize towards having them met, leading to accessing more adaptive emotional experiences.

Transformation of emotional pain – restructuring the GAD dynamic

CBT models of working with clients with GAD focus on shaping the worry process into a more adaptive form, exposure work with the avoided emotions (and situations that may be evoking them), and promotion of pleasurable but hitherto avoided activities. Chronic avoidance strategies are thus targeted and chronic vulnerability is overcome through reassessment of the danger and the building of tolerance for uncomfortable experiences, together with the expansion of coping strategies, which allow clients to endure threatening situations. In our approach, we focus on overcoming avoidance strategies through highlighting the client's agency in them and the personal cost of maintaining them. We transform chronic vulnerability with new adaptive emotional experiences through a sequence of emotional processing steps (cf. Pascual-Leone & Greenberg, 2007; Timulak & McElvaney, 2016).

Our transformation model (Timulak & McElvaney, 2016) thus offers a somewhat overlapping, but also distinctively different, model of overcoming GAD difficulties. All the therapeutic work is done in the context of a caring, compassionate, real relationship, which facilitates the client in overcoming avoidance. The authentic relationship offered provides a corrective emotional experience to the interpersonal experiences that so often lead, or contribute, to the development of GAD symptoms (see Chapter 5).

We see the worry process, considered to be a defining feature of GAD, as a secondary process, deployed in an attempt to cope with underlying idiosyncratic emotional vulnerabilities. Our aim is to focus on this underlying vulnerability, being guided by the assumption that transformation of underlying, chronic, maladaptive, emotion-schemes (sadness/loneliness, shame, and primary fear) would make clients more emotionally resilient and therefore less likely to engage in worrying, and other forms of emotional and behavioral avoidance. Our learning suggested that anxiety processes are firmly engrained (cf. Le Doux, 2015) and that, although secondary, they need to be worked through in way that would increase the likelihood of "rewiring" the established pathways and neural circuitry currently involved in constructing anxiety. Thus, an important step in transforming generalized anxiety involves the transformation of the worry process, and other means of attempting to avoid the underlying vulnerability processes.

Chapter 7 will highlight work with the worry and avoidance process. The beginning of that work involves bringing these to awareness and highlighting their function (i.e., to protect from both the outside threat and from overwhelming internal emotional experience). The second step involves increasing awareness and experience of the cost (toll) of the worry process and avoidance. In the case of the worry, it is typically anxiety and tiredness, and in the case of avoidance, it is typically missing out on important aspects of life (e.g., freely engaging in enjoyable activities). Once the toll is highlighted, the need to get a break from it is articulated and the client is encouraged to stand up for that need (i.e., stand up to the worry/emotional avoidance or pursue the hitherto avoided activity). The work also focuses on the generation of compassion to the aspects of the self that suffer from the toll of the worry and emotional/behavioral avoidance. This process is repeated several times to support it, and homework activities may be suggested to consolidate it and bring it to life outside the therapy session.

The essence of the work with clients with GAD difficulties is, in common with EFT approaches to treating various other psychological difficulties, focused on overcoming the underlying vulnerability, that is, core, feared, chronic, painful emotions. Work with the core pain consists of several steps (see the full volume description in Timulak, 2015 and Timulak & Pascual-Leone, 2015). After the avoidance is overcome, the therapist helps the client to stay in touch with the underlying painful emotions (loneliness/sadness, shame, and primary fear/terror), to be able to tolerate them, differentiate the aspects of this painful experience in language, hold a reflective stance towards them, build a capacity to regulate them, and not experience them as self-defining. The therapist then helps the client to articulate the unmet needs embedded in those chronic painful emotions and clearly express them. Finally, the therapist helps the client to generate alternative, adaptive experiences (*compassion* and a healthy boundary setting *protective anger*; see Figure 4.1, see Chapter 8) that back up the unmet needs and function as an antidote to the chronic painful emotions.

The compassion and protective anger thus generated respond to "the unmet needs by conveying a sense of acceptance and validation (counteracting shame), love and connection (counteracting loneliness) and an offer of protection and generation of resolve (counteracting fear)" (Timulak & McElvaney, 2016, p. 46). These emotions and corresponding self-organizations are generated in the client, however, compassion is also provided by the therapist through his or her empathic, warm, and caring relational stance. Similarly, protective anger is not only facilitated in the client through the therapist's skillful interventions, but is also interpersonally validated by the therapist's presence (see Chapter 5). Experiences of generating and letting in compassion bring corrective healing experiences of connection, acceptance, and protection that balance the chronic wound and vulnerability (core pain). They subsequently lead to a healthy adaptive *grieving* that is characterized by a "letting go" quality (although still hurtful, past emotional wounds are not that debilitating and can be grieved; see Pascual-Leone & Greenberg, 2007; Timulak, 2015). The generation of protective anger in the client and through the therapist's relational affirmation build the inner sense of value, a sense of deserving, and a new resolve to face the feared triggers/situations. The process of generating protective anger thus leads to experiences of empowerment and, over time, towards a sense of a more resilient self.

The process of overcoming avoidance, touching on the chronic painful emotions, articulating unmet needs, and generating the adaptive emotions of compassion and protective anger, is repeated regularly in the therapy process and steps are taken to consolidate this type of emotional processing by the client (homework). The therapeutic relationship serves as an important interpersonal support in consolidating these types of experiences. The client's feared, avoided, chronic, self-defining, core painful emotions and the self-organizations based on them are thus counterbalanced. Emotional flexibility and emotional resilience are developed, leaving the client internally stronger, more confident, and more trusting of the self (Pascual-Leone, 2009). Clients now recover more quickly from upsetting triggers, and are no longer worried about potential triggers or potentially difficult situations to the same extent as before. This helps to decrease emotional and behavioral avoidance strategies, as well as problematic self-treatment. Some general tenets of the transformation model of GAD difficulties are captured in Box 4.1. We also bring a brief example of the articulation of Robert's (from Chapter 2) difficulties, as well as a brief description of the process of emotional transformation (see Box 4.2).

Box 4.1   Transformation of chronic feared and avoided painful feelings in EFT for GAD difficulties – some important tenets of the transformation model.

Understanding GAD difficulties:

- GAD difficulties can be understood as a dynamic of specific idiosyncratic triggers that bring (or potentially could bring) chronic painful feelings (loneliness/sadness, shame, and primary fear).
- In the context of those triggers the person engages in the self-treatment process that can either exacerbate core painful feelings (e.g., self-criticism) or want to prepare for them (e.g., self-criticism, self-worry) or avoid them (self-interruption) or master them (e.g., rumination).
- The person is apprehensive of (potential) triggers of emotional pain and engages in emotional and behavioral avoidance.
- The most typical emotional response to the (potential) triggers of emotional pain is global distress, an undifferentiated secondary emotional experience, characterized by a mixture of feelings that may contain hopeless, helplessness, irritability, reactive anger, anxiety, somatic symptoms, et cetera.
- The core feared underlying feelings are centered around experiences of sadness/loneliness, shame, and primary fear (terror and panic).
- The chronic feared underlying painful primary feelings signal that important needs are not being met – these are needs, for example, for connection, closeness, or love (linked to sadness/loneliness), for example, for acceptance, acknowledgment, recognition, or validation (linked to shame), and, for example, for protection, safety, or security (linked to primary fear).

Transforming GAD difficulties:

- An important part of transforming GAD difficulties is the overcoming of avoidance processes (through highlighting the person's agency in them and their cost).
- The core feared painful chronic feelings then must be accessed and the client has to be helped to be able to bear those feelings.
- The unmet needs embedded in the core painful chronic feelings have to be articulated.
- Compassion and protective anger directed at the core painful feelings (and unmet needs) are then generated and experienced.
- The therapeutic relationship plays a pivotal role in it.
- Grieving of the past wounds then ensues, as well as experiences of a more empowered self.

Box 4.2 Robert's difficulties

Triggers

Past. For example: Death of his father in an automobile accident. Father's high standards. Overall mother's emotional unavailability and critical nature.

Current. For example: Conflict with ex-wife. Lack of access to son. Business collapse. An important aunt passed away. Judgment by others. Close ones being vulnerable.

Self-treatment

For example: Self-criticism (I am a failure, I deserve to suffer, I must suffer alone, I deserve punishment, etc.). Worry (e.g., about potential further tragedy).

Global distress

For example: Hopeless, helpless, anxious, irritable, somatic symptoms.

Apprehension/Anxiety

For example: Of tragedy, further loss, conflict, others' judgment, unexpected (business) problems, social situations/judgment.

Behavioral avoidance

For example: Not going to work, avoiding social contact, withdrawal, distraction.

Emotional avoidance

For example: Constant worrying, use of humor to avoid pain, shutting down, trying to distract himself, jumping into secondary anger.

Core pain

Loneliness/sadness based. For example: Losses amplify feelings of sadness and loneliness.

Shame based. For example: He feels worthless. He has failed his father and family. He is unlikeable. He is letting down his son.

Fear based. For example: Robert is terrified of further trauma.

Unmet needs

For example: To be connected, to be loved, to be accepted, to be safe and protected.

Conclusion

Here we present our understanding of GAD difficulties. We describe how the distress is linked to specific, idiosyncratic past and current triggers. We explain how clients commonly present with undifferentiated global distress. We explain how they struggle with problematic self-treatment that compounds the distress and pain brought by the triggers. Clients suffer with anticipatory anxiety linked to the potential triggers, and this leads them to engage in behavioral and emotional avoidance as a means of avoiding core painful feelings. We describe in detail the nature of clients' core emotional pain (core pain) that typically consists of variations of sadness/loneliness, shame and primary fear. We then describe the unmet needs linked to the core painful feelings, for example, to be loved/connected, validated/accepted, safe/protected. We then focus on the process of emotional transformation and the transformation of the GAD dynamic. This process consists of differentiation of global distress, overcoming of emotional avoidance, clarifying painful triggers and problematic self-treatment, accessing core painful feelings, articulating unmet needs, and responding to them through the generation of compassion and protective anger.

Part II

Building blocks of delivering EFT for GAD

Chapter 5

Therapeutic relationship promoting emotional transformation

This chapter begins the part of the book which focuses on emotion-focused therapeutic work with GAD sufferers. The foundation upon which EFT with people with GAD difficulties is based, is broadly the same as in EFT for any other psychological difficulty. It is based on the development of a trusting relationship between therapist and client, and the use of that relationship, not only to provide a safe environment, conducive to allowing client expressions of vulnerability in session, but also to provide a corrective, healing interpersonal/emotional experience.

Emotion-focused therapy is a *relational therapy*. It builds on the tradition of client/person-centered therapy (Rogers, 1951; 1961), which means that the therapist offers a genuine, authentic way of being and relating to the client in therapy. This chapter will outline what is meant by EFT as *relational therapy*. An EFT therapist aims to offer a relationship that will build the client's trust in the therapist, thereby allowing the client to search inwards and explore their emotional experience, reflect on it, and disclose it to the therapist both directly, and in the experiential tasks of therapy. The therapeutic relationship is thus a necessary precursor to any future therapeutic activity. Without trust it is unlikely that the client would be able, or willing, to engage in the exploration, expression, and sharing of experience, which is essential for therapy.

The supportive relationship offered by the therapist in EFT is also seen as a potentially powerful healing agent. While the relationship, and the associated therapeutic presence, can have a soothing effect on the client and may also contribute to emotion-regulation, it can also offer the client an opportunity for transformatory experiences (Timulak, 2015). As we saw in Chapters 2 and 4, a lot of the feared triggers impacting clients with GAD difficulties are linked to idiosyncratic, interpersonal experiences of rejection invalidation, shaming, bullying, negligence, et cetera. The emotionally salient, therapeutic relationship has the potential to serve as antidote to those invalidating and interpersonally hurtful experiences through providing a corrective emotional experience (Greenberg & Elliott, 2012).

Authenticity

A prerequisite for relational psychotherapy is authenticity on the part of the therapist (cf. congruence in Rogers, 1961). The therapist's authenticity is an essential component in building trust. EFT therapists are encouraged to be real with their clients, not to hide behind a façade of professionalism. An important feature of authenticity is the therapist's self-awareness and understanding of their own processes and emotional states (cf. Lietaer, 1993). Additionally, while striving to be authentic, it is important that the therapist cultivates certain characteristics, conceptualized as therapeutic presence (cf. Geller & Greenberg, 2012). This may take the form of self-focused practices that would allow the therapist to recognize and acknowledge internal experiences, but be able to put them aside temporarily (this may happen perhaps before the session starts, but if necessary, it can take place during the session).

Authenticity may have also an interpersonal dimension. For instance, EFT therapists are ready to communicate to the client, when they are moved by the client's story, that they have been profoundly affected. Similarly, EFT therapists are aware of their own insecurities and while they do not burden the client with them, they do not try to hide them, as this would be inauthentic. For instance, if the client, in session, asked how I felt (LT), I would share if I felt comfortable as well as if I felt a bit hesitant. Obviously this occurs with the client's welfare in mind. Therapist disclosures are, therefore, based on a complex judgment of the situation at hand and an assessment of what the best therapeutic course of action might be (cf. Timulak, 2011).

Warmth and emotionally attuned empathy

EFT therapists openly show that they care for their clients. Interpersonal warmth in the therapist is a particularly cherished quality by clients undergoing EFT (cf. Timulak *et al.*, 2017). The effect of this warm, caring presence is further deepened by the therapist's empathy, which is particularly focused on emotional aspects of the experience. Indeed, clients with GAD symptoms (and indeed any clients), report that they appreciate feeling understood by the therapist (cf. Timulak *et al.*, 2017). While many therapies see empathic attunement as an important part of therapeutic work, empathy in EFT is an elaborate, sophisticated mode of engagement on the part of the therapist, particularly focused on the emotional processing of self–other and self–self related experiences.

EFT differentiates a full range of empathic interventions (Elliott *et al.*, 2004; see Chapter 3). These interventions are further fine-tuned by the therapist using pacing (e.g., leaving a space for vulnerable experience to form), vocal quality (e.g., using a soft gentle voice when addressing vulnerability, versus using a firm, validating voice when supporting anger), and a focus on experiential/bodily felt aspects of experience (e.g., *I can imagine it must ache in your body*). Additionally, the therapist attends to the balance of empathic exploration (where the therapist wants to unfold the experience) and communication of empathic understanding (where the therapist acknowledges what he or she understands from the client's disclosure), the constant use of empathic conjectures (an EFT therapist uses the knowledge of human emotional experience to conjecture the client's experience – for instance, in shame people may feel worthless and small, with the action tendency to hide and disappear, and all of this can be used by the therapist in the verbal offer attempting to capture his/her understanding of the client's experience), the provision of empathic emotional coaching (EFT keeps a balance between focusing the client inward on his or her experiencing and expressing what is felt emotionally outwards, and this balance deepens the client's emotional experience and in turn the therapist's empathy with it), et cetera.

The goal here is to help the client to access emotional experience, pay attention to it, express it for him or herself and to the therapist and then for the therapist to communicate his/her concerned and personally invested understanding of this experience to the client. This not only provides the client with an experience of being connected to by another human being (the therapist), but it also helps the client to modulate the experience and use it for further reflection and emotional processing (cf. Watson *et al.*, 1998). The impact is thus relational (*I am being understood, I feel cared for, I matter to somebody, that somebody is compassionate, caring towards me*), but also promotes self-healing processes such as better tolerance of painful emotional experiences, an increased capacity for reflecting on those experiences, and an ability to articulate the unmet needs contained in them.

Corrective relational experiences – witnessing

The relational nature of EFT is also revealed in the client's use of the therapist's relational offer in emotional transformation. While a caring presence and empathy, focused on exploration and understanding, allow the client to access and tolerate primary painful emotional experiences and help the client to articulate hitherto unmet needs, the differential use of the therapeutic relationship is meant to support emerging adaptive experiences. As later chapters will reveal and, as is articulated in other EFT writing (e.g., Timulak, 2015), core painful feelings are first accessed and tolerated in therapy, next, the embedded unmet needs in them are articulated, and then adaptive emotional experiences, such as compassion and protective anger, are generated to respond to the painful feelings (and the unmet needs in them). As has been stressed previously (Timulak, 2015), it is important that compassion and protective anger are self-generated. It is also important that these are supported by an authentic therapist's compassion towards the client's present, evoked in-session vulnerability, and through the therapist's validation of a just and protective anger.

As stated, the therapist does not hide behind the façade of professionalism, but rather is willing to reveal his/her own frame of reference and express a caring, compassionate stance directly to the client. Thus, the therapist may reveal that he or she is genuinely moved and touched by the client's pain and suffering, but may also offer his or her perspective on the adversity the client has experienced and which may be at root of the client's vulnerability, for example, speaking towards the client's expressions of emotional injuries when neglected by her mother:

Therapist (speaking to an emotional, very upset client who has expressed in an empty chair dialogue with her mother how she suffered when mom was neglectful and hurtful towards her): *Yeah. But ultimately it shouldn't have happened. Yeah?*

Client: No.
Therapist: I'm telling you. Yes?
Client: Yeah.
Therapist: ... And I'm powerless to go back in time.
Client: Mmm.
Therapist: But you shouldn't have gone through it. Yeah? Nobody should. It's not only that it's you. Yes? No girl.

...

Client: No one should have.
Therapist: Yeah.
Client: No one should have. And I'd love to be able to turn back the clock ...
Therapist: Yeah.
Client: ... and do something. Move a few things.

...

Therapist: Yeah. But you have it in your heart [experiences of love and connection]. Yes? When you sit here. You also gave it to your children as well. Yes?
Client: I hope so.

Therapist (referring to the client's self-criticism): You deserve to give it to yourself as well. I know it's sad in one way. Yes? Because it's important to get it from outside as well. Yeah?

Client: It's so hard to let go of the, the negative.
Therapist: Yeah.
Client: It's so hard. And it's so hard to let go of the anger [towards mother].

The experience of being authentically met by their therapist at the moment of touching on core, painful feelings is transformational and corrective for clients (Greenberg & Elliott, 2012). Where there was once neglect, rejection, and attack, there is now caring, attending, and validating from a kind other. As this happens in the context of high emotional arousal (see Chapters 8 and 9), these experiences are poignant for the client and contribute greatly to shaping their emotion schemes (cf. Lane *et al.*, 2015). The therapist's presence provides a sense of deep human connection in the face of suffering. It also has a regulatory function, as these experiences shape the structure of emotional memory. The therapist's caring presence is internalized and may serve as a buffer against upset in times of vulnerability in the future.

Ruptures repairs and safety building

Despite the EFT therapist's efforts to provide a deeply caring and validating presence that, in essence, counteracts the client's previous, interpersonal, emotional injuries (particularly the ones that led to the development of emotional vulnerabilities), some clients may be so interpersonally vulnerable that they are hugely sensitive to the therapist's natural incongruities, vulnerabilities, artificialness, empathic misattunements, and errors. In such cases it is very important that the therapist is aware of the fact that clients tend to feel vulnerable in therapy sessions and often notice aspects of their therapist's behavior, which are experienced as sub-optimal by them (cf. Rennie, 1994; Timulak & Iwakabe, in press). This suggests that the therapist should be continuously striving to build an atmosphere of inquiry regarding the client's experience, probing for any difficulties that the client may experience in therapy. The detection of any such difficult experiences is an opportunity for the therapist to help the client to articulate and express them, while validating the hurt/sensitivity from which they stem (cf. a very good description of working through ruptures in the therapeutic alliance can be found in the seminal work of Safran & Muran, 2000).

When working through alliance ruptures, it is very important that the therapist takes ownership of their responsibility and apologizes (and/or acknowledges own responsibility) for any potentially overlooked impact of his or her interventions or behavior on the client (Rhodes, Hill, Thompson, & Elliott, 1994; Safran & Muran, 2000; Timulak, 1999). Such ownership and probing for client discomfort, combined with a non-judgmental atmosphere, which encourages the client to voice his or her difficulties, is a prerequisite for working through such misattunements. This can be achieved through the therapist's communication of a deeper understanding of the client's hurt evoked by the therapist's action. The therapist empathically explores and communicates understanding of that hurt in the context of the client's idiosyncratic vulnerabilities and sensitivities, present in the client's unique personal story. Elliott *et al.* (2004) provide a useful description of working with alliance ruptures in EFT for therapists in training.

Tasks and goals agreement

In addition to the authentic caring and the provision of corrective relational expe riences, the client's trust in the therapist is also developed through recognition of the therapist's expertise. This expertise is also revealed in the therapist's skilled empathic attunement to affect, and adroit co-articulation of the client's experience, in the client and therapist co-constructed narrative. The expertise, however, also shows in the way the therapist eases the client into therapy in a way that builds trust and allows the client to go along with the therapeutic process. Traditionally, this more technical aspect of the therapeutic relationship is conceptualized in psychotherapy as the work on the therapist and the client's agreement on the tasks and goals of therapy (Bordin, 1979).

The EFT therapist builds trust by orienting the client to the therapeutic process, offering guidance and appropriate explanation. Clients with GAD symptoms may be particularly ambivalent about accessing their emotional pain. Some clients may be avoidant and only wish to talk about symptoms of anxiety or depression without linking them to those aspects of their life which leave their innermost needs unmet. In order for therapy to work, the therapist has to understand how clients conceptualize their difficulties and what they expect from therapy. Research suggests that if therapy is clearly and transparently explained, and if the process of easing the client into therapy respects the client's preconceptions and tries to meet the client in a way that makes sense to them, then clients may benefit from therapy to a greater degree (cf. Wampold & Imel, 2015; Swift, Callahan, & Vollmer, 2011).

Clients with GAD difficulties may struggle with the idea that experiencing painful feelings in therapy can eventually lead to having less emotional pain in their life. Avoiding emotional pain, and the situations that may cause it, is characteristic of their functioning. It may well be that they experience emotional pain more intensely than non-GAD sufferers and are particularly sensitive to emotional upset (cf. theories of Mennin, 2004; Newman & Llera, 2011). Furthermore, many clients believe in the protective function of worry. Therapists need to, therefore, acknowledge these beliefs and their protective function. They may, however, also highlight the cost of these strategies. If it is done in an empathic manner and, primarily through the clients' own experiences of that cost, the clients may have a greater appreciation of the EFT rationale for working with GAD difficulties (see previous chapter).

The therapist, especially in the early stages of therapy, acknowledges the client's global distress, and inquires about the client's understanding of their difficulties. The therapist explores the client's expectations from therapy, their hopes and fears, and asks about previous experiences of therapy (paying particular attention to what did and did not work in them). The therapist then explains, in language that best meets the client's understanding, the mechanisms of therapy, the therapeutic process, and the dynamic in GAD difficulties. Indeed, some clients may actively inquire about their diagnosis and the therapist may need to offer a common sense EFT conceptualization of GAD difficulties that fits with the client's current, personal situation (see description of an example in Box 5.1). The therapist needs to explain to the client, in language that matches the client's thinking about his or her own difficulties, how accessing and evoking painful feelings may eventually lead to feeling better, more at peace, freer, stronger (Greenberg, 2011).

The therapist is transparent about his or her conceptualization of the client's difficulties. The therapist is willing to both discuss his or her understanding of the client's difficulties and also to share his or her thinking about how to best address and transform those difficulties (we will look at the use of case conceptualization in the next chapter). In such discussions the therapist verbally checks whether the description he or she offers makes sense to the client, but is also attuned to non-verbal cues. Therapist and client engage in similar discussions throughout the therapeutic process, as it is important to ensure that the client is engaged in the therapeutic process, but it is also important in terms of making sense of the therapeutic experience (Grafanaki & McLeod, 1999), which can help to consolidate any changes arising from therapy sessions. These discussions, however, need to be balanced to avoid fruitless intellectualization, which might play into the client's potential tendencies to avoid feelings. EFT is, first and foremost, an experiential therapy.

Box 5.1 An example of a generic lay explanation of GAD symptoms and therapy.

The anxiety you experience is telling you that there is a potential threat out there. The things that you are afraid of, such as [add triggers as appropriate], are the things that you may be particularly sensitive to (because of your personal history and/or emotional reactivity) as in the past you have experienced that they bring painful feelings. You prepare yourself for potential situations like this by worrying (yourself) about how these threatening situations might come about and how you might feel when they do [add examples of worries as appropriate]. You are then (perhaps) more ready for these threatening situations, but the constant vigilance tires you and a constant engagement with potential threats makes you anxious (as thinking about threats raises anxiety of them being real). You are also trying to avoid situations which bring potential threat by doing certain things, such as [add behavior avoidance strategies as appropriate], but the cost to you from doing this is that you cannot pursue other things, such as [add as appropriate], more freely. Underneath of all of this is that in certain situations you may have painful feelings that experience drawn from your personal history leads you to believe will not resolve well, and you try to avoid those feelings, for instance, by [add emotional avoidance strategies as appropriate]. In the context of these potentially threatening situations you also treat yourself in particular ways, for instance, [add typical forms of self-criticism as appropriate], perhaps with the hope of being more resilient, but often this self-treatment makes you feel worse [add examples as appropriate].

This therapy will try to focus on those underlying feelings that these threatening situations bring. We will try to help you be able to stay with, or tolerate, those painful feelings and understand what information they contain for you. They usually tell us what we need. For instance, when we are criticized and feel belittled, these feelings may tell us that we need to feel validated and respected. When we are excluded and feel sad and lonely, these feelings may tell us that we need to feel connected to others. When we feel attacked and are scared, these feelings may tell us that we need to be protected. We will therefore try to make you strong enough to be able to stay with those feelings, to understand what they are telling you and we will then try to act on the needs they point to, here in the sessions, by bringing experiences that respond to those needs (for instance, caring compassion or just assertion), and also by figuring out how to have those needs met in the life outside. I hope that how we are together (our relationship) will be pivotal in how you can feel safe with the other person and your emotional experience, and how you can find the support, coaching, and validation in the way you need.

Given that so much of your time is spent worrying about those threatening situations and trying to prevent them, we will also focus on how to let go of some of those worries that are not necessary and how to put boundaries on them when you need to, so you can live more freely pursuing your goals.

Note. In real therapy sessions, this would have to be tailored to a particular client situation.

Relational focus in emotion-focused therapy

When providing training in EFT to various therapists whose original theoretical orientation is not humanistic (typically psychodynamic), we (LT) often encounter questions about how the EFT therapist deals with his or her relationship with the client. It appears that the question comes from a psychodynamic perspective that treats the relationship between the client and the therapist as a "lab" for exploring the client's interpersonal relating in general. This is not how EFT looks at the therapeutic relationship. The therapeutic relationship is very much in the forefront of EFT, as we highlighted above, however, it is not used to increase the client's insight into his or her interpersonal functioning, nor as a means for the client's experimenting with a new behavior. Simply put, EFT is a relational therapy where the therapist increases the client's sense of safety so that the most chronic painful emotional experiences can be brought to light and worked with. EFT is also a relational therapy in which the therapist offers a form of interpersonal relating that has healing qualities. The therapist, in an authentic caring way, conveys a deeply concerned, compassionate response to the client's pain and offers validation of emerging healthily expansive experiences such as protective anger and just empowerment (Timulak, 2015). In EFT, the person of the therapist and the relational stance they adopt, counteracts the interpersonal triggers that contributed or contribute to the feared, core, emotional vulnerability.

Questions that we have encountered in the EFT trainings we provide occasionally describe the therapeutic relationship as a representation of the client's interpersonal relating to others that can be used for the client's learning. It must be said that the client's learning about his or her interpersonal relating to others (and the therapist) is not the primary goal of EFT, nor is promotion of awareness and insight *per se*. This does not mean to suggest that these activities are not useful and therapeutic (cf. Pascual-Leone & Greenberg, 2006). Indeed, meaning making and reflecting on one's own experience, including its interpersonal connotation, is an important component of EFT, however, it needs to stem from transformational emotional experiences rather than from detached intellectualization.

Virtually all client emotional experience has interpersonal connotations and the therapist, naturally, reflects on this (e.g., if the client feels abandoned, he or she feels abandoned by someone, and it is particularly based on this someone's behavior, as perceived by the client). If some of this is mirrored in the relationship with the therapist, one option for the therapist is to reflect on this and allow it to inform their empathic response to the client. The rule here, however, is that the therapist is guided by the poignancy of what he or she tries to capture and articulate, and its relevance to the stage of emotional processing. For instance, sometimes pointing out the parallel between what is being explored in the other relationship with the therapeutic relationship may increase arousal and, as a result, increase access to chronic painful emotions. Sometimes, an interpersonal experience with the therapist, for instance, speaking directly to the therapist from an affirmed position of pride (e.g., *I am proud of myself*) may help the client to consolidate his or her new emotional experience and corresponding self-organizations. The primary goal for the EFT therapist is thus "emotional transformation", and "rewiring of problematic emotion schemes", and any interpersonal observations or guidance are used to facilitate access to core painful emotions, their articulation and productive use, and eventually their transformation.

Empathic observations pertaining to the client's interpersonal interactions, that the therapist may wish to share with the client, have to be offered in a way that would not leave the client feeling criticized or judged. Any such observations should be offered when there is a sense that they are either in, or at the edge of, the client's awareness. Obviously, this may be at times aspirational, as the therapist cannot fully control for the impact of his or her well-intended empathic interventions. For instance, this may occur when the therapist's empathic responses capture some of the client's potential instrumental emotions directed at the others (see Chapter 3). For instance, the client may not be fully aware that his or her angry outburst may be his or her way of dealing with insecurity. Conjecturing something like this on the part of the therapist may be quite difficult, and may be dependent on the context, stage of therapy, stage of the transformation process, and the quality of the overall therapeutic relationship.

Nevertheless, the therapist has to maintain a non-defensive, open way of relating that allows the client to express any disagreements and protests. It may not be possible to avoid occasional misattunements, particularly with clients who are vulnerable and highly interpersonally sensitive. The therapist's awareness of this sensitivity, however, may help him or her to be attuned to picking up on any potential ruptures and to work through the situation accordingly (see above).

Relational dynamic and GAD difficulties

Some clients with chronic anxiety issues require a great deal of interpersonal reassurance, which they experience as soothing. For these clients, the therapeutic relationship may begin to fill the role of an external, soothing agent that they seek out to soothe their distress. They may be worried about losing this type of reassuring support and may have difficulty letting go of the therapist and therapy. This is why it is so important that the therapist not only provides a soothing presence, but also assists the client in building emotional resilience, inner strength, longing for anxiety-free functioning, and independence. We will discuss this aspect of therapy and the therapeutic relationship in Chapter 9.

Conclusion

This chapter addresses the nature of the therapeutic relationship in EFT. It recognizes the importance of authenticity in the relationship and the provision of emotional warmth and emotionally attuned empathy. The nature of the therapeutic alliance is further considered in terms of offering clients a corrective relational experience while attending to, identifying, and then addressing any potential alliance ruptures. We also look at the role of the goals and tasks of therapy in relationship building. We explore the role of the therapeutic relationship in therapeutic work. The chapter closes by addressing how therapists might best attend to issues relating to the therapeutic relationship, which may arise due to the nature of the GAD dynamic.

Chapter 6

Conceptualizing GAD through the feared core pain

In addition to being a necessary condition for therapy to occur, a good therapeutic relationship is also an important active, healing, agent in treatment. The actual therapeutic work is very much informed by the client's idiosyncratic difficulties and the therapist's tailored therapeutic strategy, which attempts to address and transform those difficulties. The therapist's understanding of his or her client's difficulties, and the corresponding therapeutic strategies employed to transform those difficulties, is captured in the therapist's case conceptualization. Case conceptualization (or case formulation) is an important part of emotion-focused therapy (EFT).

Initially, EFT theorists, following a humanistic tradition, were reluctant to formally conceptualize their clients' difficulties. It was believed, as suggested by Rogers (1951), that this type of activity could potentially hinder the therapist's efforts to establish an authentic, caring, and nonjudgmental relationship with his or her client. As humanistic psychotherapies evolved, however, and in the dialogue with other traditions, such as psychodynamic and cognitive behavioral (Greenberg & Goldman, 2007), EFT theorists increasingly tried to describe what guides their thinking in an ever-evolving interaction with their clients. The detailed descriptions of the therapist's operations by leading theorists, served as a basis for the training of future EFT therapists. The work of several authors (Greenberg & Goldman, 2007; Greenberg & Watson, 2006; Watson, 2010) has culminated in a book, which tries to capture all of the steps and considerations the EFT therapist takes into account, globally, in his or her treatment strategy, as well as in moment-to-moment interaction. Goldman and Greenberg (2015) thus provide an extensive discussion of EFT formulation principles, gathering together various considerations that EFT therapists take on board when meeting and working with clients. Before we move to our case conceptualization, using the transformation model of working with GAD difficulties, we will briefly discuss Goldman and Greenberg's work.

Goldman and Greenberg (2015) divide their thinking about an individual client's presentation, and the steps, which need to be taken to transform the client's distress, into three stages. In the *first stage,* they focus on the client's narrative and emotional processing style. Here, they recommend that the therapist builds the relationship and focuses on assessing whether EFT is an appropriate treatment for the client's presenting problem. The focus is on narrative, with an emphasis on attachment and identity history, and emotional resources. It is important to attend to poignant, painful experiences (Goldman and Greenberg – see also their previous writing – which refers to a "pain compass" as a guiding principle of what therapy needs to focus on). The therapist also assesses the client's emotional processing (e.g., experiencing, vocal quality, emotional arousal, and productivity, etc. – see Chapter 3). Finally, this stage focuses on the emergence of the client's narrative (themes) related to attachment (relationships) and identity (self-appraisal)-based experiences.

The *second stage* of case formulation focuses on the identification of core (maladaptive) emotion schemes and the differentiation of secondary emotions, primary emotions, associated needs, and the identification of any blocks to accessing emotions. Finally, Goldman and Greenberg's (2015) *third stage* focuses on traditional EFT markers (e.g., unfinished business, self-criticism, self-interruption, etc.) and corresponding tasks (e.g., an empty chair dialogue, two-chair dialogues, etc.), where, in response to the client's in-session presentation, the therapist initiates experiential work which addresses the markers and leads to task resolutions (cf. Elliott *et al.*, 2004). Goldman and Greenberg also provide a list of tips (micromarkers) regarding how to work with experiential tasks (2015). We will focus on work with experiential tasks in Chapters 7 and 8.

We recommend Goldman and Greenberg's work as a comprehensive summary of the issues considered by EFT therapists when working with clients. Here, however, we will focus on a more strategic way of conceptualizing the client's presentation, which may lead to the therapist's overall (case level) therapeutic strategy. In the next two chapters we will look at its implications for "moment-to-moment" in-session work. Our case conceptualization primarily captures a macro-level understanding of the therapist's thinking about the case. Obviously, the therapist at all times considers the client's emotional arousal, emotional productivity, use of narrative, et cetera. For these considerations, Goldman and Greenberg's work (2015) is an excellent guide.

Our thinking focuses more on the client's overall self-organization and emotion schemes (see Timulak, 2015; Timulak & Pascual-Leone, 2015). As presented in the model in Chapter 4, we think of triggers that bring core emotional pain (chronic painful feelings), unmet needs embedded in core painful feelings, the client's self-treatment in the context of problematic triggers, the client's secondary emotions (undifferentiated global distress), and the client's apprehension of painful triggers and subsequent emotional and behavioral avoidance (see also Figure 4.1 in Chapter 4). To avoid repeating our case conceptualization of typical issues found in clients with GAD difficulties (presented in Chapter 4), we will now focus on a case example. We presented this case in our earlier paper presenting EFT for GAD difficulties (Timulak & McElvaney, 2016). Here we provide a more elaborate description. In addition to preserving the client's anonymity by changing some client characteristics and their presentation, we also draw on other, similar cases and thus develop a composite example of a client with GAD difficulties (this also accounts for some differences in the case, in comparison to how it appears in the above-mentioned paper).

Case example

Tina (pseudonym) was a client seen in a primary care service. She was in her late forties, married, and a mother of three children (in their teenage years). Tina worked in a helping profession. She was formally diagnosed using the Structured Clinical Interview Diagnosis for Axis I disorders according to DSM-IV (SCID-I; First, Spitzer, Gibbon, & Williams, 1997) as meeting criteria for GAD, as well as for comorbid depression, the most common, comorbid diagnosis typically found to co-occur with GAD. Tina's main presenting issues included constant tiredness, high levels of worry, trouble sleeping, constantly feeling agitated, tearfulness, irritability (particularly with children), and low mood (with occasional suicidal ideation). She had some previous treatment with antidepressants, but no experience of psycho-therapy. She reported having felt tired, anxious, full of self-doubt and worry for as long as she could remember, however, the feelings had worsened over the last year, since her mother, with whom she had a complicated relationship, passed away.

Triggers

Tina referred to several events and experiences, across therapy sessions, which helped the therapist to conceptualize both her historical and current triggers of emotional pain (see Figure 6.1). This information was initially gathered through the therapist's active inquiry (particularly in the first two to three sessions), but later, it came out mainly in the context of exploring her emotional experience or in experiential tasks (see later chapters). The therapist initially asks about such events in open-ended questions: *How was it when you were growing up? How did you feel when you were eight (or nine, ten, 12, 15, etc.)? How did you feel regarding your mom, dad, siblings, peers, other important people? What was the sense inside? For how long do you remember feeling low, anxious, worried, et cetera?* The therapist may also introduce guided imagery that brings an experiential flavor to the client's descriptions (this is particularly useful if clients cannot recall much about their childhoods): *If you imagine yourself at the age [give a particular age], being at home in your [a] room, how do you feel inside? Where is mom? Where is dad? Where are your siblings? What they are doing? What do you feel towards them? What might they be thinking of you?* The therapist may encourage the client to share anything that comes to mind; it is not necessary that the client provides an absolute truth. The therapist wants to encourage associations, which may become increasingly available to awareness as the client tries to remember. The therapist is not interested in rational analysis here. The therapist may inquire where the client sought comfort when he or she was emotionally distressed in the past, when he or she was growing up.

Start...

NEGATIVE SELF-TREATMENT

I do not deserve love/ Something is wrong with me/ Worry something will happen and I am responsible

TRIGGERS

Historical: abusive mother, sudden death of her dad, ostracized socially
Current: judgment, rejection by close ones and broader social circle

BEHAVIORAL AVOIDANCE

I have to make sure that nobody would get upset – I could be rightly judged and rejected

SECONDARY EMOTION: GLOBAL DISTRESS & REJECTING ANGER

Hopelessness, helplessness, upset, overwhelmed, anxious, tense, irritated, agitated

EMOTIONAL AVOIDANCE

Worry about potential judgment and rejection; My feelings and needs are not important. Bad feelings will be unbearable

ANXIETY/ APPREHENSION
Triggers/core pain will be unbearable

PHASE 1
Approaching emotions and exploring distress

CORE PAIN – primary and painful emotions
Loneliness – I do not feel loved
Shame – I am fundamentally flawed, I do not deserve love
Fear/Terror – Something terrible will happen that will find me unprotected

PHASE 2
Working through primary maladaptive emotions

UNMET NEEDS
To be loved (connected)
To be accepted
To be safe

COMPASSION

Enacted compassion from self, imagined father, husband, and eventually mother

GRIEVING/LETTING GO

It should not have happened, it is remembered, it pains, but it is in the past

PROTECTIVE ANGER

Standing up for self against dismissive imagined mother and other abusive figures; standing up to the self-critic and worrier

RELIEF
I feel calm and light

AGENCY – EMPOWERMENT
I feel strong and confident

PHASE 3
Facilitating emerging adaptive emotions

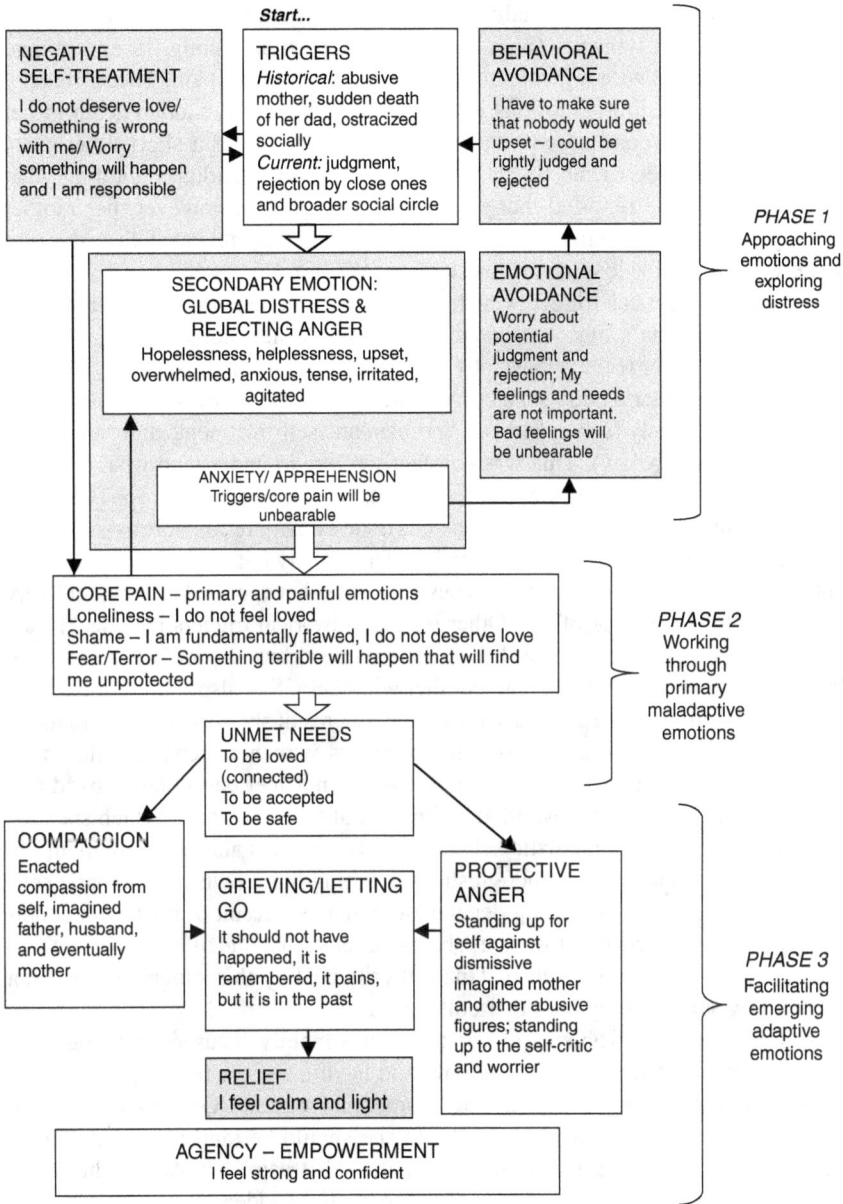

Figure 6.1 Tina's case conceptualization and transformation (Timulak & McElvaney, 2016)

Note. From Timulak, L. & McElvaney, J. (2016). Emotion-focused therapy for generalized anxiety disorder: An overview of the model. *Journal of Contemporary Psychotherapy*, 46(1), 41–52. Reprinted by permission of the publisher, Taylor & Francis, doi:10.1007/s10879-015-9310-7, and from Timulak, L. & Pascual-Leone, A. (2015). New developments for case conceptualization in emotion-focused therapy. *Clinical Psychology & Psychotherapy*, 22(6), 619–636. Adapted by permission of the publisher, John Wiley & Sons, doi:10.1002/cpp.1922

In Tina's case, our conceptualization identified a number of historical triggers, that is, events that typically (on a regular basis) or significantly (in exceptional circumstances, but with a great strength) brought emotional pain. These triggers, which produced painful emotions in her, included the early, sudden death of her father. She was around seven years old when he died after a short illness; she could still recall seeing his body, and her lack of understanding regarding what had happened. She reported that she missed him greatly, however, her mother quickly remarried. Imaginary dialogues later in therapy revealed that she was acutely aware of this loss at various stages of her life.

The main historical trigger, which brought chronic experiences of upset and invalidation in Tina's life, was her relationship with her mother. From early on she could remember feeling constantly criticized and generally disliked by her. She perceived her mother's criticism as very contemptuous and hurtful. It left her with a sense of continuously feeling bad (see "problematic self-treatment" and "core emotional pain" parts below). Tina was constantly trying to understand what could be the driving force behind her mother's contempt, but was unable to do so. The recent loss of her mother (current trigger) made this issue even more palpable as she clearly had a sense of unfinished business with her. Tina keenly felt the loss of her mother, but also felt very strongly that she had never received her approval and was still very hurt by mom's treatment of her. Other relevant historical triggers included Tina's recollection of being adored by her father's parents, but also of being separated from them by her mother who had conflict with them. She also felt her mom (and stepdad) preferred her stepsiblings to her, and as a result she was not close to them.

Tina's current triggers included her conflicts with her teenage children, in particular, her two daughters, by whom she did not feel particularly loved and respected and whom she "rewarded" with a lot of resentment, for which she then blamed herself (see problematic self-treatment). She was also worried about her husband's health and felt as though she was letting him down (problematic self-treatment) due to him becoming dependent on her as a result of his health condition. She also worried about work as she had a sense that one of her superiors was not happy with her performance. Tina felt criticized by this supervisor, and not particularly supported by her other colleagues.

Her worries (see problematic self-treatment) mainly focused on being criticized by people at work or in the family and having a sense that she was failing as mother, wife, and colleague. When something was not OK around her, she felt that it was her responsibility and that she should be (and fully expected to be) blamed – see the next part on problematic self-treatment. Among her other potential current triggers lay a fear of any potential sudden loss (particularly of people to whom she felt close); she also feared any further experience of the profound loneliness, which had accompanied her all her life.

Problematic self-treatment

The therapist could observe several problematic features regarding Tina's self-treatment in the context of pain-provoking (triggering) situations (see Figure 6.1).

Since self-worry is the most defining feature of what we currently understand as GAD, we first look at this aspect of Tina's functioning. Tina's worry revolved primarily around potential social or interpersonal situations in which she might be judged, criticized, and/or blamed, that is, situations that were particularly painful for her in most of the interactions she could remember with her mother. She worried she would be criticized by people close to her, but also by people in authority, or eventually any people including ones (such as neighbors) who could see some shortcomings in her performance (e.g., *My house is not clean, they will see it; I will be criticized for not doing my jobs properly; my husband will not be happy that I am not at home in time; I will not look after the children sufficiently and it will show on them in school; My boss will be really unhappy about something I overlooked and will shout at me in front of my colleagues; My colleagues will not talk to me, because they realize that I am weird; I will be too tired to provide for my family; People will notice who I am and will not like me; etc.*).

Closely linked to the self-worry was Tina's sense that she was fundamentally inferior and flawed. She was unforgivingly self-critical and highly self-contemptuous (*I am weak, stupid, nasty, psycho, weirdo, etc.*). She had self-doubt derived from the belief that there had to be something awful inherent in her, to have been so disliked by her mother (*It had to do something with my personality, I had to be a bad daughter*). Given that she considered her mother's behavior on some level to be very inappropriate, she questioned whether she could be "normal", as her daughter (*I have some of my mother's madness in me*). Tina criticized herself for her parenting (*It's my fault my children turned out as they did*), for her looks (*I look ugly*), as well as for her work performance (*My co-workers wouldn't praise me if they knew what I was really like*). The negative self-treatment was strong (she would be grinding teeth) and would almost have a self-harming quality in so far as she would want to punish herself. She constantly verbally attacked her character (*I am selfish*).

The therapist could also observe so-called, secondary criticism (cf. Greenberg, 2015) in which clients criticize themselves for having mental health difficulties. Tina would attack herself for having such difficulties (e.g., *you are a psycho*), and would try to coach herself to "mental health" (*I should be strong, I should not be depressed, I have no right to feel tired*). She also disliked some interpersonal symptoms of her GAD difficulties in her interactions, particularly with her children (*I am a control freak*). Another problematic self-treatment was self-interruption of her emotional experience, which we will describe below.

All the problematic self-treatment was either spontaneously visible in Tina's narrative in therapy sessions, or it was enacted and further expanded upon in experiential two-chair dialogues (see Chapter 8). Here, the therapist, at an appropriate marker (e.g., self-criticism), initiated a two-chair dialogue in which Tina enacted the critical part of her self in one of the chairs and directed the criticism towards the experiencing self, imagined in the Other chair. These dialogues also unfolded the nuances of her problematic self-treatment, their emotional quality (e.g., contempt, harshness, relentlessness), the manner (e.g., self-doubt, self-attack, self-criticism), as well as their narrative nuances, for example, what it is she actually chastises herself for. This unfolding also served to increase Tina's self-awareness and self-understanding regarding how she treats herself, its function, and how it contributes to her distress.

Global distress (secondary emotions)

The starting point of Tina's presentation was an undifferentiated global distress present across therapy sessions, often as a base from which the therapeutic work in a given session evolved (see Figure 6.1). As therapy progressed, this global distress was present for shorter periods of time (Keogh, Timulak, & McElvaney, 2014). The main forms taken by global distress in Tina's case were constant anxiety (*I feel constantly threatened, but I do not know by what*), low mood with high levels of hopelessness and helplessness (*I feel horrible and it will never change*), agitation (*I am running on constant energy*), and tiredness (*but I am totally tired*). She reported experiencing this type of distress outside of sessions, in her day-to-day life. Tina slept very little, which contributed to her tiredness. During sessions Tina also presented with many physical symptoms of global distress such as feelings of nausea and a tightening sensation in her throat. She also reported having similar problems outside the sessions. Tina was constantly tearful, resigned, and withdrawn, without hope that anybody could respond to her distress. Indeed, she often spent time in bed, feeling bad about herself, trying to hide from others. In addition to feeling so resigned, she also reported that she was very irritable and easily became angry with her teenage children. This corresponds with rejecting anger in Pascual-Leone & Greenberg's (2007) conceptualization, which we see as theoretically at the same level (secondary emotions) as global distress.

Anticipatory anxiety and emotional/behavioral avoidance

Thinking about Tina's presentation, informed by the conceptual framework presented in Chapter 4, made the therapist sensitive to her apprehension of the potential situations (triggers) that brought painful feelings (see Figure 6.1). She dreaded situations in which she might be criticized (e.g., by close ones, neighbors, relatives, superiors, and colleagues at work) or in which she would have a palpable experience of failing in something (like parenting). She was also afraid of any sudden trauma and/or loss, any situation reminding of her of the loss of her father. Tina also tried to distract herself from her feelings of loneliness. These factors fueled various forms of behavioral and emotional avoidance.

For instance, within sessions, Tina had quite low emotional arousal, despite the poignant nature of the stories she related. She regularly changed topics to distract herself. She also laughed off and dismissed her distress (e.g., *It is selfish to feel this way*). When touching on her vulnerability she often got agitated and mobilized secondary anger (*Why did you do this to me?*). She also pushed herself out of vulnerability (e.g., *Cop on, get on with it*), and described how outside of the sessions she resorted to comfort eating or a having an alcoholic drink to sooth herself. We could also see that she used worry to escape from her experience (this corresponds with Borkovec's theory of worry as cognitive avoidance).

Emotional avoidance was closely linked to, and on occasions fueled by, behavioral avoidance. For instance, Tina constantly kept busy, to not experience uncomfortable feelings, particularly of loneliness/sadness (*Well it, it stops me, this, this kind of carry on stops me from bursting into tears if you like*). To avoid shame she placated others, tried to do what she perceived others might want. Her people-pleasing behavior extended to therapy, where she came across as very compliant. Tina kept her house and her workplace in a state of perfection, so as to avoid any criticism. She tried to limit interaction with her children to avoid feeling that she was failing them. She tried to avoid any potential interpersonal confrontation (*Anything to keep the peace*). She feared any sudden trauma or loss, and consequently overprotected her loved-ones against potential disaster. The therapeutic work on avoidance in Tina's case is described in Chapter 7.

Feared core emotional pain

The therapist's main focus, from early on in therapy, was to access the client's chronic, feared core, painful emotions (see Figure 6.1). It quickly became clear that many of the emotional experiences that Tina attempted to avoid in life involved shame-based emotions. She typically expressed that she felt *worthless*, that there was something *fundamentally wrong with her*. These shame-based feelings appeared in tandem with her self-critical (contemptuous and harsh) self-treatment and in the context of existing, or potential, trigger situations in which she was attacked, criticized, and put down. Their chronicity was clearly linked to the constant put-downs Tina remembered experiencing from her mother. The experienced shame was totally self-defining and early on in therapy she was not able to tolerate it at all. When she touched on it she collapsed to hopelessness and helplessness (global distress). She also tried to avoid it as much as she could.

Closely allied to Tina's experiences of shame were related feelings of profound loneliness from which she tried to escape. The chronicity of her loneliness was linked to a sense of isolation within her family fueled by mom's rejection of her and the degree to which she felt overlooked by her siblings and everyone else in her family. Even her paternal grandparents, who were perhaps the only protective factor in her environment, eventually succumbed to pressure from Tina's mother, and broke contact with her. Tina's experienced loneliness came to the fore in early sessions, but was particularly profound when she had imaginary dialogues with the deceased father whom she lost so early in life. Again, she felt threatened by the full experience of loneliness, due to a fear that she would not be able put herself back together if she allowed loneliness to come. Loneliness was also linked to her longing to have had a closer relationship with her mother (historically) and her children (currently).

Finally, at times in the therapy sessions Tina also touched on experiences of primary fear. This was particularly linked to the potential experience of losing a loved-one (similar to how she suddenly lost her father). She dreaded being overwhelmed by experiences that she would not be able to handle and that would destroy her. These were linked with experiences of seeing her loved ones in any potential trauma (children and husband) whether social (e.g., husband's loss of job) or health related (herself, husband, and children). She could link this to a chronic, historic sense of not having anybody who would have been protective of her when she was growing up.

Tina was very successful in her avoidance of these feared feelings. She spent most of her time in everyday life avoiding any internal experience of shame, loneliness/sadness, or fear, trading it off for constant agitation, alertness, hyper-vigilance, and thus also apprehensive anxiety. In therapy sessions, it was difficult for her to tolerate her inner experience of those feelings. The therapist had to spend a lot of time helping her bear this type of experience without running from it or feeling totally overwhelmed by it (see Chapter 8).

Unmet needs

Tina's chronic, core, painful feelings pointed to the unmet needs embedded in them (see Figure 6.1). In the context of experiential work these were also more clearly articulated. She clearly longed for acknowledgment and support (*I need to get a bit of praise*) and love (*I so much want to be loved*). She specifically pointed to a chronic longing for receiving love and acknowledgment from her mother (*I missed the affection, the love, just what a mother should be doing*). The loss of her mother a year before the start of therapy signaled that this long-lasting and unfulfilled need would remain unfulfilled. Longing for connection and apprecia-tion was thus deeply frustrated.

Tina also wanted to be accepted and acknowledged, originally, by her mother, and now, by the emotionally salient (e.g., husband, children, colleagues) others in her life, but ultimately, also herself. She repeatedly went back to memories of interactions with her mother to see whether there were any glimpses of love and validation. It could also be implied from her shame-based feelings that she wanted to have an experience and inner sense that she was "all right" and that there was not anything wrong with her. She also longed for inner confidence that she had value, and that this value could be seen by others.

Apart from the need to be loved, to be connected to, to be valued and acknowl-edged, it was visible that Tina wanted to feel protected and soothed in the context of her primary panic. Her insecurity longed for a sense of safety and protection, or an inner strength that would offer her self-support. She chronically missed having a protector in her life and had a sense that she had never developed a capacity to stand-up for and protect herself. All those needs emerged in the course of therapy. During therapy, the therapist facilitated articulation of these unmet needs in the context of immediately-felt, core, chronic, painful feelings and then used the needs to orient the client toward an adaptive response to those needs (see Chapter 8).

Transforming core emotional pain and apprehensive anxiety

The first part of Figure 6.1 (up to and inclusive of the unmet needs section) points at the therapist's thinking regarding how he or she might understand the client's self-organization dynamic in the context of the feared triggers. The second part of Figure 6.1, from unmet needs down, rather captures the therapist's strategy and what helped to transform chronic core painful feelings of shame, loneliness, and fear. The therapist's overall strategy is then informed and captured in Figure 6.1. The therapeutic work is fully integrated into the relational offer on the part of the therapist, which builds a healing therapeutic relationship by providing a caring and compassionate presence, delivered through skillful empathy attuned to Tina's emotional experience, using empathic exploration and communication of empathic understanding.

Initially, the therapist tried to help the client get some regulation and soothing for the global distress she was in (particularly in early sessions, but also later sessions; often at the beginning of the session or when the client collapsed into global distress after touching core pain – see Chapter 8). The therapist then also tried to help the client to have an awareness of her emotional and behavioral avoidance, and of the cost that this problematic self-treatment entailed for her (see parts of Chapter 7). The therapist also works experientially with GAD characteristics such as worry and avoidance (and did so in the case of Tina as well), which we will explore in Chapter 7. The main work, however, focused on accessing core painful feelings, making them more differentiated and bearable for Tina. This enabled her to allow herself to feel them without being totally overwhelmed (see Chapter 8), articulate the unmet needs embedded in core painful feelings (see Chapter 8), and eventually respond to the unmet needs through compassion (self-compassion and interpersonal compassion from the therapist) and healthy protective anger (self-generated by Tina and validated by the therapist; see Chapter 8). This was generally achieved through experiential work in EFT transformational tasks such as (self–self) two-chair dialogue for problematic self-treatment and (self–other) empty chair dialogue for emotional injury (see Chapter 8).

The experience of feeling adaptive emotions responding to the unmet needs present in the chronically felt painful (maladaptive) emotions has a transformative effect that needs to be repeated over and over in therapy, as was the case in Tina's therapy. These transformative experiences led to spontaneous grieving of the pain she had to go through (although now with a more "letting go" quality), but also to a sense of empowerment and inner resilience (see the bottom of Figure 6.1). We will track this transformation process in Tina's case in more detail in later chapters (Chapters 7 and 8).

Chronicity and personality features: Some considerations

Our experience when working with clients with GAD difficulties reveals that when clients also meet criteria for what are conceptualized by the DSM as personality disorders (as assessed, for instance, by SCID-II; First, Gibbon, Spitzer, Williams,

& Benjamin, 1997), the work can be potentially more complex. This is true in particular if the clients' presentation and difficulties meet criteria for DSM categories in Cluster A (e.g., Paranoid) or Cluster B (e.g., Borderline), as these clients may be more vulnerable, fragile, and sensitive to trust issues. Here the short course of therapy (16–25 sessions) focusing on GAD symptoms may be insufficient as such clients may benefit more from long-term support. The fact that their presentation meets criteria for these personality disorders suggests that they are particularly vulnerable to emotion dysregulation and may experience particularly chronic core painful feelings of being abandoned, lonely, judged, and rejected.

The real therapeutic work, therefore, needs to focus primarily on those areas and may require stepwise approximations, carefully approaching those vulnerable feelings (cf. Pos & Greenberg, 2012). The work should focus on building inner resources to help the client bear the distress and difficult interpersonal experiences. The therapeutic work is expected to take much longer, although a briefer course of therapy may provide some form of support and contribute to building resilience. It is likely, however, that these clients will seek further support. For a dedicated account of the work with clients with this type of difficulty, see Pos and Greenberg (2012). We will spend time discussing issues of "comorbidity" in Chapter 9, which describes the process and phases of therapy. We will also focus on problems with the regulation of secondary, and particularly primary, core painful emotions in Chapter 8.

On the other hand, as mentioned above, it is quite typical to find clients who meet criteria for GAD, who also meet criteria for one of the Cluster C (anxious and fearful disorders) personality disorders (see Chapter 2). These types of difficulties indicate to the therapist the degree and perhaps also the persistency of avoidant behavior. Therapeutic work may require different levels of approximation and the focus may need to be on highlighting the cost of the avoidance, outlining what is being missed by the client due to the avoidance, and working on mobilizing the client's natural desire for a fuller, more engaged life (see Chapter 7). Again, expectations of what can be achieved in short-term therapy may be limited as the client's cautiousness and avoidant behavior are firmly ingrained traits and patterns of behavior. Clients also have firm beliefs about the advantage of such behaviors in providing a much sought after sense of security. We will discuss this issue more in Chapter 9.

Use of case conceptualization

While classical humanistic therapy, such as client-centered therapy (Rogers, 1951), was hesitant about the therapist spending time conceptualizing the client's difficulties and formulating a strategy for therapy, out of fear that it would impair the therapist's authenticity, EFT is more explicit regarding the use of conceptualization/formulation in informing therapeutic strategy (cf. Goldman & Greenberg, 2015; Timulak & Pascual-Leone, 2015). This increased usage of conceptualization in EFT evolved out of the recognition of its usefulness in harnessing the client's exploration and transformation processes. As most of EFT's clinical writing developed out of process research, and principal EFT theorists were also process researchers, naturally occurring research observations and reflections began increasingly to influence clinical practice. This was also our experience (hence this chapter).

The here presented conceptualizing framework, as well as other EFT writing on case formulation (e.g., Goldman & Greenberg, 2015; Greenberg & Goldman, 2007; Greenberg & Watson, 2006; Watson, 2010), mainly serve the therapist's understanding of his or her overall therapeutic strategy. It informs the therapist's thinking about the therapy in between the sessions, but it also informs the therapist's general direction in therapy and broadens the therapist's attention to the phenomena uncovered in the process of therapy. While on some level it may appear as very technical, and potentially as being in some way a hindrance to the therapist's authenticity, the opposite is true. A therapist's skills are internalized over the therapist's career and what was once a technical skill, over time, becomes a part of one's professional persona, while remaining authentically caring towards, and present with, the client. Indeed, the therapist's skillfulness, which may include clarity regarding what is happening in therapy and where the therapy may be heading, may be an important part of building the client's trust in the therapist and therapeutic process (Diamond, Diamond, & Levy, 2014).

While the case conceptualization described above is something that the therapist engages in internally, it informs the therapist's reflections on the therapeutic process that are potentially shared with the client, and it informs any psychoeducational teaching that the therapist may engage in, in therapy (see also Chapter 9). Indeed, the EFT therapist encourages the client's meaning-making of the experience in therapy as an important trajectory in the therapeutic process; one in which the therapist may want to pause the client, and highlight what just happened (for instance, the therapist may point out to the client the level of self-contempt present in the expressed self-criticism and the devastating effect that it may have on the client). This may contribute to the client's making sense of his or her experience (that is, being co-constructed with the therapist), thereby contributing to the broadening of the client's awareness of their own self–self and self–other processes in generating particular emotional experiences. The natural space for sharing the therapist's reflection, informed by the therapist's case conceptualization, is towards the end of the sessions, when the therapist asks the client to reflect on the therapeutic work in the session (on what happened in the session, e.g., in an unfinished business dialogue). Here the therapist may offer his or her understanding, informed by the framework presented in this chapter.

We also recommend the therapist use the framework presented in Figure 4.1 when making notes from the session. Indeed, this framework was used in this manner in a number of studies (e.g., Dillon *et al.*, 2016; O'Brien *et al.*, 2017; McNally *et al.*, 2014) to track the client's process in individual therapy sessions. We would not, however, recommend that the framework be used for the flow-chart type of learning seen in CBT. We consider this could potentially lead to intellectualization, which might become an obstacle to first-hand, fresh, experiential exploration. However, we used a simplified framework and theory of what occurs in somebody who is diagnosed with GAD, when the client inquired about their condition. In such cases, it was used in a more abstract form, rather than specifically tailored to the client, again, perhaps out of concern that it would prevent therapeutic work rather than facilitating it.

While we are cautious about the flow-chart teaching, we would encourage therapists to use the framework, or even better, parts of it, in reflecting on what happened in the session, at important junctures in the session and at end points of the session. We would also encourage therapists to use the framework in devising potential homework for the client (see Chapter 9). The framework should be at hand for the therapist if the client inquires about the therapist's understanding of the client's difficulties and the therapist's understanding regarding what needs to happen in therapy in order for the client to overcome his or her difficulties. Finally, the framework, together with the overall EFT theory, should be a general guide for the therapist that can be leaned on when providing rationale for therapy, early on in therapy, or in the induction to therapy (see also Chapter 9).

Conclusion

This chapter outlines how, over time, EFT has adopted the practice of developing case conceptualizations (or formulations) as a means of guiding the therapist through the work of therapy. A key text is used to illustrate how case formulation of experiential therapy is used in the pursuit of elaborating an understanding of the client's presenting difficulty. We then outline our own approach to case conceptualization, a more strategic way of conceptualizing the client's presentation, which may guide the therapist's overall therapeutic strategy. The approach postulates several important domains of reflection that the therapist employs. These include triggers of emotional pain, global distress that is on the surface of the client's pain, problematic self-treatment that represents an unsuccessful effort to deal with the self in the context of the triggers, apprehension and anxiety linked to the triggers that also lead to emotional and behavioral avoidance, and the underlying core pain and unmet needs. We also briefly mention transformative processes, such as self-compassion and protective anger, that respond to the core pain. A case study is presented and then used to take the reader through our conceptualization.

Chapter 7

Overcoming avoidance – working with worry

As Chapters 4 and 6, make clear, the main therapeutic work in emotion-focused therapy (EFT) for generalized anxiety disorder (GAD) difficulties lies in transforming underlying chronic painful emotions (emotion schemes), which are feared by the client who seeks to avoid them by engaging in worry, mainly concerning potential, threatening triggers and the emotions they may bring. Indeed, when we began the EFT for GAD project we assumed, theoretically, that transformation of this chronic underlying vulnerability would lead to the client overcoming their chronic apprehension, anxiety, and worry. We assumed that clients would begin to trust their internal capacity to process difficult triggers and the emotions they bring. We theorized that, as clients became more emotionally resilient, they would no longer need to fear the situations that currently preoccupied them. As the research evolved, we realized that we had underestimated the problems of chronic worrying and profound emotional and behavioral avoidance.

As we started to review our cases and reflect on our ongoing work, we identified two reasons why we needed to focus on the worry, and emotional and behavioral avoidance. We recognized that the worry presentation (in particular) was so dominant in clients that it was impossible to ignore. We learned early on that many clients, who acutely felt the emotional impact of their worry, appreciated having some direct sense of mastery and control over this process. We could also clearly observe that the worry process leads an almost autonomous life and is so ingrained that even when clients felt particularly confident and resilient inside, it did not take much for them to succumb once more to the worry process, should a potential trigger emerge. It appeared that years of worrying had led to the worry process becoming particularly ingrained (wired in), in a complex situational-habitual manner (as it appears with corresponding ingrained patterns at the level of neural circuitry-connections, e.g., Hilbert *et al.*, 2015; Li, Cui, Zhu *et al.*, 2016). We therefore started to examine this process, and with the creative use of established experiential techniques (tasks), we started to develop a model of working with the worry (Timulak & McElvaney, 2016) and study its application (Murphy *et al.*, 2017).

Working with worry in EFT

Several EFT authors (Elliott, 2013; Greenberg, 2015; Timulak & McElvaney, 2016; Watson, Timulak, & Greenberg, in press) describe a tentative use of two-chair dialogue for working with worry. Our research group also examined it empirically across our initial EFT cases for GAD difficulties (Murphy *et al.*, 2017). This empirical work, and our clinical observations, informed the model presented in Table 7.1. Below, the model is described using clinical examples.

I Marker of worry

Typical in-session presentations of the worry marker contain the clients' worrying and feeling exhausted, or may contain descriptions of recent worries that prevented the client from participating in everyday activities, and caused trouble with sleep, leading to experiences of profound exhaustion and debilitating anxiety. The client might say: *Last night I could not sleep. My partner is traveling on a business trip and she needs to drive a long distance. I kept worrying that she might have an accident and die. I started to worry about the impact of it on our children. I started to worry about how I should prepare her for the journey, what I needed to tell her and perhaps suggest she might use some alternative, safer, means of transport, for instance, the train.* The client may describe such worries and become agitated in the session, which offers an excellent opportunity to make the worry the focus of the session.

Table 7.1 Steps in the worry dialogue (Timulak, 2017)

	Experiencer chair	Worrier chair
1.	Marker – worrying, exhaustion	
2.		Enactment of worrying – experiential quality
3.	Accessing and differentiating anxiety and tiredness (potentially also core pain)	
4.	Articulating and expressing need for freedom, for less limited life	
5.		Probing for compassion – seeing the pain and unmet need (highlighting function of worry)
		A) If no compassion coming – go with the increased worry (unable to control)
		B) If compassion is coming – savoring it experientially and expressing it
6a.	Building protective anger, setting boundary to the worry	
6b.	Letting compassion in – savoring it experientially, but still insisting on the boundary	

The worry is sometimes embedded in other problematic forms of self-treatment. For instance, it may be closely linked to self-criticism. The client may worry that they will fail in some way, or that they will be judged, or that they will not perform appropriately, because deep down they "believe" that they are a failure, weak, inadequate, et cetera. Such beliefs are expressions of chronic self-criticism. In such cases, the worry dialogue may oscillate between the critic (we explain how to work with self-critical processes in Chapter 8) and the worry dialogue. Indeed, in our early attempts to work with GAD clients, we noticed that dialogues often overlapped because, when we asked the client to enact self-worrying (e.g., *I will harm my children*), they could easily switch into the critic (e.g., *I am a horrible parent*).

Given that work with the critic is so well described in EFT literature (e.g., Elliott *et al.*, 2004; Greenberg *et al.*, 1993) there is the danger that the therapist may focus solely on this aspect of the client dynamic. EFT therapists are trained to listen for markers of the self-critical process, and thus, they may have a tendency to distil the critic into the worry, particularly because the worry and the critic are commonly found together (we are currently running a project which investigates the interaction of the critic and the worry self-treatment, Toolan, 2017). This is not necessarily a big problem. Therapy needs to focus on the self-critical processes, as they are typically central to the clients' core, chronic, painful, primary, maladaptive feelings. However, it may become a problem if the worry is overlooked entirely in therapy. Our experience suggests that if we want to transform clients' chronic worrying, this process must become an explicit focus of therapy. Clients have to have more understanding of their worrying, more control over it, feel capable of letting go of it, and the ability to respond and stand-up to the worry.

Another self-process that resembles worry is rumination (see Chapters 2 and 4). In worry, however, the client is concerned with preventing, or preparing for, potential threats that could bring painful feelings (i.e., protective function). In rumination clients repeatedly go over painful situations and experiences that have already happened, hoping perhaps to make sense of them, master them, learn from them, get some reassurance, et cetera. The main distinction is that the worry process is driven by a future-oriented fear of triggers (and the emotion they bring) whereas, in rumination the person perpetually revisits a situation that has already taken place. The common feature in both processes is an attempt to get some sense of control. In both cases the process is mostly unsuccessful, as the endless preparation for future threats (worry) is, in and of itself, anxiety provoking, which leads to hyper-vigilance and exhaustion in the client. The endless analyzing (rumination) of the painful situation causes distress, and any learning (meaning-making) from the repeated, re-analyzing of the situation is upsetting and prevents respite from the situation. Although we are not primarily focusing on work with rumination here, clients with GAD difficulties may be prone to rumination. Again, ruminations can be linked to other self-processes such as self-criticism, for example, *I go over, over, and over the situation I failed in.* Work with self-ruminating may resemble work with worry, described below, however, there are some differences. While the worry process wants to protect from threat, rumination wants to achieve a sense of mastery that might offer some reassurance. Rumination, like worry, can be linked to self-criticism and thus may incorporate the punitive element of going over one's own mistakes.

Another self-process, similar to worry, is obsessional thinking, as in what is currently recognized as obsessive-compulsive disorder (OCD). In obsessions (see Chapters 2 and 4), the person is "intruded" upon by thoughts or images signaling danger (e.g., dangerous bacteria). The person does not have a sense that he or she can in any way control the thoughts of threat, and may be uncertain of their origin, hence the sense of being intruded upon by such thoughts or images. Although conscious control is not recognized, one could speculate that thinking of or imagining potential dangers fulfils a similar function to the self-protection against potential threat found in the worry process, which is a somewhat slower and more deliberate process of either staying safe, or acting in a way that would ensure greater safety. Although work with obsessions is not described here, there are attempts to describe this type of work from an EFT perspective (the work of Robert Elliott and Catalina Woldarsky). We did not encounter this type of problem in the clients with GAD difficulties that we worked with, but we would postulate that the therapeutic work would broadly follow a strategy similar to the one highlighted here for working with worry (see also below).

Another self-treatment process resembling worry is self-panicking, or self-scaring. This is particularly visible in panic disorder, for example, *You are getting a panic attack, you are going to faint,* in specific phobias, for example, *This sound of the plane is strange, something is wrong* (fear of flying); social phobia/anxiety, for example, *They judge me, they see how inadequate I am.* Variations of self-panicking that may include self-worrying are sometime referred to as *anxiety splits* (e.g., Elliott, 2013; Greenberg, 2015). Given that clients with GAD difficulties often have other comorbid anxiety difficulties, variations of the anxiety splits are quite common. While we are focusing here on the work with worry, these self-panicking, self-scaring processes have to be addressed in therapy if they are part of the client's presentation and we briefly comment on some of those anxiety-producing, self-treatment processes alongside the description of the worry dialogue.

2 Enactment of worrying – experiential quality

Once the worry marker is established, the therapist presents the two-chair worry dialogue task to the client. Typically, it is not the first chair work (see Chapter 9) that the client has engaged in, in therapy, as the therapist may have done some tasks earlier in therapy that focused more directly on the client's core chronic painful feelings, for example, two-chair task for self-criticism or an empty chair dialogue for an interpersonal injury (traditionally referred to as empty chair task). We will present these tasks in the next chapter. So, if the client is already familiar with two-chair tasks the therapist's explanation of the task may be brief. If this was the client's first exposure to the chair dialogue, the therapist has to explain the task in a bit more detail (we will talk more about the overall therapy strategy and the use of chair dialogues in Chapter 9). The therapist may then say something along these lines: *So, this is how you worry yourself ... Let's have a look at this. We will try to set up a dialogue. We will bring in this chair* (referred to as the Worrier chair), *if you could please sit here and be that part of you, that voice inside of you that expresses those worries and if you could express those worries to this part of the self and worry her (him). Make him/her* (points to the original client's chair that we refer to as the Experiencer chair; cf. Greenberg *et al.*, 1993) *worry about ...* The therapist always tweaks his or her instructions so they would match the client's presentation and would be accessible, in language that the client would understand. The first chair-work dialogue should not come as a total surprise to the client. From early on (from the first session), the client is socialized to EFT by being told that the therapy works with imaginary dialogues, in which the client is asked to enact parts of the self or other people from their life in order to access emotional experience and generate adaptive experiences that would counteract chronically painful experiences.

Once the therapist explains the task, he or she coaches the client in enacting the worry fully: *Let's do it. Let's have a look how you do it.* The exchange may appear as follows (a portion of this exchange overlaps with an example in Watson, Timulak, & Greenberg, in press):

Therapist: *Okay, so come here and now be you. This is the worry part, yeah, somehow you worry yourself. So, let's have a look at how you worry yourself, yes, do some of it.*

Client [in the Worrier chair]:   *How do I make myself worry?*

Therapist: *Yeah, be that voice inside that expresses the worries. Just do it.*

Client [enacting the worry]:   *But are you ready that if they do say it to you about not getting that report finished this week, are you ready for confrontation* [in work]? *Um.*

Therapist: *Okay.*

...

Client [enacting another worry]:   *Did you sort out everything for John's* [boyfriend's] *birthday? Have you got enough money for that ... for his birthday present?*

....

Client: *Um ... will he like his birthday present? Um ... have you spent too much money on the birthday? Um ...*

...

The therapist coaches the client to express their worries to the point where the client fully goes with the task and the worry is enacted in a way that conveys its experiential quality (urgency, a sense of agitation, insistence, control). Sometimes, even early on in the dialogue, the therapist may probe for, or try to capture the function of, the worry, although this is more commonly step 5 (The therapist: *So you do it in order to ensure that she does not make a mistake as she would not be able to bear the consequences? Perhaps an upset boyfriend or boss at work?*). The relationship of worry with the self-critic may come to the fore at this stage as well (*You had better do everything right, because they will find out what a fraud you are*; Toolan, 2017). Early on in therapy (see Chapter 9) the therapist and the client may fluidly change from worrier to the critic dialogues at this stage (2) of the dialogue, later switching back to the critic dialogue, which may be more directly linked to the core painful emotions (e.g., shame). This happens as the client spontaneously worries him or herself about potential painful triggers (e.g., rejection by others) and criticizes him or herself for why that trigger is painful (e.g., because the client is weak or deserving of rejection, etc.). Overall, however, it is important that each of these processes (self-worrying and self-criticism) is looked at and worked on independently. It is therefore important that therapy contains several, purely worry-focused dialogues, despite the fact that the client may at any point switch from worry to the critic. The therapist therefore must be disciplined to stay on the worry task (highlighted in Table 7.1) in order to address and transform the worry process.

In the case of markers similar to worry, such as self-scaring or self-panicking, the therapist may use a variation of this task, in which the client enacts the panicking part of the self, as illustrated in this example:

Therapist: *So how do you make him* [pointing to the Experiencer chair] *panic, yes? Play the panic attack, yes. How would you panic him?*

Client: *I just keep panicking and say when you went into this room, hardly anybody knows you. You're going to get so panicky and anxious that you are just going to have to get up and leave and everyone around will look at you.* [Here the panic is linked to social anxiety and the underlying unbearable shame. The therapist, however, focuses specifically on self-panicking – see the therapist's next response.]

Therapist: *Okay, but I am the panic attack. You are here. So, like I'm uncontrollable and I'll overwhelm you.* [The therapist encourages the client to enact the panic attack that is taking over the client, over the client's body.]

Client: *Yeah.*

Therapist: *Yes, tell him, do it, enact it. Almost as if you were the panic attack. I'm powerful and uncontrollable, I will take over.*

Client: *I'm stronger than you.*

Therapist: *And I'll embarrass you, yeah, do it.*

Client: *I'm stronger than you. I control you. I will panic your body, I will make your legs go limp, I will bring the tension in your chest, I will scare you.*

So, while the worry process looks at potential future threats, the self-panicking (that often happens in everyday life out of the client's awareness) is immediate and focused on triggering the bodily symptoms of panic in that moment. Some clients with GAD difficulties co-present with other anxiety splits (Elliott, 2013; Greenberg, 2015), so there may be times in therapy when the therapist may also facilitate a self-panicking dialogue (see Chapter 9 about dialogue variations when working with clients with GAD difficulties). In general, however, while worry dialogues are central to therapy and are repeatedly engaged in with the clients with GAD difficulties, other variations of similar anxiety and fear producing dialogues are engaged in rarely, and only with clients that specifically present with markers for them.

3 Accessing and differentiating anxiety and tiredness (potentially also core pain)

After the client enacts and expresses the worry process in its full experiential quality, the therapist asks the client to change seats and return to the Experiencer chair (the default chair that the client sits in, in therapy). The therapist then initially probes for the impact and the toll of the worry:

Therapist: *Come back here* [pointing to Experiencer chair] *… see what happens inside when you get this. What happens inside when you get this flow of thoughts and worries?*

The client then has an opportunity to focus inwards and see the impact the worries have on him or her. The impact of being subjected to the enacted worrying is then typically seen in the client's experiences of tiredness, exhaustion, and anxiety. The therapist tries to slow the client down, so that he or she might fully feel and notice the unpleasant impact the worries have on him or her, inside his or her body, on his or her internal experience. The therapist focuses and paces his or her interventions so that the client might at first focus inward, on the experience, articulate it in language, and then express it to the Worrier chair. The dialogue may then look as follows:

Therapist: *What happens inside when he/she* [pointing to the Worrier chair] *worries you here and now?*
Client: [slowly] *… I feel tired, exhausted.*
Therapist: *It's just tiring, exhausting. Yeah?*
Client: *It's tiring* [looks deflated]. *I just feel shut down and exhausted.*

Therapist: *And what does it do to you inside if she* [the worrier] *goes around and around?*

Client: *I feel overwhelmed, tired, and scared.*

…

Therapist: *If you go to that tiredness. Yes? How does it feel there?*

Client: *If I go to that tiredness, I'll go to sleep.*

…

Therapist: *It feels like it's just never ending tiredness.*

Client: *It's just 24 hours a day.*

Therapist: *Just try it for ten seconds to feel that tiredness. Yes? Don't run away from it.*

Client: *I don't have to try, I feel it.*

Therapist: *Okay. It's there. Okay.*

Client: *It's here.*

The experience of anxiety, tiredness, exhaustion, pressure, and so on is typical of this stage of the worry dialogue. At times the clients may also touch on the core pain that they are trying to avoid, by over-preparing for the pain provoking triggers. This is perhaps due to the associative nature of human emotional functioning, as the content of the worry is never too far from the triggers and/or problematic self-treatments that bring the emotional pain (e.g., the worry, *I am worried that they will reject me,* can easily trigger experiences of *feeling rejected*). The client may thus move from more symptom-oriented (secondary) distress to more poignant and clearly articulated core painful feelings (such as loneliness/sadness, shame, or primary fear). The following brief example illustrates how a more chronic, core feeling of shame may surface in the context of the worry dialogue:

Client: *It is so tiring it's unbelievable.*

Therapist: *Yeah. But it's almost like "I'm totally taken over by you"* [taken over by the worry] *or something? Yes? "I can't even see what I need", "I'm just kind of, eh, constantly behind. I have to do something. I'm dragged actually". Yeah?*

…

Client: *Because it's* [the worry] *always there.*

Therapist: *Yeah.*

…

Client: *The worry is always there.*

Therapist: *Yeah.*

…

Therapist: *Okay. So tell her. Yes? You're constantly there. Yes?* [The EFT therapist always makes sure that the client attends to inner feelings, names them, and expresses them – cf. Greenberg, 2015.]

Client: *Yeah … It's trying to keep a lid on you so that everyone else can't see me falling apart.*

Therapist:	*Yeah. Yeah. Yeah. I see. So it's like, "You almost make me fall apart but I can't afford to fall apart". Yes?*
Client:	*Yeah. Yeah.*
Therapist:	*Because I have to be there for others.*
Client:	*Yeah. And the constant …*
Therapist:	*But it's just that extra pressure or something?*
Client:	*That's exactly it.*
Therapist:	*Yeah. And the feeling is like what you are saying. It's like pain. Yes? And something like total tiredness and total …*
Client:	*Tiredness and anger and … anger at myself for being so irrational, for being so …* [a hint of self-criticism].
…	
Therapist:	*So it's like, "Anger at you that you make me worry constantly," or something?*
Client:	*Because you're worrying constantly* [speaking to the Worrier chair] *… it's making me not a nice person.* [Crying. Here the client touches on a more core experience, shame of who she is.]

The client's touching on shame in this example is very fleeting. Often in the first round of the dialogue the client stays at a more symptom level. The core pain is more likely to be activated if the worrier does not soften (stage 5A; cf. Murphy et al., 2017). In any case, if the therapist touches on more central chronic painful feelings, linked to self-judgment or painful interpersonal triggers, typically, the therapist would then initiate the task, which focuses more directly on this core issue (see Chapter 8 for the description of intrapersonal and interpersonal tasks used in work with core pain). In general (see Chapter 9), we prefer to work at a deeper level. Worry is a process in which the client attempts to prepare for potential, unbearable situations and emotions (a more superficial process); the deeper level process, however, concerns the one that evokes those unbearable emotions (chronic problematic emotion schemes). There are, however, exceptions from focusing on a deeper level of processing. As we need to make sure that the worry process is sufficiently addressed and transformed in therapy, we also focus on it by following the task outlined in Table 7.1 to completion, several times in therapy (see task completion principle in Greenberg et al., 1993). This requires balance, an ability to discern which process to follow at which time, and we will discuss it more fully in Chapter 9.

We have commented on the other forms of problematic self-dialogues that heighten anxiety, such as self-scaring and self-panicking. Here we note that these forms, at this stage of the dialogue, usually bring a more acute experience of anxiety, such as panic symptoms (stage 3). So, rather than being tired and anxious, the client may feel sheer panic or terror. In such a case the therapist does not need to deepen the process but rather may help the client to stay with panicky feelings (for instance using deep breathing). This may accelerate engagement with stage 4.

4 Articulating and expressing need

Once the toll of the worry is fully experienced by the client, and expressed to the part of self imagined to be in the Worrier chair, the therapist focuses the client on what he or she needs as he or she feels the impact (toll) of the worry. At this point, clients often articulate that they need a break from their worries, greater freedom from them, and that they need to have a sense of freedom and of freer living in general (Murphy *et al.*, 2017). The therapist encourages the client to express these needs to the part in the Worrier chair that instills the worry. The exchange may look as follows:

Therapist: *Okay. What do you need when you feel so tired? What do you need from her* [pointing to the Worrier chair]? *She's* [the worrier] *so scared that she kind of tenses you. She controls you. And you take it on.*

...

Client: *I need her to be quiet.*
Therapist: *Tell her.*
Client: *Be quiet.*
Therapist: *Okay.*
Client: *Just let me be ...*
Therapist: *Okay. Let me be.*
Client: *Give my brain a break.*
Therapist: *Give my brain a break. Tell her ...*
Client: *Give my brain a break.*
Therapist: *Yeah.*
Client: *Be quiet. Just be quiet. Just stop talking. Leave me ... On my days off let me have a day off.*
Therapist: *Okay. Okay. So this is what I need. Yes?*

The articulation and expression of the need is then often further worked on in step 6A (see Table 7.1) as the articulation of the need for freedom from the worry often helps to generate the assertive, protective anger that helps to keep the worry process at bay (or can help to stop it once the client catches him or herself in the midst of it). Similarly, as in the case of working with the worry, the articulation of the need is an important process in working with other anxiety triggering processes such as self-scaring or self-panicking. In those instances, the client articulates and expresses the need to be free from the self-scaring and/ or self-panicking process.

5 Probing for compassion

Once the client has articulated and expressed the need towards the worrier, the therapist asks the client to return to the Worrier chair and instructs the client to look at the experiencer and see the client's pain (the cost of the worry) and the need for a break or freedom from the worrier. The therapist asks the client to see what they feel inside, towards that pained part of their self that was just accessed and enacted in the Experiencer chair. The therapist does this with the hope that seeing the pain and the heartfelt need for a break from the worry might elicit compassion (softening of the worry) in the part of the client accessed and enacted in the Worrier chair. The therapist is thus checking-in for a potential softening. An example of such checking-in is provided here:

Therapist: *Okay. Could you swap now* [to the Worrier chair]*? So now as a worrier. Okay? This is the worry in you. Okay? Almost what's the response from inside? You see her saying: "I need you to stop", "I can't bear it anymore. I have my ... I'd like to have kind of time on my own with my partner". Yeah?*
Client: *Mmm.*
Therapist: *"I need you to stop." What's your response from inside to that?*

Essentially there are two types of scenarios following this (5A and 5B in Tale 7.1). Particularly in the early dialogues, the clients (in the Worrier chair) do not soften (5A) and may express incapability of letting go of the worry. Another more likely outcome is that they feel threatened by the demand, as they associate the worrying with the provision of safety, leading them to escalate their efforts to worry the self, which is sitting in the Experiencer chair. In such a case the therapist goes with the escalation, allows it and highlights it and its function. The escalation will be used in step 6A for building the protective anger in the Experiencer chair that would allow the client to set a boundary to the worry. The articulation of the function of the worry may serve potentially as a stepping stone to a potential, later, softening of the worry (e.g., *I cannot stop, not because I want to scare you, but because I want to protect you*). An example of escalation and unraveling the function of the worry may look like this:

Client: *If I stop* [making you worry] *what'll keep you going?*
Therapist: *Okay. "So, I can't stop." Yes? Tell her. "I can't stop."*
Client: *I can't stop because if I stop your life will stop.*
Therapist: *Okay.*
Client: *Your, your drive will stop. Your determination will stop. Your "get up and go" would stop. And you won't get out of the bed* [The function of the worry].
Therapist: *Okay. So it's like, "I'm making you work". Yes? "I'm, I'm making you function."*
Client: *I'm keeping you going.*
Therapist: *Okay. Tell her. "I'm keeping you going."*
Client: *I'm keeping you going. I'm keeping you ... I'm getting you out of the bed in the morning so as you can fix all these things. So as you can ...*
Therapist: *Okay. Be on top of things.*

Client:	*Be on top of everything and be awake and moving. That's ...*
Therapist:	*Okay. But it's almost driven by fear that you could fall apart. Yes? If I wasn't kind of managing you or if I wasn't ...* [highlighting the function of the worry].
Client:	*Yeah. I'd ...*
Therapist:	*You and others would fall apart. I mean the, the whole place. Yeah. The whole family would fall apart. Yes? If I wasn't there.*
Client:	*Yeah.*
Therapist:	*Pushing you and pushing you.*
Client:	*And fight with ... Keeping you on top of all the goings-on in the house and with the three kids and ... keeping your, keeping your mind going.*
Therapist:	*Okay. So I can't give you a break. Yes? Tell her. I can't give you.*
Client:	*So I can't give you a break. I can't let you stop.*

The alternative scenario in this stage of the two-chair task for worry is that the client (in the Worrier chair) is capable of softening, or is at least willing to try to soften, and shows the self in the Experiencer chair some compassion. Sometimes the client may express an inability to stop worrying, but regrets the impact the worry has on the self in the Experiencer chair, and may say something like *"please ignore me if you can"* or *"please help me let go"*. Occasionally the client in the Worrier chair recognizes that this part of his or her self (the worrier) is problematic for others as well; sadness may come and the sense of isolation that the client in the Experiencer chair may need responding to in some supportive way. An example of a tentative softening may look like this:

Therapist:	*So do you want to be on her side* [hinting at the voice quality expressed by the client]?
Client:	*Yeah, I mean, yeah.*
Therapist:	*So tell her, yes, I want to be on your side.*
Client:	*I want to be on your side.*
Therapist:	*Okay, okay.*
Client:	*I mean, if it means that you won't behave recklessly.*
Therapist:	*Okay, okay, so this is my fear, yes, it's like I don't want to be stopping you, but I care about you, yes. I have to see that you are safe or something, yes, or that you are not harming yourself, yeah.*
Client:	*Yeah.*
Therapist:	*But it's so difficult for me to let go, yes, because I can't trust that you will not harm yourself or something, yeah.*

Here we can see a tentative softening. There is a sense expressed that *I do not want to make you tense and scare you, because I see it is harming you, but nevertheless I need you to be safe, I need some reassurance that you will be safe.* The quality of expressed softening varies. However, in therapies which are progressing smoothly, it is increasingly direct with a more "letting go" quality of the worry, and less reassurance seeking.

6B Letting compassion in

If compassion is expressed, the client is asked to return to the Experiencer chair (step 6B) and is encouraged to let in the compassion, savor it, and feel the potential relief it brings. This may be a more complex process, as clients may be reluctant to let in any feelings of being cared for. Their self-criticism, the sense of undeservedness, may be obstructing it. The therapist must empathically validate that hesitation, but ultimately needs to empathically encourage the client to give it a try, and attempt to let the caring in. An example may look as follows:

Therapist: *Okay, see if you can let it in? Her saying she feels warmth towards you. What's the sense inside when you hear it?*

Client: *I don't know really, are you sure?*

Therapist: *Okay, it's like I don't trust it fully. It feels nice, but it's like I am not used to it or I wouldn't expect it.*

Client: *I am not really used to it at all, no.*

Therapist: *But it feels nice, yeah.*

Client: *Yeah.*

Therapist: *Okay and it's important to be able to admit it, yes, even though it's difficult, it's cringing in some way because you are not used to it, yeah.*

Client: *Yeah.*

Therapist: *So what's the feeling like inside?*

Client: *I suppose it's calm as well, you know.*

Therapist: *Okay, so it's very nice, yeah.*

These stages (5 and 6B) of the two-chair dialogue (probing for compassion) may not be present in the dialogues addressing self-scaring or self-panicking. Compassion is typically not provided by the part of the self that scares the client, but rather, comes potentially from an imagined, caring significant other. In the work with self-scaring (such as self-panicking in panic attacks), it is much more important to build protective anger and the sense of a self that cannot be scared. The promotion of protective, boundary-setting anger is also crucial in self-worry dialogues.

6A Promoting protective anger

Any resistance to softening, and escalation of the worrier, can be used by the therapist to build protective anger in the Experiencer chair. So, while the therapist probes for compassion in the worrier when the pain is expressed, and wants to see whether there is any softening towards the self in pain in the experiencer chair, the therapist does not panic if softening fails to appear. The therapist simply highlights the drama of not softening, and amplifies the rejecting stance and re-imposition of the worry process by the worrier. This escalation and re-imposing of the worry will then be used in the Experiencer chair, to which the therapist invites the client. While compassion and softening come from witnessing the pain the worrier brings, protective anger comes in response to the highlighted problematic treatment (mistreatment), as a healthy protection against it.

The therapist may therefore encourage a protective response and increase the likelihood of it emerging, by highlighting the mistreatment; by asking the client to see what they want to do in the face of mistreatment. If the client is unable to stand up for the self, the therapist approximates the assertion to illustrate what the client may be capable of, for example, by facilitating expression of what they would wish to do, had they the power to stand up to the worry. The anger also often comes with articulation of the need (see point 4). An example may look like this:

Therapist: *She is saying she won't stop. What is your response to that? Will you let her do it to you?*

Client: *... No. It is too much to take. I have had enough.*

...

Therapist: *I have had enough of worries. So I have a right for you to let go of worrying me. Yes?*

...

Client: *Yeah.*

Therapist: *Yeah. Tell her.*

Client: *You don't ... How would I say it? I do have the right for you to let go. I ... I can manage myself. I'm not going to break at the slightest thing.*

If the client is unable to stand up to the worrier, the therapist may ask the client to express this inability, and see how it feels to be overpowered by the worrier. The therapist may then invite the client to check-in and see what their feelings are when they are defeated by the worrier (e.g., *How is it inside when s/he – the worrier – overpowers you and insists that s/he will worry you and scare you?*). Clients typically respond by stating that they do not like it (*it feels horrible*). If clients are then asked what they want, they are more likely to generate self-protective responses, particularly if the therapist respects that they are unable to, but focuses rather on what they need and what they would wish for if they had the power. The therapist may creatively look for the ways, with the client, that would help him or her to reclaim the space they need. This process can be illustrated in John's dialogue:

Client: *It's not nice, like. It's, like, it's not nice knowing that I could be this way for the rest of my life, you know.* [Expressing hopelessness of being unable to stand up to the worry.]

Therapist: *Yeah, this would be extreme now, yes, what I'll say, but trying whether it fits. I will be your slave. Tell him.* [The therapist here uses a paradoxical intervention. The therapist wants the client to check-in and see whether they are okay with the total collapse and submission. This typically has the opposite effect, as the experience is unpleasant and very much against what the client experientially needs. Consequently, clients are able to discern that this does not feel good for them, and start to fight for themselves.]

Client: *Yes, I'll be, I'll be your slave too. I cannot stand up to you.*

Therapist: *See how it feels. Do you really want to be his slave? I want to be your slave. Tell him* [checks for the internal impact of expressing resignation and submission].

Client: *No, obviously not. I don't want to be your slave. Like, I obviously want to be free to do what I want with, with my life.*

Therapist: *Say it to him. I cannot say to you that I will be your slave.*

Client: *I can't be your slave. I need to be my own person.* [The client is starting to stand up to the worrier, stand up for the self.]

Therapist: *It's like, I don't want to be your slave, yes? Tell him.*

Client: *I don't want to be your slave. I want to be me. I want to live my life. I want to do things. I want to express myself and do, have a normal life* [further assertion].

Therapist: *Yeah, say it again to him. I want to be me, yeah.*

Client: *I want to be me.*

Therapist: *Yes, say it again.*

Client: *I want to be me.*

Therapist: *How does it feel when you say that?* [The therapist wants the client to savor the experiencing of standing up for the self; cf. Timulak, 2015]

Client: *I feel a little bit more confident in myself, stronger.*

Therapist: *Yes, say it to him. I feel stronger.*

Client: *I feel stronger. I feel more confident.*

Therapist: *Yes, so if you will be kind of enslaving me, what will be my response? What would your response be if he keeps doing it?* [The therapist wants to further facilitate the assertion.]

Client: *Try and fight him back.*

Therapist: *I will fight you back. Say it to him* [further assertion].

Client: *I will fight you back.*

Therapist: *What is the sense inside?*

Client: *It's just I feel a little bit more confident, a bit stronger about everything myself, you know.*

The in-session experiences of protective anger in the context of worry, naturally lead to a sense of being more in charge, confident, and not at the mercy of the worry process. The sense of having sufficient power to fight the anxiety-producing worries, functions as an antidote to anxiety. Where there is anger and a sense of internal power, there is less space for fear and anxiety. The client feels more expansive, strong, powerful, and consequently feels less fearful, weak, and anxious.

Our clinical experience suggests that the work with protective anger is crucial in overcoming anxiety. While the experiences of compassion in the sessions provide a sense of protection, they also imply that there is a danger. On the other hand, the experiences of protective anger show the client that he or she can face the anxiety-inducing worries (self-scaring, self-panicking). Coupled with the experiences of standing up for the self in transformative work (see Chapter 8), they contribute to the overall sense of empowerment and resilience.

Developments in the worry process across dialogues

Our experience using worry dialogues suggests that in a brief 16 to 20 session-long EFT treatment for GAD difficulties, the client engages in three to five worry dialogues (Murphy *et al.*, 2017). In general, we observed progress across the dialogues with clients more likely to soften the worry, and stand up to the worry, in later dialogues. Indeed, O'Flynn and Timulak (2016), studied this tentatively on a small sample of early and late dialogues using the Worry Resolution Scale that they developed (see Table 7.2) and could see that in the last worry dialogue in therapy, the clients were faster in achieving higher stages of resolution, and spent more time in those higher stages of resolution. (Although we are, in general, trying to avoid thinking in terms of "resolution" as we do not think there is a once-off

Table 7.2 The stages of the Worry Resolution Scale (O'Flynn & Timulak, 2016)

1. **Description of worry** Client implicitly or explicitly expresses worries or other fear-based avoidance process.
2. **Enactment of worrier** Client enacts worrier by actively worrying the experiencer through doubting/scaring/undermining et cetera.
3. **Deepening/impact of the worry** Client expresses the impact or toll of the worry at a superficial secondary emotional level, for example, expressions of exhaustion or hopelessness. May touch on deeper core pain.
4. **Articulation of unmet need** Client expresses the need for compassion and/ or a break from the worrier and begins to stand up to the worrier by expressing protective anger towards worrier.
5A) **Softening/compassion (in worrier)** Client expresses emerging compassion in response to the distress elicited in the experiencer.
5B) **Assertive anger (in experiencer)** Client expresses emerging protective anger against the worrier.
6. **Reflection and integration** Healthy emotional expression is reflected upon. Role of the worrier and the importance of developing compassion and/or assertive anger is discussed.

resolution in this process, we keep the word to be consistent with other, similar EFT scales that are used for research purposes, cf. Elliott *et al.*, 2004.) This suggests that the dialogues have to happen repeatedly, and that clients appear to enjoy greater progress in them, as they are repeated. The relationship between this in-therapy session progress and changes in the worry process outside of therapy sessions needs to be further tested. Similarly, the relationship between the progress in the worry dialogues across the therapy sessions, and overall therapy outcomes also warrants further investigation. A project looking at this relationship is currently being run in our lab.

Reflection on the task and the use of homework

Traditionally in EFT, as the work on a particular task (such as two-chair dialogue for worry) ends in the session, the therapist and the client take time to reflect on the experience. When reflecting on the task or tasks, as at times (as we will see in later chapters), the client may be engaged in more than one task in the session, it is important that the reflection is firmly rooted in the actual experience generated during the task. We want to avoid intellectualization. The reflection on the experience in the task can help the client to make sense of the experience and integrate it into a personal narrative. It can also provide a base for the potential use of homework.

Greenberg and Warwar (2006) have presented several ways of using homework in EFT. Although we are not prescriptive, and as therapists differ in their personal style in using homework, we recognize that some therapists and many clients find homework useful. Homework can bridge in-session experiences with life outside of therapy sessions. In general, we propose two main types of homework (cf. Greenberg & Warwar, 2006). The first type is *awareness-promoting homework* in which the client notices processes that they became aware of in therapy, in their everyday life. In the case of the worry dialogue this can be homework in which the client is instructed to pay attention to situations in which they worry and are also encouraged to observe what immediate impact it has on them. The second type of homework is *experimentation with new experiencing or behavior promoting homework*. This can also be conceptualized as *consolidation* homework as clients may want to mark some of the changes they experienced in therapy. In this type of homework, the therapist and the client try to reflect together on what could help the client to carry on in-session changes that they experienced in therapy, for example, what would help them to stand up to worry outside of the session, what would help them to soften the worry when it comes, or how they might engage in activities that they previously avoided because of their worries (e.g., attending a social event).

Inspired by the work of Serine Warwar (2015), we developed a framework (see Table 7.3; Timulak, 2017) that can be used towards the end of the session as a basis for reflection on the worry dialogue. The framework is a basis for reflection that may help to both increase awareness and also consolidate the work. The

Table 7.3 The framework that can be used to reflect on the Worry Task and as a base for homework (Timulak, 2017)

Parts enacted in the Experiencer chair	Parts enacted in the Worrier chair
	– **How do I worry myself?** (increasing awareness of the ways the client worries him or herself) – **What drives my worries?** (focusing on the underlying fears of the painful triggers, see Chapter 6 on case conceptualisation)
– **What impact the worrying has?** (highlighting the emotional toll of the worry) – **What do I need in the face of the worry?** (articulating the need with regard the worry)	
	– **What do I feel towards the impacted part of me?** (bringing a reminder of compassionate experiences that may help let go of the worry)
– **How can I face the worry?** (a remainder of the resolve in the session to face and fight the worry)	

questions in Table 7.3 *How do I worry? What drives my worries?* can be used by the client to make sense of the experience in the task but also as homework for increasing their awareness during the week regarding how worry happens and how it manifests.

Furthermore, observing the impact of the worry (typically exhaustion and anxiety) may increase the client's awareness of the toll of the worry. Focusing on what the client needs, how he or she can face the worry, and how he or she feels towards the impacted part of the self can lead to experiments with consolidation of potential in-session gains. The client and the therapist may think of activities that can help the client to let go of the worry (e.g., *When I catch myself worrying, I will breathe and will try to calm my panic by being compassionate towards the upset that the worry brings*) or activities that support the client's capacity to establish boundaries to the worry (e.g., one client imagined/externalized the worrier as a thing that talked to him and was exhausting him and he actually got angry at it and did ignore it). We encourage therapists to be creative and attempt to explore options with their clients, to find what would best suit the client. Often it is the client that spontaneously reports what they tried in-between sessions.

Working with self-interruption in EFT

Clients with GAD difficulties use a variety of strategies to avoid feared emotional experience (see Chapter 6). Over-preparing for potential threats (triggers) in the form of worry (and then acting on the worry in the form of behavioral avoidance) is one way clients avoid core painful emotions, although the cost of it is exhaustion and constant anxiety (cf. Newman & Llera, 2011). Another way, well-described in EFT literature is self-interruption (cf. Elliott *et al.*, 2004; Greenberg *et al.*, 1993). Self-interruption often shows in the form of various tensions through which clients attempt to limit potential felt-upset. They are literally tensing to brace themselves for the impact of the feared trigger or upsetting experience. Sometimes self-interruption appears in the context of other tasks, particularly empty chair tasks, in which clients engage in a dialogue with an imagined, significant other and are unable to stay with, or express, a particular experience out of the fear of the experience or the other's imagined response.

There are several ways of working with interruption. Often self-interruption is noticed by the therapist, but may not be focused on, as simply following and evoking the salient emotional experience may override the interruption. When the interruption becomes significant enough to prevent or stifle productive emotional processing, the therapist may bring it to awareness. The therapist may include his or her noticing of the client's interruptive process in his or her empathic response, although obviously not in a way that would make the client feel judged. Sometimes, this may help the client to deliberately bypass the interruption. Habitual interruptions may also become the focus of awareness or experiment homework. The therapist may, for instance, suggest small exercises, such as asking the client to watch a moving film, paying attention to how they become tearful, and how they stop themselves from crying. Clients are encouraged to try not to stop themselves, and to allow the tears to come (see Timulak, 2015).

When self-interruption is so central a process that it becomes a focus of the session (or overall therapy), EFT has a well-established task; a two-chair dialogue for self-interruption (Elliott *et al.*, 2004; Greenberg *et al.*, 1993) that the therapist can engage the client in. EFT focuses on the emotional experience (rather than on ways of suppressing it) and uses many evocative tasks, which on their own, may be sufficient to overcome the self-interruption. Consequently, the self-interruption task is used relatively infrequently and mainly with the clients that consistently engage in self-interruption (emotionally overregulated clients). In our experience with clients with GAD difficulties, while we observed various strategies for emotional avoidance (see Chapter 6), we very rarely used the full-fledged self-interruption task. It is a task that an EFT therapist needs to be familiar with, but may use infrequently or may use only parts of (e.g., bringing to the client's awareness how they stop their experience).

Since this task is well-described in other EFT literature we will only briefly summarize it here. We also offer our version of the task in the format of a table (Table 7.4). Please note that while this table is informed by the task description in Greenberg *et al.* (1993) and Elliott *et al.* (2004), it is presented somewhat differently. We somewhat redesigned it for didactic purposes to align it with other tasks that we present in this book and with the transformation model presented in Chapter 4. We also emphasize the role of compassion and protective anger in bringing change to the self-interruption processes. In addition to the fact that the task does not have a one-resolution point, it is, rather, an example of productive

Table 7.4 Steps in the Self-Interruption Dialogue (Timulak, 2017)

	Experiencer chair	Interrupter chair
1.	Marker – stopping oneself, tension	
2.		Enactment of interruption (highlighting its function and what drives it, e.g., fear of the emotional experience and/ or expression)
3.	Accessing and differentiating the impact of the interruption (tension)	
4.	Articulating and expressing the need for freer emotional experience and expression	
5.		Probing for compassion – seeing the impact/cost of the interruption (highlighting the protective function of interruption)
		A) If no compassion is coming – go with the increased interruption/ tensing/suppression
		B) If compassion is coming – facilitating resolve to let go of protection
6.	Building the resolve to set a boundary to the interruption and experience emotions more freely, allowing the emotional experience and expressing it	

processes that have to be further supported by repeated use of this, or other tasks in therapy, in order to increase the client's emotional flexibility and resilience (see Chapter 1 and Pascual-Leone, 2009, and Timulak, 2015).

The task starts with the identifying of the marker, stage 1 in Table 7.4. As already said, these types of markers may be present throughout the work with clients with GAD difficulties, the therapist has to make a decision about the salience of any interruption and whether there are other ways to overcome or bypass it (e.g., the use of evocative empathy or the use of some other evocative task). Once the therapist negotiates with the client and they decide to engage in the self-interruption task, the therapist asks the client to enact the interruption in the Interrupter chair, stage 2 in Table 7.4 (e.g., *How do you stop yourself from feeling? Actually do it. Stop yourself.*). After the vivid enactment, the client is asked to return to the Experiencer chair, and the therapist guides him or her to attend inwards (e.g., *What happens inside when you get that?*) to see what impact the interruption has, stage 3 in Table 7.4. It typically brings tension, muscle-aches, sometimes a sense of constriction, or even a headache. The client is asked to attend to the felt impact, articulate it in the narrative, and then express it to the Interrupter chair.

After sufficient differentiation in stage 3, the client is asked to articulate and express the need with regard to the interrupter, stage 4 in Table 7.4 (e.g., *What do you need from this part of yourself?*). Often at this point, particularly if the self-interruption task is done in the context of other tasks such as empty chair task for emotional injury (see Chapter 8), the client spontaneously moves to stage 6 in Table 7.4, and mobilizes the need to feel and express emotions. This is followed by actually allowing the interrupted emotions to come, and expressing them. If the self-interruption task is enacted as a stand-alone task, the therapist may facilitate stage 5 in Table 7.4, that is, the therapist may ask the client to sit in the Interrupter chair, look at the impact the interruption has on the client in the Experiencer chair and see what he or she feels towards the thus impacted self (e.g., *What do you feel towards that tensed part of yourself?*). A softening (compassion) may occur at this moment and the client in the Interrupter chair may feel caring towards the tensed self (in the Experiencer chair) and express a caring feeling and perhaps a resolve to let go of interrupting the experience and its expression (stage 5B in Table 7.4).

Early on in the dialogue (and therapy), it is, however, more likely that the client will be unable (or unwilling) to stop the interruption process out of fear of the experience and may actually escalate the process of interrupting (see stage 5A in Table 7.4). The therapist respects this, highlights the escalation, and then proceeds to stage 6 (e.g., *What is your response to that interruption right now? What do you want to do with it?*) or to stage 3 (typically earlier in the dialogue or earlier in therapy; e.g., *What happens inside when you get that right now?*). The client now either feels a greater toll of the interruption or starts to assert him or herself against it. The whole process is very fluid and does not always follow the linear stages as highlighted in Table 7.4 (which is of course the case with all tasks). The therapist thus patiently tracks the client, and creates experiential opportunities for the client to move along the highlighted stages, while respecting where the client is, and how much he is capable of moving on. As said before, there may be very good reasons for the interruption and this needs to be respected.

Self-interrupting may come in a variety of forms and may, at times, be very subtle. It may appear in the form of withdrawal or resignation to protect oneself from the hurt. The reader may find a good example of work with self-protection, which can be conceptualized as an interrupter, in Les Greenberg's video (*Emotion-Focused Therapy Over Time*; Greenberg, 2003, session 2), in which the client talks about the inner wall protecting her from getting hurt. The function of the self-interrupter is often to protect (similarly to worry and some types of self-criticism). This function must be acknowledged and understood, which also allows the client to more freely experience the cost of it.

As with other tasks, the work in the self-interruption task is also reflected upon by therapist and client in the session, as the task ends. Homework may be devised by the therapist and the client if they feel that it would enhance or consolidate the in-session work. The framework presented in Table 7.5 may be used for the reflection and/or homework.

Table 7.5 The framework that can be used to reflect on the self-interruption task and as a base for homework (Timulak, 2017)

Parts enacted in the Experiencer chair	Parts enacted in the Interrupter chair
	• **How do I stop myself from feeling?** (Increasing awareness of the ways the client stops him or herself from feeling) • **What drives my efforts to stop my feelings?** (Focusing on the underlying fears of the painful emotions, see Chapter 6 on case conceptualization)
• **What impact does the interruption have?** (Highlighting the emotional toll of the interruption) • **What do I need in the face of the interruption?** (Articulating the need with regard to the interruption)	
	• **What do I feel towards the impacted part of me?** (Bringing a reminder of compassionate experiences that may help let go of the interrupting process)
• **How can I face the interruption?** (A reminder of the resolve in the session to allow and express emotion)	

Overcoming avoidance in Tina's case

Tina was quite an emotionally overregulated client. She downplayed the importance of emotions, tried to laugh them off if they were painful, and generally tried not think about them. The therapist was aware of this, and occasionally acknowledged it, but primarily focused on the underlying emotional experience. Tina and the therapist engaged in four worry dialogues (sessions four, eight, 14, and 15). Many of Tina's worries centered around being judged (e.g., by colleagues, neighbors, and close ones) as being inadequate, a failure, and ultimately, unlovable. This led to exhaustive overcompensating and over-compliance on Tina's part. Her worries were linked to self-criticism (e.g., *Something will happen and I will be responsible. Something is wrong with me. I am unlovable. I am worthless*), which led to overcompensation and perfectionism. The worries left her feeling sick in the stomach, tense, on edge, anxious, agitated, et cetera.

In the dialogues, Tina recognized the controlling nature of the worry (preventing potential "dangerous" unpredictability). Her softening was visible, particularly in the last two dialogues in which she admitted that she wanted to let go of the worry because of the impact it had on her and others (but felt this was impossible). She realized that her controlling behavior (driven by the worries) was not liked by those around her (her children) and drove them away. She softened into sadness and was filled with vulnerability in the Worrier chair.

She then expressed compassionate understanding from the Experiencer chair towards the vulnerable worrier, however, this did not mean that she would not clearly express the need for a boundary against the worry, the need to feel free of the worries and anxiety.

Conclusion

This chapter, which focuses on working with avoidance processes in therapy, details how worry is worked through in EFT. A comprehensive model of working with worry is presented and is illustrated using clinical examples. A worry resolution scale is outlined and recommendations are made regarding the optional use of appropriate homework tasks. Other anxiety processes such as self-scaring and self-panicking are also briefly introduced. The chapter also illustrates how to deal with self-interruption processes, which may occur when working with clients with GAD difficulties. Again, an adapted model of working with self-interruption is introduced. Finally, the worry and interruption processes are illustrated using a case example.

Part III

Transformative work

Accessing and transforming core emotional pain

A focus on accessing and transforming core chronic painful emotions is central to all work in EFT, and this applies to EFT work with clients with GAD difficulties. So, while the work on emotional avoidance (see previous chapter) is important, it mainly addresses the processes that prevent the client (and the therapist in therapy) from accessing, processing, and potentially transforming chronic pain. The work on emotional avoidance can therefore be conceptualized as a stepping-stone to more crucial in-depth work. This does not necessarily mean that the work on avoidance (such as self-interruption) sequentially precedes the more in-depth work, which focuses on the core painful feelings (see the next chapter where we discuss the sequencing of therapeutic process). Rather, avoidance is focused on if it is an obstacle to assessing chronic painful feelings, which need to be responded to and transformed in therapy.

The most important aspect of therapeutic work with any clients experiencing emotional suffering, including clients with GAD difficulties, is to address the core of their suffering, which consists of core problematic emotion schemes, eliciting chronic painful emotional experiences and dominant problematic self-organizations. As we said in the previous chapter, it was our expectation, when we started the development of the EFT for GAD project, that if we could address and transform this chronic vulnerability, the client's propensity to worry would automatically decrease. The issue proved to be more complex than this, but it did not change our thinking on the centrality of working at the level of core pain in therapy for the treatment to be transformative and impactful. Also, as our observations of the dynamic revealed by clients in therapy suggest (see Chapter 4), the worry and emotional avoidance processes served the function of preventing the client from experiencing the worst-feared core, painful feelings in their everyday life (i.e., sadness/loneliness, shame, and fear/terror).

In this chapter, we will try to illustrate the work at the level of the core pain on the basis of our observations of working with clients with GAD difficulties, particularly through the use of experiential tasks developed in EFT (Greenberg et al., 1993; Elliott et al., 2004). We first look at the overall therapeutic strategy process, regardless of whether the therapist uses the tasks or not (see Box 8.1, and also Chapter 4, Box 4.1, the part on transformation of GAD difficulties). We then illustrate the process, specifically using tasks. Finally, we illustrate the process in the case of Tina.

Accessing, differentiating and transforming core emotional pain

The capability of the client to bring their most painful feelings to therapy sessions is a function of several factors. Some of those factors are client factors, such as forms of emotional processing (over-regulated and under-regulated access to emotions and the use of emotional avoidance), capability to trust others (the therapist), overall levels of distress (whether they are manageable or not), et cetera. Other factors are on the therapist side, for example, the capability to form a safe therapeutic relationship that invites vulnerable emotional experiences (see Chapter 5), the level of expertise required to allow the client to feel safe enough to touch on the uttermost vulnerable feelings, et cetera. Given the differences in presenting issues among clients with GAD difficulties, their levels of distress and their capability to attend to, access, and process emotions, the therapist has to adjust his or her interpersonal style and the way he or she is helping the client to process emotions, accordingly. Although the therapist adjusts the strategy depending on the client's presentation, in general, he or she follows the strategy articulated in Box 8.1.

1. Establishing safety. As described in Chapter 5 on the therapeutic relationship, the EFT therapist is always warm, compassionate, empathic, and transparent with the client. With clients that are more cautious about the therapy process, the therapist may need to spend more time explaining the process to them, including some discussion of the therapist's own actions, so that such clients might build an understanding of what therapy is about. Overall, however, the therapist has to help clients to experience how letting go and touching on vulnerable emotions, in the presence of a caring and empathically attuned other, brings a sense of being looked after and, optimally, a felt sense of relief.

Box 8.1 The process of accessing, differentiating and transforming emotional pain (cf. Timulak, 2015).

1   Establishing safety (relationship, client control, clarity).
2   Regulating the client experience.
3   Focusing on what is most painful (in the context of triggers and self-treatment).
4   Staying with the pain – overcoming avoidance.
5   Tolerating the pain and differentiating the aspects of vulnerable experiences in attention, awareness, and language.

6   Articulating the unmet needs.
7a   Eliciting compassion and being able to let it in and grieve what is or was missed.
7b   Facilitating protective anger and savoring the sense of empowerment.

All steps rely on (a) relational processes in which the therapist contributes to accessing, differentiating and transforming the core chronic painful feelings, for example, by providing safety and guidance, but also healing compassion and validation of protective anger and (b) the client's intrapsychological processes in which the client builds the capacity to stay with the painful feelings without avoiding them, being able to articulate the experience and unmet needs, and respond to those needs by self-compassion and protective self-assertion.

2. Regulating the client's experience. The therapist attempts to establish the sense of safety so the client can focus on the most vulnerable of experiences early on in therapy, but also consistently throughout the therapy. A part of feeling safe for the client has to do with the fact that the experience is not too dysregulating. This is achieved by the client and therapist's continuous effort to articulate the experience in language, which has a regulating function (e.g., Barrett, Wilson-Mendenhall, & Barsalou, 2014). The therapist's guiding may also help here if the client becomes more dysregulated. The therapist may invite the client to breathe (and be calm through breathing) or may introduce some experiential techniques such as clearing a space or self-soothing (see below).

On the other hand, if clients are not in touch with their emotional experiences the therapist may invite them to slow down their exploration and focus inwards (see below for related tasks). The therapist also uses evocative language when empathically responding to the client's experience. The therapist may encourage the client to dwell on certain experiences, or stay with the memory of them, or to imagine aspects of the explored situation in order to evoke emotional experiences and memories.

3. Focusing on what is most painful. The general strategy here is to focus on that which is the most emotionally painful for the client to bear. What lies underneath the undifferentiated distress, expressed as a general sense of helplessness, hopelessness, irritability, and anxiety? What needs are not being met in the client's life? What are some of the disappointments they experience? And, specifically for clients with GAD symptoms, what experiences might they have if the scenarios they most feared came to life? For instance, if a client is afraid that her children will be unprotected on the school trip, what could happen to them (perhaps dying or getting sick, or feeling alone and unsupported) and how would this make the client feel (an experience of sheer terror and trauma, feeling responsible/

guilty for not protecting them, feeling ashamed of letting them down)? These primary feelings are the ones that the EFT therapist wants to focus on.

4. Staying with the pain – overcoming avoidance. Once those painful feelings come to the fore in therapy, the therapist wants to stay with them and help the client refrain from avoiding them (see previous chapter as well) by shifting topic, downplaying those feelings, dissociating from them, or focusing on superficial symptoms (such as anxiety). The therapist wants to elaborate the narrative accompanying them (cf. Angus & Greenberg, 2011), and wants the client to be able to stay with those feelings and inspect them. If the client systematically avoids emotional experiences, the therapist may also initiate the self-interruption task.

5. Tolerating the pain and differentiating aspects of vulnerable experiences in attention, awareness, and language. Once the chronic feelings, linked to the triggers, feared by the client, are accessed and the client can stay with them, the therapist focuses on differentiating them. The therapist, through empathic exploration and process guidance, facilitates the client in differentiating aspects of their emotional experience in awareness and language. For instance, the therapist invites the client to unfold the emotional experience. The therapist may invite the client to inspect the memories to which the chronic painful feelings are linked, the situations that trigger them, how it is to feel those feelings, and examine what the client does with them (usually avoids them, cuts them off, or feels overwhelmed by them). For instance, in the example of the fear surrounding the children's school trip (see point 3); the roots of this fear may be in the client's experience of feeling unsupported as a child and now, identifying with his or her own children, fearing them potentially feeling insecure. This fear can also be linked to the client's propensity to feel inadequate and tendency to self-blame (e.g., *if the kids suffered it must be my fault*). The same fear of something happening to children on a school trip may also be linked to sheer terror of staying with imagined trauma which brings a memory of how overwhelming other traumatic experiences in the client's life have been (e.g., when she lost her mother suddenly). The therapist and client slowly explore various aspects of the experience, stay with it, allow the client to experience it, and help the client to bring to awareness various aspects of the changing experience, ultimately co-constructing articulation of this experience in language.

6. Articulating the unmet needs. Once chronic feelings are differentiated, the therapist focuses the client on the unmet needs embedded in them, which signal what was and remains unfilled. As explained in Chapters 4 and 6, these unmet needs are usually needs connected to experiences of sadness and loneliness, shame, and fear/terror; that is, needs for love and connection (e.g., *I want to be connected and loved*), needs for validation and acceptance (e.g., *I want to be valued and not doubted*), and needs for protection and safety (e.g., *I need reassurance and the soothing presence of the other*). The therapist can help to articulate those emotions by asking what the client needs or needed, in the context of poignantly felt chronic, painful primary feelings, when he or she feels (or felt) profoundly alone, judged, insecure, et cetera.

7a. Eliciting compassion, being able to let it in, and grieve what is or was missed. Once the needs are articulated and expressed, the therapist validates them and tries to help the client to access the internal resources that would respond to them. The therapist also provides a relational presence that validates those needs and is compassionate towards them (see Chapter 5). The internal resources consist of emotional experiences of self-compassion, and of experiences of being capable of letting compassion in. The therapist facilitates the client's process so that the client might feel those experiences in the session. For instance, compassion is often elicited by witnessing one's own pain (e.g., *What would you wish for that girl that just lost her mother? What would feel good to provide her with?*). The client needs to be frequently encouraged to let in that compassion on the other side, for instance, with process guidance that invites the client to try to let compassion in (e.g., *If you were that little girl for the moment, how is it to hear that? Can you try to let it in?*).

Expressing compassion and letting it in leads spontaneously to a grieving process (cf. Pascual-Leone & Greenberg, 2007). It is as if the safety offered by the compassionate presence has allowed more difficult memories to come to the fore. The therapist facilitates grieving by allowing the client to recount what was, or is, difficult. The therapist can offer a compassionate and caring presence to further facilitate grieving. Active expression of understanding-communicating empathy is very important here.

7b. Facilitating protective anger and savoring the sense of empowerment. As the therapist facilitates experiences of compassion, their savoring, and subsequent grieving, he or she also facilitates a more self-affirming stance in the client, stemming from recognition of the validity of their needs and their ownership of them (e.g., *I deserved to be protected, accepted, and loved*). The therapist facilitates this by highlighting the mistreatment or adversity the client went through and pointing at what treatment would have been deserved or right (e.g., *Is it natural that a girl who needs her mom so much loses her? What does that lonely girl deserve? Is it okay to doubt somebody like this?*). The therapist tries to amplify any healthy affirmation that occurs and brings the client's attention to how standing up for the self feels (e.g., *What do you feel inside as you say this was unfair, what happened?*). At this point clients often feel a sense of power, confidence, resilience, or entitlement. The therapist then can help them to savor the sense of standing up for the self, a more empowered sense of self that is particularly important in anxiety problems which can lead the person to avoid and mistrust their own resilience. Suddenly, the client can be freer, more expansive, and confident. For instance, in the small example of the school trip, the client may come to experiences such as, "*I did the best for them. I gave them lots of love. I am confident in how I provide for them. I am a good mother. I am a good person. I did not deserve to lose my mom.*"

The whole process of accessing, differentiating, and transforming core emotional pain has two main pillars. One (a) relational, in which the therapist provides an expert presence that allows the client to feel safe and soothed enough to bring up the most feared aspects of their experience, with the therapist helping to differentiate those experiences and articulate unmet needs, supported by the therapist's genuinely compassionate stance, and their validation of the client's emerging empowerment (*I see what you went through, you did not deserve to go through it,*

I value you and what you went through, and I witness not only your pain, but also your bravery and resolve). The second pillar (b) is more intrapsychological in so far as the client learns how not to run away from the painful feelings, but rather, develops his or her capacity to stay with them, tolerate them, and differentiate them in awareness and language. The client becomes increasingly able to recognize their needs and respond to them with inner self-compassion, self-validation and self-affirmation, or a healthy boundary-setting anger.

Obviously the process, outlined briefly above (and summarized in Box 8.1), is complex and overcomes many hurdles across multiple iterations (we talk about some of them in the next chapter [see also an extensive description in Timulak, 2015]). The majority of this transformative process in EFT happens in the context of experiential tasks (Elliott *et al.*, 2004; Greenberg *et al.*, 1993) that are particularly suitable for accessing, differentiating, and transforming the core emotional pain underlying many GAD difficulties. We are going to look at the role and use of those tasks in the following pages.

Transformative process in tasks

The hallmark of EFT work is the use of various experiential tasks (cf. Elliott *et al.*, 2004; Greenberg *et al.*, 1993). EFT tasks fulfil various roles (see Chapter 3). Many have transformative elements. For instance, the worry and other anxiety-tackling tasks, as well as the self-interruption task presented in Chapter 7, can also be understood as transforming the anxiety or interruption processes. However, by emotion transformation we primarily understand the transformation of core chronic painful feelings (core pain) in therapy. From that perspective, the tasks presented in Chapter 7 focus on targeting and transforming processes that allow the client to avoid core painful feelings.

Preparatory tasks

As we explained in Chapters 4 and 6, we see transformation of the feared core pain as the main focus of work with clients with GAD difficulties. Several tasks (apart from the worry and interruption task) as conceptualized by the EFT authors (cf. Elliott *et al.*, 2004) can be, and typically are, used in EFT in the process of transforming the core feared emotional pain. Some of those tasks can, however, be conceptualized as preparatory tasks, as they themselves are not focused on emotion transformation (changing emotion with emotion). These tasks can rather help the client to engage in the therapy process. For instance, establishing safety (point 1 in Box 8.1) is helped by the therapist's general, relational, empathic style, and empathic validation (see Chapter 5), and has also been described in task-format (cf. Elliott *et al.*, 2004 and the *empathic exploration task* and *empathic affirmation task* – see Chapter 3).

Regulation of highly aroused emotions, important for the client's capability to engage in a productive therapeutic process, may be also accomplished in an experiential task. While, as a default, the therapist may want to help a dysregulated client by his/her own calming presence and process-guiding on a micro-intervention level, for example, promotion of regular deep breathing, the therapist can also introduce a *clearing a space* task (cf. Elliott *et al.*, 2004). An example of a clearing a space task with a client with GAD difficulties is presented in Timulak (2015). The client in the example is flooded with various issues that worry and upset her. The therapist, using empathic exploration and communication of understanding as well as process guiding, asks the client to (see also Box 8.2):

1 *Pay attention inward* – typically to the middle of the body where we feel things. The therapist does it slowly so the client can stay with the sense inside, and may also encourage the client to close his or her eyes. The therapist uses exploratory language to guide the client inside (e.g., *See what is the sense inside. How does it feel inside, in the middle of your body?*).

2 *Describe the bodily feeling* (e.g., the sense of tension in the middle of the body) to the therapist (e.g., *If you were to describe that feeling inside, what is it like?*). The therapist is empathic, using a slow pace to allow the client to dwell on the feeling.

3 The therapist then invites the client to *give a name to the feeling*, to label it. Optimally, the name/label captures both the detailed felt-quality (e.g., *a tension as if an iron ping-pong ball was in my chest*) and the outside event the feeling relates to (if known or clear to the client). For instance, the sense of the ball inside is related to the fact that my elderly mother is on a trip abroad without my constant protection. The therapist then empathizes with the description (e g , *The iron ball inside, here in my chest, somehow related to my mom being unprotected*).

4 Next, the therapist invites the client to imagine *putting the feeling aside* where it would feel comfortable. For instance, he or she may say: *If you were to put that feeling (the iron ball inside your chest) somewhere aside, where would it feel good to put it? Some people wish to put it close to them, some people would wish to put it to a box, some people further away. Where would it feel right?* Once the client nominates a place the therapist invites him or to imagine that it goes there, for example, *Now imagine that that feeling, the iron ball related to your mom being unprotected is going there. Can you imagine that? Does it work?* The therapist waits for the client to confirm that the imagination worked.

5 Sometimes the client with anxiety struggles to let go of the feeling, as they believe that by letting go of the feeling they would be exposed, vulnerable, or unprotected. For instance, the client may not want to let go of the iron ball as it reminds her to check on her mother every hour of the day. The therapist may then suggest putting the feeling close by, within reach: *Okay, the feeling will not disappear, we will just try to put it a bit aside, within your reach so you could get to it, if needed. Where would you put it? It is just for a*

moment, it is not for good. You know that the feeling like this can come back very quickly.

6   Once the client is capable of imagining that the feeling has been put aside, and confirms this to the therapist, the therapist invites the client to *focus inside again* (the therapist may also stress the physical distance between the feeling and the client): *So we put that iron ball there, next to your chair on the ground. It is there and you are here. What is the sense now inside?* Typically, the client reports some shift, and change to the feeling.

Early in the task, the client may actually feel a temporary worsening at step 5, as clients with anxiety issues often panic when invited to let go of some anxiety-provoking issue in this way. In this case, the therapist would focus on the worsened/changed feeling and again repeat steps 1 to 5 (*pay attention inward, describe the feeling, name it, imagine putting it aside and check inwards*). Steps 1 to 5 are repeated, in any case, for as long as the client can identify something upsetting, that they recognize impacts on his or her feelings in the middle of the body (where we "feel things"; most typically around the solar plexus, where a complex network of nerves of the sympathetic system supporting flight-or-fight responses is situated). The process is repeated until the client has a sense of relief inside his or her body. It is not fully established why this task brings relief and calm, but, we speculate, it may have something to do with the client's perception of their increased capability to regulate their own feelings.

It is our experience that the use of this task, while very fitting for clients with GAD difficulties, is rare and we would recommend using it only if the client is so dysregulated that they cannot focus on the underlying core issues and the therapeutic process at all. If the client is unable to sit in the session, then it may be helpful to use this explicitly regulating task. Some clients really like it, find it useful and report using it at home with some success (cf. Timulak *et al.*, 2017). The guide presented in Box 8.2 could potentially serve as a guide for homework. However, we believe that the use of the task is much easier when experienced with another, trained person.

Box 8.2 A variation of the clearing a space task (Timulak, 2017 on the basis of Elliott *et al.*, 2004).

1   Pay attention inward.
2   Describe the bodily feeling.
3   Give a name to the feeling (label it).
4   Imagine putting the feeling aside where it would feel comfortable.
5   Once the feeling is aside, invite the client to focus inside and check again.
6   Repeat steps 1 to 5 until the client experiences a sense of a shift (relief).

Another task that can be used to help regulate highly aroused global distress is a "superficial" *self-soothing* (expression of self-compassion) task (Timulak, 2015). Later in the chapter, we will talk about self-soothing in the context of the two major experiential tasks used for transformation of core emotional pain; problematic self-treatment, two-chair work (self-evaluative split in Elliott *et al.*, 2004) and self–other, unfinished-business, empty-chair work. However, self-soothing can also be used before the client has reached the differentiated, unfolded core painful feeling, but is distressed on a more general level. Usually, these are experiences of hopelessness and helplessness, irritability, and general anxiety. Sometimes intervention such as this can be used towards the end of the session, if the client is very dysregulated, to provide some experience of calm. They can also be used earlier on in the session if the client is so dysregulated that they cannot use the session productively.

In this task, the therapist asks the acutely distressed client to think of a person who possesses qualities that would allow the client to show their distress to them, e.g.: *It is so upsetting and rocky inside. I am wondering who comes to mind that would be there, who would see what you are going through? Who comes to mind that would be there for you?* The nomination of a person by the client should come from their personal experience, through association (who comes to mind?), rather than through rational analysis. The nominated person can be from any time (e.g., a former friend, deceased grandparent, teacher): *Who comes to mind? Who would have that quality? It does not have to be a person that is available to you in everyday life, they can be from the past too.*

Once the client nominates the person, the therapist asks them to enact them in the Other chair: *Please come to this chair and be your grandmother. What does she feel towards John there* [the client's name]*? What would she wish for him? What would she offer him? Please do it.* The emphasis is on enacting the caring attitude, the offer of well-wishing, with a soothing quality. Although the client is enacting a caring other, in fact, he or she is generating those qualities within him or herself in the moment. This may occur, due to the client having internalized some of those very qualities that are being attributed to the nominated person.

Once the soothing and caring quality is fully enacted, the therapist asks the client to return to the original chair, and encourages the client to let in the soothing quality from the imagined other, caring person: *Could you come back here? How is it to get that "I like to play with you, I love you, I care about you, you can come to me with your worries, I will stand by you and will make those bad things disappear"? What is the sense inside when you get that?* If the client is able to let some of the care in, and expresses that he or she feels somewhat calmed, the therapist encourages the client to bathe in that calming presence, and express how it feels inside to be calmed by the enacted soothing person in the Other chair.

In both of these tasks (clearing a space and self-soothing), that promote emotion regulation, the therapist can spend some time with the client to explore the resources the client has available, which may provide a calming experience and support emotion regulation (for instance, walking the dogs or cycling, etc.). The therapist then encourages the client to ensure that they avail of those calming activities outside the therapy session. This is something that can be planned as homework.

The emotion regulation hopefully becomes less of a problem as therapy progresses. The client internalizes the therapist's calming, caring, and compassionate presence as well as their own experiences of self-compassion and emotional resilience. As previously outlined (Timulak, 2015) building protective anger and an increased sense of assertiveness in therapy, contributes to a sense of internal solidity and resilience. This resilience decreases the propensity to dysregulation. We believe that this is especially so in clients with GAD difficulties, where healthy anger helps to build and develop the expansive, confident self, in place of the fearful, overcautious, and avoidant self.

Accessing primary underlying emotions in tasks

Empathic exploration, which is a default position for the EFT therapist, can also be conceptualized as a task (cf. Elliott *et al.*, 2004; see also Chapter 3). The EFT therapist invites the client to focus on emotionally salient experiences in the session. The therapist, in his or her empathic responses, tracks the client's perceptual field (triggers), internal experiences (bodily and emotional), needs, and action tendencies (implicit in the experience) as well as the creation of meaning from the experience. In an act of therapeutic collaboration, the therapist co-constructs the client's symbolization of the felt experience and helps to create meaning from the experience. The therapist uses empathic exploration interspersed with empathic communication of understanding. To build the experience the therapist uses empathic evocation, empathic conjecturing, and, at times, process guiding, while always checking whether the emerging symbolization/meaning fits the client's experience (cf. Elliott *et al.*, 2004; Chapter 3).

Empathic exploration focuses on acknowledging secondary emotional experiences, while deepening and differentiating primary emotional experiences. As explained earlier in the book, this type of process can be productive on its own, as differentiating the experience and symbolizing it with language not only brings conceptual clarity, but also produces felt shifts in experiencing (commonly a sense of relief and/or determination – cf. Elliott *et al.*, 2004). Again, *Learning Emotion-Focused Therapy* by Elliott and colleagues (2004) provides an excellent presentation of empathic exploration as a task for the therapist to follow.

Another task that can serve the purpose of differentiating the experience and symbolizing it in language is *Systematic Evocative Unfolding* (Elliott *et al.*, 2004; Greenberg *et al.*, 1993; Rice & Saperia, 1984; see also Chapter 3), developed by Laura Rice in her programmatic research. In EFT, this task is traditionally described in the context of the marker of puzzling, problematic experience. Indeed, clients with GAD difficulties may be describing events in which they were particularly surprised by their inner reaction. Here, the situation that brought the puzzling emotional reaction is focused on by the client and the therapist. The therapist asks the client to take him or her back to the situation and then, go slowly, chronologically through the perceptions, and internal reactions to these perceptions, in the situation. The task starts with the overall context or background, and the client's feelings at the beginning of the situation. The puzzling reaction then becomes clearer as the client tracks what trigger (stimulus) brought which particular, internal emotional reaction and how the client's own construal of the trigger was implicated (cf. Rice & Saperia, 1984).

For instance, a client with GAD may describe a situation in which she attended a family function to celebrate a family member's birthday. At some point during the celebration she felt very uncomfortable and upset and had to leave the premises. She was very puzzled by this reaction. The therapist invites the client to go slowly through the situation and their inner experience as though it were a slow-motion movie: *Okay, could you take me through what was happening and how you felt inside? Can we start with just before you went to the event? Where were you? What was happening there? How did you feel inside? You can even close your eyes and take me through it as if it is happening right now.* The client then describes (optimally in the present tense) how she is in her bedroom, unsure what dress to put on. She also feels subdued and is not particularly enthusiastic about going to the celebration. The therapist empathically follows the client, but also encourages her to continue: *so what happened (what is happening) next?*

The client then describes how she gets to the event, slowly describes how she initially feels awkward fitting in, then realizes she is not drinking like the others. Others are becoming more cheerful and she cannot connect to their gaiety. She starts to think about all the tragedies that have occurred in the family (including people who have died and are not here with them today). She then looks at the happy faces of her relatives and starts to think: *How they can be so happy when we had so much trauma?* She starts to feel very upset (angry, sad, and hopeless) and feels she needs to run from the pub. After she calms down, she does not remember why she fled the pub and why she was so upset. As she recounts it to the therapist, they both focus on the feeling of anger, sadness, and hopelessness, the upsetting feeling inside: *I cannot connect to others' gaiety, because I miss my loved ones and because I am traumatized by what happened.* This then becomes the focus of further empathic exploration.

Another EFT task that can be used to differentiate a particularly unclear felt experience is *focusing*. The task comes from the work of Eugene Gendlin (1981; 1996) and in EFT is used to address particular markers of the client's in-session experience, such as "unclear felt sense" (cf. Greenberg *et al.*, 1993; Elliott *et al.*, 2004; see also Chapter 3). Bits of focusing can be (and often are) used as a part of the overall therapist's repertoire of empathic interventions, used to promote the client's self-exploration (e.g., *What is the sense inside as you say that?* or *If you were to speak from that feeling, what would it be saying?* etc.). Indeed, any of the steps described in the focusing task (cf. Elliott *et al.*, 2004) can be used in this way. Furthermore, the described focusing attitude (attention to internal experience, cf. Elliott *et al.*, 2004; Leijssen, 1990, 1998) captures the quality that the therapist is attempting to facilitate and promote in the client throughout therapy.

Focusing can also be used as a stand-alone task. In the context of working with clients with GAD difficulties we have found that some clients have difficulty staying with the internal focus on their experience. In such situations, and when clients have an unclear experience, the therapist can use the task to unfold the experience. It is optimal if the unclear felt sense has a bodily feeling to it, centered in the middle of the body. Clients with GAD difficulties commonly refer to other bodily symptoms such as tensions in their arms, neck, or back. These are not optimal for focusing work as they typically stem from long-term, possibly self-protecting (self-interrupting) postures, in which clients brace themselves from (social) danger, push themselves through the tiredness, et cetera. Given that these feelings are not acute, fresh, unclear feelings, but rather somatic, muscular symptoms linked to the client's overall problematic functioning, they are not a good option for a focusing task.

The focusing task overlaps with the clearing a space task. The first three steps (see Box 8.3) are identical: the therapist invites the client to (1) *pay attention inward* to the middle of the body where the client has the unclear felt sense; then asks the client to (2) *describe the bodily feeling* to the therapist. The therapist empathizes with the feeling, allowing the client to dwell on the feeling; and then (3) invites the client to *give a name (label)* to the feeling, again optimally capturing both the detailed, felt quality and the aspects of the outside event the feeling relates to (if known or clear to the client).

The next steps are somewhat different. Rather than putting the feeling aside, the therapist asks the client to (4) *check-in inside* to see what happens to the feeling when aspects of it are named (labeled, symbolized in language). Typically, the felt quality shifts somewhat. The therapist then (5) asks the client to *repeat steps 1 to 4*, this time attending to a shifted, felt quality or a different aspect of the felt experience. The process continues until the client differentiates the originally unclear felt experience (at the level of primary emotions). This is usually accompanied by a sense of clarity, but also a sense of relief and/or determination that accompanies the clarity. When the feeling is well differentiated, the therapist can also encourage (6) the client to check for *the need* attached to the feeling (e.g., soothing, understanding). The articulation of the need sometimes brings soothing and calming. At other times, the therapist may encourage the client to imagine that they are getting a caring response to the articulated need, which may bring a soothing experience.

Box 8.3 A variation of the focusing task (Timulak, 2017 on the basis of Elliott et al., 2004 and Gendlin, 1981; 1996).

1   Pay attention inward.
2   Describe the bodily feeling.
3   Give a name to the feeling (label it).
4   Check-in inside to see what happens to the feeling when aspects of it are named.
5   Repeat steps 1 to 4.
6   Optional – check; what does the differentiated feeling need?

Transformation tasks

While the tasks that we presented above are important tasks in therapy, they are not focused on the core therapeutic process in EFT, emotion transformation (changing emotion with emotion). There are two major EFT tasks that are primarily used to bring about transformative experiences that help to restructure the client's problematic emotion schemes. These two tasks allow the client to access the core chronic painful primary feelings of sadness/loneliness, shame, and primary fear (cf. Timulak, 2015), while at the same time bringing countering emotional experiences such as pride, love, and healthy protective anger. The imaginary and experiential nature of these tasks makes them really evocative and vivid, so the experience for the clients is typically very authentic and very close to real-life dialogues.

The two tasks that we are talking about are self–self, two-chair dialogue for problematic critical self-treatment (self-evaluative or self-critical split, Elliott *et al.*, 2004; Greenberg *et al.*, 1993; see Chapter 3) and the self–other empty chair dialogue for an interpersonal emotional injury (classically referred to as unfinished business, Elliott *et al.*, 2004; Greenberg *at al.*, 1993; see Chapter 3). One of the tasks, the self–self, two-chair dialogue, refers to the task which addresses the form of problematic self-treatment that often presents itself in the context of a threatening trigger, for example, *my children will be (or are) upset* (trigger in the case conceptualization presented in Chapter 6), *so it is all my fault. I am a horrible mother and horrible person* (problematic self-treatment – see Chapter 6).

The other task, the self–other empty chair dialogue, refers primarily to interpersonal emotional injuries that often have historical origins, for example, a dismissive treatment from the mother, typically expressing perceived messages like: *you are a bad person, you failed me as a daughter, you are a failure* While the emotional injuries are important factors in developing chronic painful feelings (problematic emotion schemes), the problematic self-treatment in the context of those injuries compounds the injuries; although historically it could be understood as an attempt to mitigate the injury (e.g., *I criticize myself in order to improve, so that my mother might eventually approve of me* – cf. Chapter 4 and also Timulak, 2015). We are now going to have a look at the processes in these two major therapeutic tasks.

Self–self (two-chair) dialogue for problematic (self-evaluative) self-treatment.

This task is initiated in the session at an appropriate marker, which generally appears in the form of the client's self-criticism, self-devaluation, self-contempt, self-attack, et cetera. Self-harming behavior can also be an expression of self-criticism, although this issue is more complex (cf. Sutton, 2007; Chapter 4). As we discussed in Chapter 4, problematic self-treatment may have several functions. It may be an effort on the client's part to shape themselves, so they might win a positive response from the other (e.g., *My mom will love me if I become a better girl*).

It may represent non-acceptance of the self, in so far as the person fears that they may lose connection with the other (e.g., *If I don't excel, nobody will be interested in being with me*), or it may be an internalization of the perceived judgment of others (e.g., *they hate me, so it must be true that I am weird*), et cetera (see Chapter 4). Although we can often see that problematic self-treatment wants to better the person, it does not help, and leaves the person feeling put down, ashamed, embarrassed, worthless, resigned, et cetera. Paradoxically, although critical and contemptuous self-treatment leads to feeling bad, at times it can also be sought out by the person, as they may feel relief through obtaining the "deserved" punishment. The "deserved" punishment can sometimes bring a physical pain (in self-harm) that leads the client to feel distracted from the "psychological" pain and thus, paradoxically, may bring temporary relief.

The therapist's work in two-chair dialogue for problematic self-treatment (self-evaluative split) has been described in classic EFT texts, such as Greenberg *et al.* (1993) and Elliott *et al.* (2004). Here we describe it in the context of work with clients with GAD difficulties, and across the stages that are commensurate with our conceptualization of therapeutic change, presented in Chapters 4 and 6 (see Table 8.1). The marker of self-criticism found in clients with GAD is often close to their self-worry. Indeed, we are currently in the process of tracking self-critical messages within self-worry dialogues in a sample of clients with GAD symptoms. It appears (Toolan, 2017) that the worry dialogues are closely linked to the self-criticism, as in the above example, which shows worrying about children's welfare, because *I am a bad mother*. Given that clients with GAD difficulties commonly meet criteria

Table 8.1 A variation of the two-chair dialogue for problematic (self-evaluative) self-treatment (Timulak, 2017, on the basis of Elliott *et al.*, 2004)

	Experiencer chair	*Critic chair*
1.	Marker – self-contempt, negative self-treatment present	
2.		Enactment of criticism – harsh, poignant, main message, experiential quality
3.	Accessing and differentiating core pain	
4.	Articulating and expressing unmet needs	
5.		Probing for compassion – seeing the pain and unmet need
		A) If no compassion is coming – highlight rejection (message and mistreatment in it as well as function of it)
		B) If compassion is coming – savoring it experientially and expressing it
6a.	Building protective anger, setting boundary	
6b.	Letting compassion in – savoring it experientially	

for other "disorders", such as depression or social anxiety, it is likely that there are some self-critical processes that are not closely linked to the worries and go beyond the triggers that the client is attempting to avoid (this is, however, an empirical question that will need to be answered by future research). Regardless of whether the worry and self-criticism are linked or not, the process of working with self-critical (and similar) processes is, more or less, the same. In situations when self-criticism is linked to the self-worry, it is important that in the process of therapy we target both self-worrying as well as self-critical processes (see Chapter 9).

Table 8.1 delineates six stages that the therapist tries to facilitate when working with the client's self-criticism. The therapist's facilitation of the process is flexible and creative, so the stages are only tentative. The task can also be embedded within other tasks, which we will discuss in the next chapter.

1 Marker stage

Once the marker of self-criticism (in its various forms) is present in the session, the therapist may propose examining this process in the two-chair task. It is important that the therapist spends some time introducing the task, in the lead-in, prior to commencing, so that the client is clear about what type of self-treatment process they will be focusing on in the task (e.g., *So this is how you attack yourself, so this is how you put yourself down*). Also at times, the self-critical process may be co-occurring with self-worry, in which case the therapist has to make a strategic decision regarding which to focus on first (see the next chapter).

An example of a marker stage, a prequel to the dialogue, may look as follows. The female client reports that nobody in her family respects her (trigger). Rather than being angry with family members she starts to attribute the reason for this problem to herself.

Client:	She [her daughter] *won't even listen to me. She pulls a face when I am trying to talk to her.*
Therapist:	Like, "I despise you", or something almost like this, yes?
Client:	*Or my son. We seem to have made a mess of everything because …*
Therapist:	Yeah.
Client:	*I take the blame for that because …*
Therapist:	Okay. But it is almost like then I criticize myself [empathically, as if speaking for the client], *that not only she is bad to me but it is also my responsibility.*
Client:	Yeah.
Therapist:	Because I, I was supposed to, you know, to parent her in a way that she wouldn't be like this.
Client:	Yeah.
Therapist:	It is my failure, or …
Client:	*That's right, and then I'd be trying to be nice to her, like, "Could I make you something darling? Will I do you a hot water bottle for bed?" and I'm running around after her trying to make her happy,*

you know? [Here we can see the client's avoidance, as well. She is afraid of the daughter's criticism.]

Therapist: *But it's almost like, eh, "How can you* [the daughter] *be so reject-ing?" or something? "I, I want this somehow remedied," or some-thing? "If I did something wrong ... "*

Client: *Well, that's it, because I do absolutely everything for them. I've told you that before, probably too much* [a hint of self-criticism here]. *I do everything. I try to keep everybody sort of happy. I try.*

Therapist: *So, somehow it is so painful to get that rejection from her, so you are trying to please her. But there is also that self-doubt: I did something wrong.* [Self-doubt is an example of problematic self-treatment, self-criticism.]

Client: *Yeah, it is all my fault.*

Therapist: *So this is how you criticize yourself. It is all my fault.*

Client: *Yeah. It is all my fault.*

Therapist: *It is all my fault. Could we look at that? Could we look at what hap-pens when you criticize yourself like that? We touched on it several times already.*

2 Enactment of criticism stage

Once the therapist and the client have settled on the marker, and have agreed that they are going to have a look at the self-critical process, the therapist asks the client to enact the self-criticism. At times, this can also be done through the, so called, attributional split (cf. Elliott *et al.*, 2004; Greenberg *et al.*, 1993), in which the dialogue may start with the other's judgement (in the example above it could be the daughter's judgment). When working with self-criticism, the emphasis here is on the experiential quality the self-criticism brings, for exam-ple, self-contempt visible in the client's face (the therapist may say, *And you pull your face. What is the message in this expression? Is it like I despise you?*). It is also important to distinguish between a more superficial self-criticism (e.g., *you should not be depressed*) and a more primary self-criticism that judges the self on a personal level (e.g., *you are stupid, you are a failure, you are selfish, you are unworthy, you are a bad person, you are selfish*, etc.).

The therapist facilitates the client in accessing this personal self-directed judg-ment. The client is facilitated in expressing the self-criticism fully, so the full quality of the self-attack is clearly present. It does not have to be present for a long period of time, however, as the point is not in having the client hurt him or herself, but rather to bring out in the open what usually happens inside for the cli-ent. Once the therapist senses that the self-attack is at its peak, the therapist asks the client to change seats and follows up with the instructions for the next stage (see below). It is also good if, at this point, the therapist meta-communicates with the client about what is happening in the session, for example, *So this is how you attack yourself.* This can also help clients increase their own awareness of their own self-critical process.

An example of this stage can be seen in the following exchange:

Therapist: *If you come here* [pointing at the Critic, chair]? *Yes? You can come.*
              So you will be that critical part, eh, critical, Gina [a fictional client
              name] *because it seems like a part of you is always not happy with*
              yourself. And this is you as well because it's almost like a voice in
              your head ...
Client: Mmm.
Therapist: *So, what are some of those reproaches, yes, or criticisms that,*
              that, eh, that almost voice inside of you? How do you make sure
              that she [pointing to the Experiencer chair] *knows that you are not*
              happy with her? Could you try to make sure that she knows you
              are unhappy with her? Because it is almost like a part of you is not
              happy with yourself. You know?
Client: *I don't like you* [speaking to the Experiencer chair] *being moody*
              and making other people in your family, um, unhappy. You
              should be able to snap out of it and not be doing it. [This is a
              more superficial level of self-criticism, as the client essentially
              criticizes herself for being depressed and not for a particular per-
              sonal characteristic.]
....
Client: *If there are any problems, it'd be down to you.*
Therapist: *Okay. Okay. So it's like ...*
Client: *Down to you.*
Therapist: *Okay. So, "It's like all your fault" Yeah?*
Client: *Yeah. It is all your fault.*
Therapist: *You're causing all the problems* [amplifying the self-criticism].
Client: *You're causing all the problems. I don't like your weakness. You're*
              very weak. [This is an attack on a more personal level.]
...

Therapist [pointing at the experiential quality enacted by the client]:   *And a kind*
              of attitude of rejection or negative ... judgment or something?

Client: *Yeah. Rejection, really. Yeah. I dislike everything about you* [pull-
              ing a face]. *How you are with others, there is something in you that*
              is repelling. [Again, this is an attack on a more personal level.]

3 Accessing and differentiating core pain stage

Once the problematic self-treatment is clearly enacted, the therapist asks the client to swap chairs and see, while sitting in the Experiencer chair, how the enacted
self-attack impacts the client's internal experience.

Therapist: *Okay. So, this is how you attack yourself. With so much contempt*
              and relentlessly, on so many levels. So what's the sense like when

you get this? How does, how does it feel inside? Take a breath and
see how it feels.

Given that the problematic self-treatment is typically some sort of self-criticism
and negative self-evaluation, such as putting oneself down, the internal experience
accessed in the Experiencer chair is typically that of *shame*. This primary experience may be hidden underneath secondary hopeless resignation (e.g., *I just feel
resigned*) or defensive anger (e.g., *So what? I don't care!*). At times, the client may
not be able to differentiate the inner response form the self-criticism and will simply agree with the critic (e.g., *You are right, I am weak*). The therapist, therefore,
has to acknowledge the client's experience, empathize with it; but must also focus
on the underlying felt-sense inside, when one is put down or made an object of
contempt, et cetera. It can help the therapist's empathic conjectures to try to imagine how the client would feel if some other person (other than the critic) attacked
him or her like this. It is very important that the client and therapist access the
underlying, vulnerable client experiences in an aroused and fresh manner. The
accessed hurt is a potential source of compassion that may be elicited in stage 5,
as we elicit compassion through witnessing the pain.

The client's focus on internal experience normally leads to differentiation of
felt experience and to, most typically, variations of shame (embarrassment, worthlessness, etc.). Given that the whole internal, chronic, painful, emotion-scheme
structure can be activated, the client may also be associatively feeling other core
painful feelings that perhaps come from past rejecting, intrusive treatment from
others. For instance, the client may feel that they failed their parent, so the feelings of shame in the face of self-attack may also trigger feelings of not feeling
loved by their parent, et cetera. The therapist may follow that pain pathway and
switch the task, for instance, into an empty chair dialogue with the client's parent
(we will discuss the movement from task to task in the next chapter). In the most
straightforward instances the core chronic painful experience stays linked to the
self-attack that was just enacted. The differentiation of the felt experience can
then look as illustrated in this example:

Therapist: *Okay. So, what's the sense like when you get this? How does, how*
               does it feel inside? Take a breath and see how it feels.
Client: *It doesn't really feel, it doesn't feel good being like that. It doesn't*
               feel good, but it releases something in me, but it's not a good feel-
               ing ...
Therapist: *What would you say to her?* [The therapist is trying to keep the
               contact with the Critic chair, so the client stays in the task.] *How*
               does it feel to get it? It's like, "I feel like I deserve it" or something?
               You're saying.
Client: *I feel, yeah, like I deserve to be ... I deserve not to be happy or some-*
               thing. That's all that I've known all, really else ... I realize that now.
               I didn't realize it. But I realize it. That's the way I've lived.

Therapist:	Yeah. Yeah. It's almost like, "I'm used to it ..." [acknowledging secondary resignation].
Client:	That's all I expect.
Therapist:	Yeah. And how does it feel? Yes? You say that "I got used to it. I almost feel like I deserve it". But I assume that it must be also unpleasant. Yes [trying to aim at the underlying feelings]?
Client:	It is very unpleasant.
Therapist:	It must be bringing almost a physical impact [focusing on the experienced quality]. Yes? This is like constantly being slapped ... "It's all your fault". But what would you say to that voice of yourself? Tell her how it feels inside when, when she's kind of criticizing you constantly. It's you. Yes?
Client:	Horrible. It's awful. Um, just being put down all the time.
Therapist:	Yeah. "I feel put down by, by you, by ..."
Client:	Put down and worthless and ... [the client touches on shame]. Awful.
Therapist:	Yeah, this is how it feels ... Okay. So go to that worthlessness. Yes? Now. Yeah?
Client:	Mmm.
Therapist:	How is it in that worthlessness? It feels like what?
Client:	It's just, um ... You're just sort of existing. You're not, eh, interested in ... You're just going through the motions of life ... but you're not really ... You couldn't care less, type of thing. You know?
Therapist:	Okay. So it's almost like "I'm losing all joy to live or anything".
Client:	Yeah. There's nothing joyous. I just don't care.
Therapist:	Okay.
Client:	I just go through the motions, and if I am with people, you laugh when you have to laugh and you ... but I just want to withdraw and hide from everybody.
Therapist:	Yeah, and where do you have that sense of worthlessness. I mean in your body. Where is it?
Client:	It's just all here, this area all the time [pointing to the middle of her body and the chest].
Therapist:	Okay. And could you speak from that feeling to the part that criticizes you [pointing to the Critic chair, trying to keep the contact and the experiential flow of the task]? Let her know how it feels inside?

4 Articulating and expressing unmet needs stage

Once the client stays with the painful emotional experience in a productive manner without running away from it (see Chapter 4), articulates it in language, and expresses it in a contactful manner to the Critic, the therapist focuses the client on what the feeling needs. This is normally in relation to the Critic with whom the client in the Experiencer chair is in dialogue (e.g., *What do you need from him/*

her [the Critic] *as you feel this*?). The unmet needs have to be, firstly, articulated (named) and then expressed to the Critic. As experiential tasks can often naturally flow from one into another (e.g., two-chair critic dialogue into empty chair unfinished-business dialogue; see below and particularly next chapter) the need may occasionally be expressed to the other imagined person. In its simple and most typical form, in the context of the two-chair self–self, critic dialogue, it is expressed to the critic as in the example below:

Therapist:	*Okay. You are feeling so worthless inside. So what would you need from her? From that voice in you telling you what's bad about you? What would you need from her?*
Client:	*I need her to say, "You're not bad, and ..."*
Therapist:	*Tell her, "I need you to tell me ..."*
Client:	*I need you to tell me that I'm doing all right and that I'm not bad and I'm not a bad mother and a bad wife and ...*

5 Probing for compassion stage

Once the client accesses core painful feelings of being ashamed, put down, weak, et cetera, and articulates and expresses the heartfelt need towards the critical part of the self, the therapist will attempt to see whether the client can access self-compassion towards those vulnerable feelings he or she accessed in the Experiencer chair. The quality of the primary vulnerable feelings accessed in the Experiencer chair (as to the level of arousal, productivity, freshness, etc.) may increase the likelihood of the client's softening towards that vulnerable part of themselves. We assume that the client is capable of being moved by the poignancy of the observed vulnerability (cf. Timulak, 2015). The process may be, however, quite complicated for highly self-critical clients who are actually threatened by their own vulnerability and become even more self-rejecting when they see what they perceive to be their weakness. Often it may be the case that the self-criticism has developed as a way of dealing with precisely this type of vulnerability (see Chapter 4), consequently, accessing it in the task actually mobilizes further self-attack. In any case, the client's response to their own vulnerability when prompted by the therapist is informative to the therapist as it tells the therapist how accessible self-compassion is to the client. Some clients struggle with being self-compassionate, some struggle with being self-assertive (self-protective in the face of mistreatment) and some struggle on both fronts. Thus, close observation of the first experiential task dialogues serves also as a source of information for the therapist's assessment of the client's processing difficulties.

Probing for self-compassion is attempted by the therapist in asking the client to sit in the Critic chair and look at the self in the Experiencer chair expressing vulnerability (e.g., *I feel worthless, withdrawn, put down, and it hurts me to my core*) and the freshly articulated unmet need (e.g., *I want you to tell me I am a good person, a good parent, I want you to be on my side and not put me down constantly*). It may look as follows:

Therapist: Okay. *If you could come back here* [to the Critic chair]. *So what do you feel towards her* [pointing to the Experiencer chair]*? I mean, towards that part of you that feels so vulnerable, withdrawn, so much longing for your appreciation?* [The therapist is highlighting both the chronic vulnerable feeling as well as the unmet need.] *What do you feel towards her? What would you wish for her?* [Asking for the feeling is a standard question, but at times an invitation to express a wish for the vulnerable part may help to access compassion particularly powerfully. The wish also points at potentiality, or willingness, as the intentions may differ from capability. At times clients wish that they could be compassionate, but are unable to access it.]

As highlighted above, there are two variations of what might happen (at times they may blend). In the first option (see *5a. no compassion expressed stage*), the client may become more rejecting. See the example from Timulak (2015, p. 134):

Therapist: *Yeah. Yeah. Okay. Could you come here* [inviting the client to the Critic chair]*? … When you see her like this here? Yes? … do you feel like you would want to kind of judge her even more or to be even harsher? For her to feel vulnerable even …* [The therapist here is almost confronting the client with the fact that she could be so cruel as to attack herself.]

…

Client: *Look at you* [with contempt in her voice].

…

Client: *Reduced you to tears again … You just … You just haven't got it in you. You just …*

In addition to having acquired valuable information about how self-contemptuous and self-critical the client can be, the therapist here can now opt to follow two processes. One way could be to highlight the rejection (e.g., *So this is how you judge her* [the self in the Experiencer chair]. *Do it a bit more*). This can help in stage 6a, where the client needs to stand up to the, now escalated, mistreatment (see below). The second process that the therapist focuses on is highlighting the function of the self-criticism. For instance:

Therapist [speaking on behalf of the client]: *I cannot look at you. I need to attack you, and I am doing it, so … ?* [Leaving the space for the client to finish.]

Client: *So you would put yourself together and would not be moaning around …*

Therapist: *And the sense is? What would happen if she was moaning?*

Client: *Nobody will be interested in you.* [Self-protective function of the
                critic shows here.]
Therapist: *You will be alone.*

Sometimes the self-criticism is an internalized message received from a significant
other (e.g., *On some level my mother had to be right, I am a bad person*). The
therapist may thus also check for the origin of the self-treatment (see the example
in Timulak, 2015, p. 134–135):

Therapist: *Yeah. Yeah. "I'll be like this to you"* [repeating the critic's words].
                *Yeah. Where does it come from? I mean, is this how you remember
                you treated yourself or somebody else kind of had this type of, you
                know, dismissive attitude or ... ?*
Client: *Growing up. If you couldn't do something they'd just say, "Well
                go away and leave it and we'll do it ourselves"... The brothers and
                sisters and ... teachers in the school and my mom.*

What matters here is the perceived function of the self-criticism, which is
generally to improve the client in some way, and thus prevent the attack,
rejection, et cetera, from emotionally significant others (see below). So,
while self-worry typically seeks to prepare for a threat coming from interpersonal (social) judgment (attack, exclusion), self-criticism at times attempts
to achieve broadly similar goals by making the self more acceptable. Both
processes here act in the service of improving the chances of the self surviv-
ing in the face of (potentially) threatening or painful triggers (e.g., acceptance
by others, rejection by others, versus appreciation and love). If the therapist
highlights the function of the critic, it can help the client's self-awareness, but
it can also potentially be a source of self-compassion in later work as traces of
self-criticism serving some historically adaptive function can often be found
(see also Timulak, 2015).

The alternative to the client not expressing compassion is when the client
expresses compassion directly (*5b. Compassion coming stage*). This can happen
in the first dialogue or in some later dialogues (we will talk about the sequence of
dialogues in the next chapter). If the compassion arrives spontaneously in the first
dialogue, it is informative for the therapist's case conceptualization and assessment (an important healing processes is potentially available to the client). The
assessment purpose is, however, secondary here. The therapist primarily wants the
client to feel self-compassion, dwell in it, and express it. The therapist wants the
client to have an experience of this type of self-relating, so it might be more easily
accessible to the client outside the sessions. The interaction may look as follows:

Therapist: *Okay. So what do you feel towards her? I mean towards that part of
                you* [pointing at the Experiencer chair], *that girl in you* [the client
                referred to how she always felt like this] *who is so withdrawing,*

feeling so worthless, longing inside to be seen and valued? What do you feel towards her? Right now, what would you wish for her?

Client: *I want you not being left out and hidden.*

Therapist: *I don't want you hiding, I want you ... what? ... What do you feel towards her? Yeah?*

Client: *Eh, I don't know. I don't feel, um ...* [starting to cry].

Therapist: *Yeah. What are those tears saying? Yes, that are coming a little bit. They say ... is it what?*

Client: *Eh. I feel caring [Therapist: towards you] ... towards you.*

6b Letting compassion in stage

Once the (self-)compassion has been expressed it is important that the client be encouraged to let it in and bask in it. For many clients with engrained self-criticism this can be an extremely difficult process. Often the self-critical process gets in the way, and a sense of either not deserving compassion or not being used to it intrudes, leading the client to become skeptical, suspicious, and resigned. The therapist must therefore facilitate the client to be able to let in compassion. This process may look somewhat like this:

Therapist: *See what happens, yes, inside, when she says to you, "I respect you".* [This is what the client expressed just few moments ago in the Critic chair towards the self.] *"I am on your side." How does it feel inside?*

Client: *I wish you did ...*

Therapist: *I wish you did. So it is almost I cannot believe it. But how does it feel? "I respect you, I am on your side, I care about you." Can you let it in?*

Client: *Um, I can't, eh, I can't accept if anybody compliments me or anything, and I'm never very good at anything like that. Do you know what I mean?*

Therapist: *Okay. So it is like, I cannot let it in.*

Client: *Mmm. I can't, I can't accept anybody being kind of really nice to me. You know?*

Therapist: *But what's the sense inside, right here, right now as she says it to you.*

Client: [A long pause.] *It's like a lift. It's good. It's a lift. It's, um, it's like I can breathe or something. I don't know.*

Therapist: *Yeah.*

Client: *I felt, I spent so much time walking around like knots inside and ...*

Therapist: *Yeah.*

Client: *But that's not there. I still feel sad but all the, eh, turmoil ...*

Therapist: *Yeah.*

Client: *If you like, is being unraveled. You know?*

Therapist: *Yeah. Okay.*

Client: *Just feels better.*

Therapist: So it's like ... *Tell her. Yes? "I feel that kind of relief or breeze."*
Yeah? *"And it feels good to hear it."*

6a Building protective anger, setting boundary stage

While accessing fresh self-compassion and being able to let it in is an important
principle of therapeutic change in the context of problematic self-treatment (see
Chapter 4), it is equally important to build the client's capacity to stand up for the
self, in the face of humiliating self-criticism and self-diminishing self-treatment.
While self-compassion is accessed through witnessing one's own vulnerability, the
building of protective, boundary-setting, anger (assertion) is facilitated by highlighting the mistreatment that the self is subjected to. Although protective anger may
occur spontaneously in the client, the most typical expression of this is visible in its
experience and expression in the context of escalated self-attack corresponding to
stage 5b, when the client is probed for compassion towards the core pain expressed
in the Experiencer, but the client in the Critic chair attacks further. In such a case,
the therapist asks the client to go back to the Experiencer chair and see what his/her
response to this mistreatment is, here and now. The therapist intentionally highlights
the mistreatment rather than focusing on the pain the mistreatment brings. So rather
than saying: *What happens inside when you get it?* (as in stage 2), the therapist may
say something like: *What is your response to that, when s/he treats you like this?*

As with self-compassion, clients often struggle to be capable of protecting
themselves and stand up for the self. Several strategies regarding how this process can be supported have been highlighted by Timulak (2015). For instance, the
therapist may facilitate the client through encouragement (e.g., *Will you let him/
her put you down like this?*), or paradoxical interventions if the client is collapsing, to which the client responds with a resurgence of fighting back (e.g., Client:
I am weak, I cannot stand up to him. Therapist: *Tell him I am weak, you can put
me down as you want.* Client: *I am weak, you can put me down.* Therapist: *Do
you enjoy it?* Client: *No.* Therapist: *So tell him, I am not enjoying it. I want ... ?*
Client: *I am not enjoying you putting me down. I want you to shut up.*). The therapist may also focus on the needs and wishes the client may harbor, even if they do
not feel able to stand up for the self (e.g., Therapist: *You're saying I am unable to
fight you. What would you wish you would do if you were able?* Client: *I would
tell you to shut up.* Therapist: *So try and see.* Client: *I want you to shut up*), and
so on. (For other examples and strategies facilitating healthy anger see Timulak,
2015 and the text below on unfinished-business tasks and the next chapter.)

Timulak (2015, p. 135–137; see also Timulak, 2014) presents an example in
which the client who was unable to stand up to her own critic, at first stood up in
an imaginary dialogue to her bullying cousin and, as she was self-asserting to the
cousin, the therapist asked her to confront her critic (again, this is a strategy that
can also be used). Although the client stood up to her cousin, she is unable to do
it to her Critic and collapses again. The therapist asks her, *"Do you want to collapse in the face of this?"* The client says no and as the therapist prompts her by
asking what she wants she starts with, *"I don't want to collapse"* and continues

with, "*I want to be seen as a person*", a few seconds later, adding "*a fully fledged adult*". The therapist then encourages an expression of this to the Critic and relationally validates that she has every right to feel like this.

In generating protective anger, we often see a typical EFT dance, in which the therapist invites the client to look inside for the felt experience, stays with it, names it (to which the therapist responds empathically), and then expresses it (as encouraged by the therapist). The building of protective anger like the development of self-compassion, is a process that works across sessions and is closely linked to a similar process in the self–other empty chair dialogue task (unfinished business) for an emotional injury (see below). We will look at the interaction of the two tasks below and in the next chapter.

Further use of two-chair dialogue for problematic (self-evaluative) self-treatment

Two-chair dialogue for problematic (self-evaluative) self-treatment is a major task that allows the therapist and the client to access and transform chronic painful emotions linked to problematic self-treatment. The task is closely linked to the empty chair dialogue task (unfinished business) for an emotional injury, described below. The unfinished business task deals with major interpersonal injuries (particularly from significant others) that we conceptualize as triggers, and that are the source of chronic painful feelings/vulnerabilities (sadness/loneliness, shame, and primary fear/terror). The two-chair dialogue for problematic self-treatment addresses self-treatment that developed in the context of these painful, and now feared, triggers The two-chair task can often, therefore, fluidly weave itself into an empty chair task and vice versa (we will talk about this more in the next chapter).

Given that problematic self-treatment is a crucial compounding factor of chronic emotional pain, the transformation of this largely self-critical process has to be fully and repeatedly attended to in therapy, so that the client might internalize a more self-compassionate and self-protective/assertive mode of self-treatment. For that to happen the client has to repeatedly experience transformation from shaming, towards self-compassion and the assertive, self-protective, sense of self, but also needs to be able to reflect on that process. The client needs to build sensitivity towards his or her own awareness of the problematic self-treatment. The client needs to be able to make sense of it, so he or she might build a new self-narrative incorporating the transformed emotion schemes and self-organizations.

This can also be achieved through in-session, post-task reflection on the processes and experiences in the task and through the use of homework. For instance, each stage delineated in Table 8.1 can be used for a particular piece of homework. Stage 1, in terms of reflection and awareness, can be used to show how the client attacks him or herself (the client can be instructed to pay attention during the week to see how they criticize themselves). Stage 2 can be similarly used to enable the client to become aware of what shape the self-attack takes (again the client can monitor the different ways they attack themselves during the week). Stage 3 can be used for reflectively identifying how the client feels in the immediate aftermath of the self-attack (again this can be monitored during the week). Stage 4 can help the client to reflect on what needs are being disrespected in the attacks on the self (for instance, the client can be asked to see how he or she could cherish and nurture those needs, e.g., to be respected, valued, etc.).

The experiences of compassion in Stage 5 can be used for planning how self-compassion could be consolidated during the week(s) following the session. The therapist and the client can explore how the client could introduce those experiences to their everyday life (e.g., what activities express self-compassion according to the client, e.g., painting class, yoga, etc.). Finally, the experiences of self-assertion and boundary setting in Stage 6 can serve as a basis for the discussion and planning of activities that support that newly affirmed part of the self (e.g., *I will give myself a break if I catch myself blaming myself. I will take more breaks during the week,* etc.). The therapist may find it useful to use the framework presented in Table 8.2.

Table 8.2 Framework that can be used to reflect on the two-chair dialogue for problematic (self-evaluative) self-treatment and as a base for homework (Timulak, 2017, inspired by Warwar, 2015)

Parts enacted in the Experiencer chair	Parts enacted in the Critic chair
	• **How do I criticize (attack) myself?** (Increasing awareness of the ways the client treats [criticizes, attacks, devalues, etc.] him or herself)
• **How do I feel when I am being criticized (treated badly)?** (Highlighting the emotional impact, often variations of shame, at times linked to other painful emotions) • **What do I need in the face of the criticism?** (To articulate the need stemming from the hurt feelings)	
	• **What drives my criticism?** (e.g., wish to improve; wish to avoid interpersonal judgment and rejection; wish to earn recognition, respect, love; a sense that I deserve to be punished, etc., see Chapter 6 on case conceptualization)
• **How can I face the critic?** (A reminder of the resolve in the session to face and fight the critic)	
	• **What do I feel towards the hurt, shamed, put down, vulnerable part of me?** (Bringing a reminder of compassionate experiences that may respond to the unmet needs in the vulnerable experience accessed in the Experiencer chair)

Self–other (empty chair) task for an emotional injury (unfinished business)

Most of the triggers of the core painful feelings are of an interpersonal nature (the exceptions are situational triggers such as illness, loss of employment, etc.). Repeated or long-term problematic interactions, particularly stemming from a developmentally sensitive time, often lead to emotional injuries that become chronic. These are experiences of interpersonal rejection, judgment, intrusion, burdening, scaring, et cetera. They are generally of two kinds, historical or recent. Sometimes it is a mixture of the two (e.g., a problematic relationship with a parent that was historically problematic, and is still problematic). Traditionally, EFT literature refers to the task focusing on experiential work with the historical interpersonal triggers that caused the emotional injury as empty chair work for unfinished business or, shortly, unfinished business task or empty chair work (cf. Elliott *et al.*, 2004; Greenberg *et al.*, 1993). This task was intended to respond to markers suggesting lingering, internally upsetting (such as hurt and resentment) feelings that were currently experienced and were often also restricted/interrupted, and were experienced in relation to a significant person in the client's life (cf. Elliott *et al.*, 2004; p. 245).

Here we will present a variation of this task (see Table 8.3) that can be applied to current as well as historical problematic relationships that evoke chronic painful feelings of loneliness/sadness, shame, and/or fear in the client. Clients with GAD difficulties generally have several interpersonal relationships that tend to stir chronically problematic, difficult to process, feelings. These can be current romantic relationships, relationships with work colleagues/bosses, relationships with siblings, other relatives, or friends. Almost all of the clients with GAD difficulties that we worked with had complicated relationships with at least one of their parents (sometimes both). These could be relationships with their biological parents, adoptive parents, or step-parents.

While therapy focuses on all interactions that stir chronic, difficult feelings, or interactions that are seen, and experienced, as a threat, stirring unbearable feelings that are better avoided, it mainly focuses on the most salient and historically significant interpersonal interactions which have led to the formation of problematic emotion schemes and ensuing problematic self-organizations. Thus, almost automatically, the main focus of therapy and the main use of the empty chair task relates to chronic feelings stirred by interactions with significant others, such as parents. So, while in a short-term therapy any emotionally salient problematic relationship can be focused on in this task, here, the emotionally problematic relationship with the parent central to the client problematic emotion schemes/self-organizations is typically focused on in a systematic manner and repeatedly.

As mentioned above, almost all of the clients with GAD difficulties that we worked with had one or other parent at the center of their chronic painful feelings (typically the mother, but in some cases, the father, or both). Unresolved painful feelings and emotional injuries experienced in those relationships are focused on, usually in a series of dialogues (see the next chapter, Chapter 9). We also observed that current or recent interpersonal interactions (relationships) that stirred painful feelings were in many cases similar to, and evoked similar chronic feelings to,

Table 8.3 A variation of the empty chair task for an emotional injury (unfinished business) (Timulak, 2017, based on Elliott *et al.*, 2004)

	Experiencer chair	Other chair
1.	Marker – unfinished business, hurt	
2a.	Expressing pain, hurt, and anger	
2b.		Enactment of harsh, hurtful other, getting core message from them
3.	Accessing and differentiating core pain – loneliness, shame, primary fear Perhaps protective anger if it comes	
4.	Articulating and expressing unmet need	
5.		Probing for compassion – seeing the pain and unmet need
		A) If no compassion is coming – highlighting rejection (message and mistreatment contained in it, highlighting the function of it)
		B) If compassion is coming – savoring it experientially and expressing it
6a.	Building protective anger, setting boundary	
6b.	Letting compassion in – savoring it experientially	

those evoked by interactions with those historical figures; although there could be some painful feelings that were not particularly linked to historical experiences (e.g., recent traumatic encounters).

Typical triggers of the core pain linked to historical triggers include experiences of being held as an object of contempt by a parent, experiences of a loss (often sudden) of a parent, experiences of a parent who was too fragile (and thus forcing the client, as a child, to assume a parental role too early), a parent being terrifying/violent, threatening, or having angry outbursts, a parent simply not being there, a parent that was constantly intrusive, criticizing, undermining, et cetera. Correspondingly, the current (recent) interactions could be with significant or important others who were judgmental, scary, contemptuous, abandoning, betraying, et cetera.

Table 8.3 delineates six stages that the therapist tries to navigate when working with clients' interpersonal emotional injuries. As with the two-chair dialogue for self-critical processes, the therapist facilitates the process flexibly and creatively, so the outlined stages should be seen as tentative. The task can also be embedded within other tasks (particularly the two-chair task for self-criticism), which we will discuss in the next chapter.

I Marker stage

The empty chair task is normally introduced at the in-session marker when the client's experience indicates that they are freshly in touch with complex unsettling feelings in relation to a salient other. The feelings are typically undifferentiated (at least in the early dialogues) or somewhat complex (a mixture of the feelings). They are known, chronically experienced, lingering, and uncomfortable. Clients may want to avoid the topic of the relationship stirring those feelings. Once the marker of a chronic emotional upset in relation to a salient other is present, the therapist may initiate the task.

2a Expressing pain, hurt, and anger/2b Enactment of hurtful other stage

As you may have noticed, there are two parts to stage 2 in Table 8.3. We use this structure, so that the reader might conceptually link the empty chair task with the two-chair task. In the two-chair task, in the second stage, the client enacts the self-attack. Here, the client starts to speak from the hurt and the therapist facilitates the differentiation of the hurt (stage 2a). However, part of the differentiation of the hurt is also an enactment of the client's perceptual field, that is, of the behavior of the other that the client found hurtful (stage 2b). The enactment of the hurtful aspects of the other, as seen by the client, will help to deepen the experience of the impact it brought to the client.

The introduction of the idea of a dialogue with the hurtful other may appear strange to the client. To some, it may appear awkward, or anxiety provoking, while others may fear that it could be too evocative. Indeed, this is one of the reasons why the task is used – so the emotion schemes and relevant self-organizations become activated in therapy and are thus more amenable to possible restructuring. As therapy progresses, clients normally get used to this and other experiential tasks. The initiation of the first dialogue with the hurtful significant other may look as follows:

Therapist: Yeah. So if you stay with her picture [the picture of the client's mother, now deceased, who was very rejecting and judgmental]. *This is what we will be doing from time to time. I will help you through it, yes? We will actually bring her almost here. Yes?*

Client: Yeah.

Therapist: *I mean almost to have a dialogue with her. It will be maybe a little bit strange in the beginning, yes? But it is rather to see what is really difficult for you. You know? To make it more alive almost. In order to change this or to come to terms somehow with it, it is sometimes important to bring it you know here. I mean to look at it. So if you stay with her picture, yes? Just if you imagine her in this chair* [pointing to the Other chair]. *What happens inside? What is the feeling like? It is like what?*

Client: *It is just like, um, I just want to choke almost. You know. It kinda comes up and it is hard.*

...

Therapist: Okay. What is the feeling if you stay with the picture of her?

Client:	*Sadness.*
Therapist:	*Okay. And we will actually try to talk to her. So it is like, "Mom, I am sad", and I am sad for what?*
Client:	*Why were you always so hurtful, I suppose?* [The question "Why?" is often where the clients start the dialogue.]
Therapist:	*Okay. So it is like that, "I am sad that you were so hurtful to me always".*
Client:	*Yeah. I have asked her, like, "Why are you always so nasty?" you know. She would look at me and just look at me and shrug and ...*
...	
Therapist:	*Yeah. Yeah so this is what was painful, yeah? So I would go like, "Mom, this is what was so painful, to get those shrugs," and so on, yeah?*
....	
Client:	*Yeah, that is it, and then, um, you would not communicate with me properly then, and always looked hurt herself.*
...	
Therapist:	*Yeah. Okay. So it is like, "You were never responsive to me?" Yes?*
Client:	*Yeah. Never. You were never responsive.*
Therapist:	*And what is the sense inside as you are saying it? Tell her.*

The beginning of an empty chair dialogue can also be characterized by a large amount of secondary anger:

Client:	*You never even wanted to know me. You didn't care what I did when I was a teenager or anything* [defensive/rejecting anger].
Therapist:	*Yeah.*
Client:	*You didn't care if I didn't come home at night. You just didn't care where I was.*
Therapist:	*Yeah.*
Client:	*You never bothered. Once I didn't inflict and ... and didn't damage your life or anything. Once you could carry on doing what you wanted to, you didn't care. You never showed love.*
Therapist:	*Yeah, So it looked like, like I felt this hole ... in me for the whole of my life, yes, and it just ...* [The therapist is aiming at the underlying vulnerability here.]
Client:	*I felt put down all my life.*
Therapist:	*Yeah, but also this, I had this longing, yes, for you to be ... more caring or something.*
Client:	*I wanted you to be more caring. I never felt you really loved me.*

As the client begins to describe the hurtful behavior of the other, early on in the dialogue, the therapist asks the client to enact that hurtful behavior (stage 2b). Essentially, it is the perceptual field of what the client saw in the other that was hurtful. Here is an example (Timulak, 2015, p. 91–92):

Therapist: *Could you come here* [pointing to the Other chair]*? And if you could be the rude mother that you remember for a moment, yes, it is just to convey the message what she was doing. Yes?*

...

Therapist: *So how would she behave? How would she deliver this rudeness to you and to others?*

Client [speaking as imagined mother]:   *She would look at you and then she would go "ththth".*

Therapist: *Okay. Do it ... And the message of it is almost like as if she is saying what? Like, "I don't care about you"?*

...

Client: *Yeah. Absolutely, all the time. I want to insult you.*

...

Therapist: *Yeah and what would be the insult? What would be an example?*
Mary: *Um. "You're very fat." "You're getting fatter."*
Therapist: *You are fat. Tell her again.*

The therapist then goes further and tries to unfold what drove those insults in the harmful behavior of the hurtful other (e.g., Therapist: *And what drives this insulting? Is it like, I am unhappy, so I want you to be unhappy?* Client: *It's like I am jealous of your freedom, of your youth, of your friends. I am unhappy and I do not want you to be happy*). Once the core message is expressed, the client and the therapist move to the next stage (see below).

At times, the problematic behavior of the significant other does not come in the form of rejection or attack, but may appear as the significant other's vulnerability (e.g., *I am falling apart from seeing you vulnerable*), or embarrassment and/or panic. For instance:

Therapist: *Be her* [her mother] *like ... It's almost like her voice in your head, that it's hers. Yes? What would she be saying?*

Client [as her mother]: *I actually know the voice from in here. It's, "Stop that now. People are looking. People are listening. No one needs ... needs to know". Um. It's ... "People have their own problems so they don't need to know yours".*

Therapist: *Okay. Okay. And what's driving it? It's like, "I want to ..." what? "I want to be proud of you as a, as a ..."* [The therapist is trying to conjecture why the mother is embarrassed to see her daughter vulnerable.]

Client: *Well, yeah. I want you to be ... independent ... the kind of woman who ... isn't weak and ... is a strong ...*

Therapist: *Okay. So it's almost like, "You're letting down my image of you", or something?*

Client [still as the mother]: *I feel panicky, embarrassed for you.*

3 Accessing and differentiating core pain stage

Once the initial hurt is experienced and expressed (in the Experiencer chair) and the hurtful or difficult behavior of the other is expressed (in the Other chair), the client is invited to come back to the Experiencer chair and see what impact the hurtful behavior of the other has (e.g., *Come back here and see what happens when s/he attacks you like this*). The therapist is now trying to facilitate the client's further access to the core chronic painful feelings. As we described in Chapters 4 and 6, these are typically feelings of loneliness/sadness, shame, and/or primary fear.

Each client has his or her own idiographic constellation of core painful feelings, emotion schemes, and problematic self-organizations built from those schemes. The therapist's goal here is to deepen the process, to help the client activate problematic emotion schemes by achieving a sufficient level of arousal. Clients may also experience and express secondary emotions; they may show some adaptive experiences, such as protective anger (e.g., to the therapist's prompt: *So what do you say back when she puts you down like this?*). The main focus of this stage, however, is to deepen vulnerable feelings that the client normally struggles to stay with, and may be desperately trying to avoid (which may be also an issue at different points throughout the empty chair dialogue). The therapist is empathic and affirmative, helping the client to stay with, and bear, these difficult emotions without being overwhelmed by them (i.e., access them in a productive way). Here is an example of touching on the core pain at this stage:

Therapist: *Yeah. Okay. Could you come here* [pointing to the Experiencer chair]*? What happens as you get that* [rejection from the enacted imagined mother]*?*

Client: *I'm still put down then. I mean, I never even told you about this, I suppose. But put down.*

Therapist: *About what?*

Client: *I, um, was only 16, like, when I kind of left home, if you like.*

Therapist: *Yeah.*

Client: *Nobody bothered. You never bothered where I was or anything. You know?*

Therapist: *Yeah. Tell her.*

Client: *You pushed me out to, eh … Was only very young. You know?*

Therapist: *Yeah. Yeah. Okay. So it's like if she was here, it's like, "You really kind of reject me, rejected me when I was weak, young, 16 …". The sense inside was that she really doesn't care* [focusing on the underlying feeling].

Client [crying]:   *I didn't feel cared for. I missed being cared for. I missed you. And I did not know why you do not love me. I had just you and wanted you to show me that you care, that you do love me. That I am OK. That I am your girl and I am okay.*

Here is another exchange that illustrates some of the process that can be seen at this stage:

Therapist:	Okay. Could you come here? So what happens inside when you get that message? [The imagined mother was expressing unresponsiveness, and claimed she was too unhappy and distressed to be capable of looking after her daughter] Yes? This is what we were getting, but now, here? Yes? When you get this message what happens inside? Yes? What's your response to it or something?
Client [speaking to the imagined mom]:	It wasn't fair.

Therapist:	Yeah. "It's like I was a kid and I should have a life as a kid." Yeah?
Client:	Mmm.
Therapist:	"I should have had, eh, a careless life, actually, as a child." Yes? Not knowing about her difficulty.
Client:	Carefree life.
Therapist:	Yeah. This is what I missed.
Client:	Yeah. I should have … I should have had the life that my best friend had. This is what I missed at home.
Therapist:	Yeah.
…	
Client:	Always, because it … She [friend's mother] was the type of mother I wanted. I missed it in you.
…	
Therapist:	So you had … "This is what I need to get, have at home" or something?
Client:	Yeah.
…	
Therapist:	Disappointment. Yes? It was like constant disappointment. Yes? Like every day hoping that it will be different from now on.
Client:	Yeah. Every day there was hope that you would look after yourself, that you wouldn't be drinking. That you would be there for me. This is what I missed …
Therapist:	And this fills me with so much sadness … and … loss.

Client [crying]:	Yeah. I missed you … I do miss you…

In this stage, clients may touch on variations of sadness/loneliness, shame, and fear (e.g., they may be terrified by the hurtful other). The therapist tries to help the client to stay with those difficult feelings, feel them, put them into words (empathize with them), and encourages the client to express them to the imagined hurtful other. In certain circumstances, if the other was very abusive, the clients may be not able to access vulnerability. In that case, the client may be asked to express the hurt to an imagined responsive other (of their choosing) and express vulnerability to them (see more on that below, in Timulak [2015] and in the next chapter).

This stage may also involve checking in for particular episodic memories (e.g., Therapist: Does any memory come up from earlier on when you felt like this?), which may be pivotal for the emotional injuries that the client is accessing and expressing in this stage. These are specific memories from childhood and adolescence. If the client remembers instances that are illustrative of when they felt the injury they are accessing, the therapist may ask the client to re-remember them and speak as though they were just happening (e.g., Therapist: *Be that 12-year-old that so much wanted your mom to like her performance* (at a school event), *who was so disappointed when she dismissed it. Be that girl right now. What is the sense inside?*).

4 Articulating and expressing unmet need

Once the feared, core chronic, emotional pain is accessed, felt, stayed with, and expressed, the therapist directs the client to the unmet needs in the core painful emotions (e.g., for love, connection, validation, protection, etc.). The guidance towards the needs comes when the client is experiencing primary core painful emotions in a productive manner (Greenberg *et al.*, 2007), that is, the client is feeling the painful primary emotion but is not running away from the emotion, is not trying to avoid it, and can tolerate it despite it being painful. The therapist usually facilitates the client to express the unmet needs to the hurtful other. At times, when the hurtful other was too abusive and/or too terrifying, the therapist can first ask the client to imagine a potentially caring other (open to the client's vulnerability) and express the need towards that person. With some abusers, such as strangers, the client may only be asked to express the need to a potentially caring other. The abuser may be just confronted with the protective anger.

The expression of the need has to be anchored in the here-and-now experience. Even though it may refer to past unfilled needs (e.g., *I needed you …*), the therapist tries to ensure that the client feels the interaction as if it was happening right now. The therapist can, for instance, use the present tense or encourage enactment as if what was needed was happening right now (e.g., *be that small girl/boy right now. What is it you need? Tell her/him?*). The here-and-now quality of the experiencing makes the experience more real and thus helps to activate involved emotion schemes (self-organizations) more vividly and more fully. An example of a heartfelt need can be seen in Timulak (2014; 2015, p. 56 and 107–108), in which the client expresses, in a poignant example, how she did not have anybody to turn to and how she needed her mother to be there when she was young. She expresses: *It's every now and then a girl needs her mom.*

Another brief example may look as follows:

Therapist [speaking on behalf of the client]: Yeah, but I … need a connection. That's why I longed all my life as a child.
Client [speaking to the imagined mother]: That's what I wanted you to be like.

Therapist: Someone to be there for me. Yeah?
Client: You never wanted to [expressing sadness and loss].
Therapist: Because this is my nature and this is what I needed from my mom, yes?
Client: Yeah. Exactly.

Or another example:

Therapist: Yeah. But inside, if you go to that vulnerability ... Yeah? What is it you need from your mom in that vulnerability?

Client: Non-judgment. Non- ... And just seeing me as someone who's going through a hard time, rather than someone who's weak or someone's who failed. Or not, not to be embarrassed by my emotion, I suppose.

Therapist: Yeah. "So I need you ..." Tell it to her.

Client: I need you not to be embarrassed by my emotion ...

Therapist: Yeah.

Client: ... By my ... I need you to support me rather than ...

Therapist: Yeah. "I need your support." Yeah?

Client: I do need your support.

...

Therapist: Yeah. What's the sense inside now as we are speaking?

Client: Just kind of sad that they [parents] don't get it, I suppose.

..

Therapist: Yeah. "It's like I'm sad that you're not getting it all." Yes?

Client: Yeah.

Therapist: Say it to her.

Client: I am sad that you're not getting it. That you're ...

Therapist: Yeah.

Client: ... You don't understand that ... I need it. That I need ...

5 Probing for compassion – seeing the pain and unmet needs stage

Once the unmet needs experienced in the context of core pain are expressed, the therapist typically asks the client to come back and sit in the Other chair and see what he or she feels towards the core pain and the expressed needs in the Experiencer chair (e.g., Therapist: *Come back here. And now be your mom. What do you feel towards her* [the client in the Experiencer chair], *being so vulnerable and longing for you to love her? What do you feel towards her, right now?*). The therapist is trying to focus the client (as the imagined significant other) on the vulnerability that was just expressed by the client (stage 3 and 4) in the Experiencer, the self-chair. It is fresh pain and vulnerability, which elicits compassion in the client enacting the significant other (*How is it to see her so vulnerable, so much longing for you to love her?*). Focusing on that vulnerability, unmet needs, and the feeling towards them, increases the likelihood of generating compassion.

Of course, whether compassion can emerge is down to several factors. Some of them have to do with the skillfulness of the therapist (who may be helping the client to access vulnerability in the Experiencer chair and then focus on that vulnerability). Others have to do with client factors. For instance, clients may vary in how easily they can overcome avoidance, access the pain, and, eventually, self-compassion. This of course depends on their overall history and other predispositions (including biological ones) developed over the course of their lives. The actual relationship with the injurer naturally plays an important role here. Some interpersonal injuries happen in the context of otherwise loving relationships, whereas others occur in relationships characterized by absence or deprivation. The client's capability to soften in the Other chair thus also provides important assessment information for the therapist about how chronic and pervasive the injury is. Moreover, eliciting compassion is a process. To feel compassionate towards the self, while enacting the injurer, may take (and usually does take) a series of empty chair dialogues. It is a process in which various aspects of the hurt (and hurtful behavior) are acknowledged and given a voice.

If the perpetrator of traumatic injury was not, and/or was not supposed to be, in a caring relationship with the client (e.g., an unknown attacker), we would not expect a softening to develop, out of enacting somebody who can only represent threat. Therefore, the dialogue would only use such a person (trigger) for stage 6a (building the protective anger) or perhaps stage 2b (if the trigger/attacker/abuser was not too terrifying and dysregulating). The softening, and enacting of the caring other would then rather, be drawn from a potential protector who was, or was not, available. In some cases, the absence of this protector could be a part of the injury, so they would also be enacted in stage 2b in a separate, albeit related, dialogue (e.g., an invalidating parent who did not believe a client's reports of childhood sexual abuse at the time they occurred). We will further discuss some of these potential nuances of therapeutic strategy in the following chapter.

Complicated relationships with significant others (e.g., ambivalent relational experiences that contain a mixture of injuries and caring, or at least some caring or potentially caring experiences) usually show some sort of transformation in the series of empty chair dialogues, wherein more softening, compassionate qualities are eventually accessed. It is, however, usually a slow and delicate unfolding process, requiring a lot of skill from the therapist (cf. Timulak, 2015). Earlier dialogues are typically characterized by little or no softening. What happens is that when the client is asked to enact the injurer and encouraged to look at their own vulnerability and unmet needs, further rejection comes (see stage 5a. *No compassion coming* in Table 8.3).

Here the therapist has to respect that suboptimal response, acknowledge it, and highlight the dramatic impact of the enacted other being so hurtful (e.g., Therapist: *So you/she* [the client enacting her mother] *cannot relate to that vulnerability and to what that little girl needs, you just feel punishing and rejecting towards her*). This unresponsiveness will later be used in stage 6a (building the protective anger). Here, the therapist can further unfold what he or she may have already begun in stage 2b., that is, what is the function of the other's unresponsive behavior (e.g., Therapist: *So it is like, I need to be punishing you ... because ... ?*; Client [speaking as mom]: *Because I am just so unhappy that I feel your* [the client's] *vulnerability as a burden*). Highlighting this function may at times serve as a building block for compassion, as it is often not that intentionally hurtful, but rather stems from the injurer's vulnerability (e.g., a parent unable to provide care). One has to be careful here, however, as the injurer's vulnerability (commonly a parent) often stifles the client's self-protection (see stage *6a. Generating protective anger*) and leads to various forms of self-interruption (e.g., *I cannot stand up to my parent because I will lose them for good or I will hurt them and they will not be able to cope*).

An example of an unresponsive reaction from the enacted significant other is visible in the following exchange:

Therapist: *Could you switch? ... Now as your Mom, yes? ... What happens when she hears this, yes?* [The client just expressed vulnerability and her lifelong longing for her mom to love her.] *What happens?*

Client: *She'd just go, "So ... I don't care what you say. I'm not interested in ya".* [Speaking to the therapist.] *"She'd just be hard. Very hard, like. Wouldn't care."*

...

Therapist: *Okay. So I really don't mind being that hurtful. Yes? This is the message.*

...

Client [still as mom]: *No, no ... regard for anybody, only myself, and I couldn't care less.*

Therapist: *So it is almost like, "I'm vicious, yes? I'm unhappy. I'm vicious."* [The client was using those words to describe mom previously.]

...

Therapist: *And I'm doing it because ... ?*

...

Client: *I'm just hard.* [The client then goes on to say that she (as the mom) is unhappy and therefore attacks her daughter, is jealous of her happiness and her carelessness, in contrast to her being unhappy, in a role that would require her to be responsible.]

Another illustrative example can be found in Timulak (2015, p. 119):

Therapist: *Could you switch now? So now, as Mom in your head. Yes? Just ... It's just in your head. Yes? What does she say to this? ...* [In the previous round the client expressed vulnerability, lack of support, and the need to be supported more.]

Client [as the imagined mother]: *"I'm sick. You ... You have to get up and do these things for yourself. I'm not able to be doing it. You're going to have to get up and look after yourself now."*

...

Therapist: *But is it really like, "I'm unresponsive." Yes?*
Client: *Yeah.*
Therapist: *"I can't understand what you're talking about." Yes? "I have no energy. I have no willingness."*
Client [as the mom]: *Yeah. "I'm not able."*

A variation of this stage (see 5b. in Table 8.3) is that the client in the chair of the other, when enacting the other, feels compassion towards the vulnerable self and the unmet needs expressed in the Experiencer chair. This usually comes from some injurers in later dialogues (particularly if they were also caring in reality). In case it is not forthcoming, and the client is only rejecting when enacting the other, it can be elicited through putting somebody more responsive to the self in the chair, including the adult self that could be more responsive to the younger, vulnerable self.

When the client is vulnerable (stage 3) and there is no softening or compassion forthcoming, the therapist stays with the rejecting response. However, within the same session the therapist may later check-in with the client in the Experiencer chair, to see who else they could go and express their hurt to (e.g., therapist: *Who could you have gone to when you would have felt like this? Does anybody come to mind? It may be somebody from the past, someone who may not be around anymore, or anybody else that could be responsive to that hurt?*). If the client nominates somebody, the therapist asks the client to come and sit in the Other chair and be that person. The therapist then asks them to see how they feel towards the client's vulnerable self, and the unmet needs that the client is expressing in the Experiencer chair.

At times, the client can be asked to sit in the Other chair, be their adult self, and look at the vulnerable emotions expressed in the Experiencer chair, particularly the ones contained in episodic memories from childhood and adolescence. For many clients, these elicit compassionate responses. Clients who struggle with self-criticism, however, may struggle with eliciting self-compassion even in such circumstances. They may be invited to imagine how they would feel in response to an imagined other, vulnerable (younger) person like them, when they felt vulnerable, for example, a child of the age they were at, when the most painful hurts from the injurer happened. Occasionally, they can be encouraged to enact the role of a parental figure (an ideal parent) and see what form the response to the vulnerable person (similar to them) in the Experiencer chair takes. Once the compassion towards the self is accessed (whether from enacting the original injurer, or the adult self, or some other person), it is important that the client be slowed down and encouraged to focus on how the expression of compassion feels, to savor the various aspects of it. This process, together with stage 6b (described below), is sometimes also referred to as a self-soothing task (Greenberg, 2015; Sutherland, Peräkylä, & Elliott, 2014).

Here is an example of compassion coming from the original injurer who, in the later dialogues, became a more responsive other (5b.):

Therapist: *Could you come here and be your Mom, but be that fragile ...* [She was sick and unable to speak.] *What would she be saying if she was able to speak?*
Client: *I think she would have said, "I love you," and maybe, "I'm sorry."*
Therapist: *Try to tell her* [pointing at the Experiencer chair], *yeah?*

Client [speaking as her mom]:   *Yeah, I'm sorry Mary. You know I love you. I always did love you.* [In reality she never said those words during her entire life.]

...

Therapist: *Yeah, and do you feel love towards her now as you are saying it?*

Client: *Yeah. Yeah.*

Therapist: *Can you tell her, "I feel that love"? Tell it to her.*

Client: *I do feel that love towards you.*

Therapist: *"I feel like I would want to hug you, that I would want to be with you more."* [The therapist refers to what the client was saying before, that in one of the last interactions with her mom before she died, she had a sense that she wanted to hug her.]

Client: *Yeah. Yeah. Yeah I would, I would want to ... It's a pity it took to the end of my life ...*

An example of compassion coming from the adult self (in the context of not having received that reaction from the injurer in that particular dialogue) towards the self from an episodic memory may look as follows:

Therapist: *So now as yourself, yes, as an adult, Catherine* [the client's pseudonym]. *Yes? If you see that 15-year old, yes? What would you say to her? Now, as an adult. What would you say to Catherine when you see yourself there when you were 15?*

Client: *Well, really you, you, what could you say? She was so sort of sad and ...*

Therapist: *Yeah.*

Client: *I know what I'd do if it was my own daughter. Like, you wouldn't expect to be treated like that. Would you?*

Therapist: *Yeah. Okay. So if I could, what would you do for her? If you could be there. Yes? She is 15 there.*

Client: *Well, I'd want to take her back home and ... give her attention and ...*

Therapist: *Okay. So, "I, I will look after you." Yeah?*

Client: *Yeah.*

Therapist: *Tell her. "I will ..."*

Client: *I will look after you.*

Therapist: *Yeah. "I'll take care of you." Yes?*

...

Therapist: *Okay. What do you feel towards her? Do you feel like you want to protect her?*

Client: *Yeah. Absolutely.*

Therapist: *Tell her. Yes?*

Client: *I want to protect you and make you happy.*

The therapist can then check-in with the client to see how they feel inside as they say those words. Here, the therapist wants the client to be aware of, and capture, the sense of feeling compassionate towards the vulnerable self.

6a Building protective anger – setting a boundary stage

If no compassion is forthcoming in stage 5 (i.e., stage 5a), the therapist highlights the negative response from the injurer and the lack of softening towards the expressed vulnerability, and asks the client to return to the Experiencer chair. Once the client is in the Experiencer chair the therapist, rather than directing the client inwards (e.g., *What happens inside when you get this?*), directs the client to see what they would do or would wish to do in the face of escalating mistreatment (e.g., *What is your response to that "I don't care"?*). It is envisaged that as vulnerability invites compassion, the highlighting of *mistreatment* increases the likelihood of fighting back (cf. Timulak, 2015). The therapist may further probe for boundary setting, protective anger (e.g., *Will you let him/her do it?*).

Many clients with GAD difficulties struggle at this point, as they are unable to stand up for themselves. The therapist may acknowledge this struggle, but still tries to help them access healthy, boundary setting anger. The therapist may try several things (see the overview in Timulak, 2015). For instance, the therapist may ask clients what they would do if they were able (e.g., *I hear that you are unable to stand up for yourself, but if you were able what would you want?*), the therapist may use a paradoxical intervention (e.g., the client collapses and the therapists ask them to acknowledge and express it and see whether they want the other to win):

Therapist [empathizing with the client]: I collapse, I am unable to face you, you have no boundary from me, you can do what you want, tell it to him [hurtful other]...

Client:	*I am unable to face you, you can do whatever you want...*
Therapist:	*How does it feel to say it?*
Client:	*Not good. Depleted inside.*
Therapist:	*Do you enjoy it? To feel like this?*
Client:	*No.*
Therapist:	*So, what is it what you want?*
Client:	*I want to be able to stand up to him.*
Therapist:	*Tell him. I want to be able to stand up to you.*
Client:	*I want to be able to stand up to you. I do not want you to treat me like this.*
Therapist:	*And what is the sense inside as you say this?* [The therapist here hopes to catch any glimpse of self-assertion that may be appearing here.]

The therapist coaches (cf. Greenberg, 2015) the client to stand up for the self. The therapist wants to help the client feel the inner resolve to put a brake on the hurtful behavior of the other. This often leads to a sense of empowerment (see Chapter 4). Accessing healthy anger is particularly important for people with anxiety issues, as the anger builds a sense of power, inner strength, and is an important antidote to fear and anxiety. It frees the clients. This is, therefore, a particularly important goal in work with clients with GAD difficulties.

An exchange in which the client asserts a boundary to her remembered, hurtful mother can be seen here:

Therapist: Okay. Could you come here [back to the Experiencer chair]? So what, what, how does it impact you now here as when she [the injuring mother] says, "I'm just vicious, I don't feel sorry. I won't apologize. I don't care about you" ... What is your response to that? ... Does it hurt now or ... or can you be stronger?

Client: It doesn't hurt me really, no. It doesn't hurt me, um, what you've done.

...

Therapist: I won't allow you to hurt me, yes? I won't allow ...

Client: I won't allow you to hurt me.

Therapist: Those vicious attacks to be hurtful [highlighting the mistreatment].

...

Client: I could never be vicious like you were anyway. It wasn't in me to be like that. I am different and I am not terrified now [asserting the difference with a resolve].

Many clients in stage 5 express a mixture of compassion and further rejection. If the client in the Other chair expressed a mixture of further rejection, but also some softening, the therapist may facilitate the client to let in the compassion (stage 6b), but also set a boundary to the hurtful aspects of the other's expression (stage 6a). The therapist does each of the two separately in quick succession. For instance, the therapist may highlight: *She* (enacting client's mother) *is saying it is hard for me to see you in pain. I wish you did not suffer. How is it to hear it? Can you let it in?* And after the client lets it in, the therapist also highlights: *But she is also saying, "I cannot accept that you did not follow what I outlined for you". What is your response to that?* (This is probing for protective anger.)

6b Letting compassion in – savoring it experientially stage

If in stage 5, the client accesses a compassionate stance (from the enacted hurtful other, caring other, or the caring adult self) towards their own vulnerability, expressed in the Experiencer chair (stages 3 and 4), the therapist then asks the client to come back to the Experiencer chair and savor how it feels to be an object of compassion. The therapist invites the client to let in the expressed compassion from the Other chair. Many clients with a high level of self-criticism struggle at this point with letting compassion in. Furthermore, clients who experienced significant long-lasting hopelessness as a consequence of the injury from the other may struggle to believe that compassion from the enacted other (or adult self) can "undo" the injury. The therapist thus has to acknowledge and validate this difficulty, as it is important to validate the suffering that the clients have endured in the past. Nevertheless, the therapist will still work hard to help them allow compassion in, as it is something they long for.

For instance, the therapist may acknowledge the client's struggle to let in compassion, by validating the hopelessness that keeps compassion out; but can still invite the client to experiment with how it feels to receive such an expression of care (e.g., therapist: *I hear that nobody was ever there, yes it is so painful ... definite ... and hopeless ...* [long pause] *But how it is to hear it here, right now, "I do care", can you see how it feels inside if you try to let even a small bit of it in?*). The therapist may also facilitate blocking of the emerging self-criticism (e.g., the therapist may say: *I hear that it is that critical part speaking, saying you do not deserve to be cared for ... we will look at this part ... but for a moment ... could you just check inside ... how is it to be told, "I care" ... here and now ... just for the moment*). In much the same way that it is important to help the client to savor the expression of compassion, it is also important for them to bathe themselves in the experience of being on the receiving end of it. This often leads to a sense of relief and often to healthy healing (see Chapter 4). Here is an example of letting in compassion:

Therapist: *Okay. Could you come here* [back to the Experiencer chair]*? So now as a 15-year-old, yes? How does it feel to get this hug* [from the adult self]*?*

Client: *It feels great. Nice.*

Therapist: *Okay. Just let it in. Yes? To see.*

Client: *Yeah. It's nice ... Yeah. I feel better. Yeah.*

Therapist: *Tell her.*

Client: *It feels good.*

Therapist: *Yeah. "I so much needed somebody like you." Yes?*

Client: *Yeah. It does. It does feel good to hear it.*

Often the reception of expressed compassion leads to further healthy grieving that has a letting-go quality (see Chapter 4; also Pascual-Leone & Greenberg, 2007). The client may let in compassion, grieve, but still be firm in setting up the boundary (stage 6a). It may look as in the segment below:

Client [speaking to her imagined mother who showed compassion]: *Always wanted to show you I love you. You knew I loved you. You knew that, but it's a pity you couldn't show some of your feelings until you got to the* [dying] *stage. That's what I wanted you to be like* [the client grieving].

Therapist: *Someone to be there for me. Yeah?*

...

Client: *I think the deep sadness in me, the sadness, that is going. But why I was so bad, I think, was because of the last couple of months, we*

> *got so close when you were in the hospital, and that, and I was there with you and I was feeding you, and ...*

...

Client: *Clinging on to me. The very last time I saw you, you were, my husband was with me and then he went out and left me with you and said, you were hanging on to my hands and I told you, "I love you," and you sort of said, "I love you too."*

...

Therapist: *Yeah. If you stay with that image, yes, of the memory of when she said, "I love you," yes? ... How it feels inside, yes?*

Client: *... Sad, I think that's another thing, you had to be on your deathbed to show any ...*

...

Therapist: *Yeah. If you stay with this image when she told you, "I love you."*

...

Client: *Yeah. It did feel good, yeah. Good to hear that* [the client is crying].

The process of self–other empty chair task dialogue for emotional injury

The process described in Table 8.3, and the pages above, is presented in linear fashion. The six stages are, however, nonlinear and the client can move backwards to processes that would be more characteristic of lower stages, et cetera. The description is also didactic, whereas at times, the stages can blur and overlap. It is also possible that the process in a particular dialogue in a particular session may get to a particular stage and not go beyond that. In such cases, the therapist tries to bring forth some constructive processes if the stage the client has stayed at does not suggest transformation. The therapist may, for instance, acknowledge the emotional injury, mark the importance of the work on the injury, and mark the importance of building healthy boundaries, while acknowledging that the client is unable to do so at this point. The therapist may acknowledge the importance of compassion and the fact that it is difficult to get it, generate it, or let it in.

The stages delineated in Table 8.3 can also be used for devising homework (see Table 8.4). The client may be encouraged to notice when vulnerability comes to the fore, outside the session (stage 1). The client may be asked to attend to clues (triggers) in the behavior of others, that are particularly difficult to encounter (stage 2b). The client may learn how to tolerate and bear the hurt, by being able to stay with it (e.g., by not avoiding it, supporting the self with breathing), putting it to language, identifying the need (stages 3 and 4). The therapist and the client can also reflect on how to seek support, and letting it in (stages 5b and 6b), and how to build determination to hold a boundary (stage 6a). For instance, several of our clients shared with us how they planned to ensure, during the coming week, that their boundaries would be respected by their colleagues, friends, and/or strangers. They subsequently reported on their successes in holding their boundaries. This further consolidated their resolve and their sense of accomplishment and inner confidence.

Table 8.4 The framework that can be used to reflect on the empty chair task (unfinished business) for an emotional injury and as a base for homework (Timulak, 2017)

Parts enacted in the Experiencer chair	Parts enacted in the Other chair
	• **What was hurtful in the other's behavior?** (Increasing awareness of the things that hurt) • **What was the implied message?** (e.g., hypotheses about the other's motivations)
• **How do I feel when I am being treated like this?** (Highlighting the emotional impact of the other's behavior, e.g., loneliness/sadness, shame, fear) • **What do I need(ed) when I am treated like this?** (Articulating the need stemming from the hurt feelings, identifying to whom need could be expressed)	
	• **What do I or the other (caring or caring part of the other) feel towards the hurt, vulnerable part of me?** (Bringing a reminder of compassionate experiences that may respond to the unmet needs in the vulnerable experience accessed in the Experiencer chair)
• **How can I protect myself when I am treated in a way that hurts?** (A reminder of the resolve in the session to face and fight the perceived mistreatment)	

Both major EFT tasks, self–self, two-chair dialogue for a problematic self-treatment and self–other empty-chair dialogue for emotional interpersonal injury, are closely intertwined and the therapeutic process can move from one to the other and back. Indeed, over the course of therapy (and sometimes over the course of a session), the therapist facilitates both tasks (one at a time, with one being temporarily interrupted) and facilitates tying up all ends (of both tasks) together at the end. We will talk more about this in the next chapter.

Accessing and transforming core emotional pain in Tina's case

Tina (see Chapter 6) progressed steadily across therapy sessions in accessing and transforming her core painful feelings (see Timulak & McElvaney, 2016). As would be expected, her initial presentation was dominated by global distress (*I just feel so wound up all the time*), which was present in the sessions throughout the therapy, but occupied significantly less session time as therapy progressed (cf. Keogh *et al.*, 2014). Although Tina battled with emotional avoidance throughout therapy (for self-worry dialogues, see Chapter 7), she was able to touch on the underlying pain and thus was more open to transformational work. The solid and trusting therapeutic relationship contributed to her being able to engage in a series of self–self and self–other dialogues.

Although she started from a rejecting anger position (*you're vicious*), she touched on and activated the core pain experientially, early on in a self–other dialogue with her deceased mother. In the face of her mother's enacted coldness, Tina felt empty and worthless and afraid (*I feel empty, worthless; I always felt afraid of you all my life*). In an early dialogue (session 3), as in the ensuing ones (in sessions five, 12, and 13) she was able to express her unmet needs (*I missed the affection, the love, just what a mother should be doing; I needed you to be there*). From relatively early on, Tina was able to protect herself against the mother's attacks in the dialogues (*I need my space; I won't allow you to hurt me anymore*). In early dialogues, she soothed herself (as mother was unchanging) by enacting the current adult self, responding to herself as a little girl (*I love you. I feel, little girl, I want to hug you*). But softening eventually came from her enacted mother too (speaking as the mother: *I know I was wrong to you in a lot of ways, but you know I love you really, don't you? I'm really sorry for the way I was with you*) to which Tina responded with forgiveness (*I forgive you*), while still holding boundaries (*I can see your faults*). She then had a sense of letting go of the wound (*It's like I'm more capable ... of letting go*) and further grieving came (*I think so, yeah, just to say I love you and I hope you're happy, just watch over us. You still make me laugh when I think of things about you*).

Tina also engaged in a dialogue with her imagined father, that allowed her to grieve the loss of him and his absence (*I'm sorry you weren't around. I always carried you inside me*). Her enactment of the dad brought forth a very caring quality from him (*he would have said: Yeah, and I am proud of you, and I love you*). She also dialogued with one of her daughters whose behavior she found rejecting and hurtful, which contributed to her sense of loneliness. Similarly she dialogued with her husband, whose enactment also brought a caring response (*I am always here for you*) that left her feeling warm. She, however, also stood up to him (*I'm an adult, grown-up woman who makes my own decisions*). She also stood up to a colleague in one of the dialogues. She also experienced caring from her imagined and enacted grandmother who, in reality, had a caring relationship with her.

Tina had several self-critical dialogues (sessions four, seven, nine, and eleven) that were introduced by the therapist at various markers of her self-criticism (*You are stupid, you're too selfish and you're hurting others; I don't like your weakness. You're very weak*). The self-criticism was closely linked to judgment by her mother, but also her daughter, husband or colleagues (some of the critic dialogues thus happened in the context of self–other dialogues; *there's got to be something that I'm doing wrong that has them treating me like that*). The self-criticism was also linked to her worries (*nobody is going to want somebody who is so weak like that*). This led to feelings of worthlessness, however she was eventually able to stand up to the critic (*I deserve to have time for myself now; ... I want you to ... lay off, really, ... let me out of this, this cage ... shut up*) that let her feel empowered (*it's good, empowered, strong*). Tina was also able to soften in the Critic chair (*you deserve it* [freedom from put-downs] *Tina, you do*), but it was much easier for her in the adult self, responding to her younger self in the context of the mother's hurtful behavior.

We have already reported (Timulak & McElvaney, 2016) that Tina's quantitative outcomes improved significantly and that she also reported in qualitative interviews that she was no longer flying off the handle, that she was less controlling, that she did not feel worthless or that she needed to be constantly perfect, et cetera. She also appreciated the relationship with the therapist and the therapist's presence (*very, very calming*). She appreciated the chair work and she admitted that talking about things from an early age (and reliving all that stuff) "*sort of unknotted all the tensions in*" her. She realized that what happened in her childhood "*was not her fault and she is worth*" the care and love.

Conclusion

This chapter focuses on how to access and transform the feared, core emotional pain in emotion-focused therapy for GAD difficulties. It delineates the stages of accessing, differentiating, and transforming emotional pain. Preparatory tasks such as clearing a space, focusing, or systematic evocative unfolding are presented. A discussion of the transformative process in EFT tasks is then offered. Particular attention is paid to two key transformative tasks in EFT: self–self, two-chair dialogue for problematic self-treatment (e.g., self-evaluative or self-critical split), and the self–other empty chair dialogue for an interpersonal emotional injury (classically referred to as unfinished business). The processes present in those tasks are discussed in the context of therapy for GAD difficulties. A framework for reflection is offered for both tasks and suggestions for homework are made.

Part IV

Practicalities of delivering EFT for GAD

Chapter 9

Adapting therapeutic strategy

The approach presented in previous chapters unfolds naturally, over time in therapy. In general, we conceptualize the provision of EFT for GAD difficulties for short-term therapy (normally 16 to 20 sessions) differently to long-term therapy (lasting a year or longer). We developed the approach presented in the previous chapters in the context of 16 to 20 sessions of therapy that was extended for to up to 25 sessions (for clinical reasons), in the case of some clients. However, we also routinely apply the approach in private work in an open-ended long-term framework. We will, therefore, comment on both formats of providing EFT for people with GAD difficulties.

It is important to be aware that EFT is an exploratory therapy, which means that it does not follow a firm prescriptive protocol of what is going to happen in each session. Therapy unfolds as client and therapist co-create a shared focus (cf. Goldman & Greenberg, 2015; Greenberg, 2015; 2016), in the context of a caring, trusting relationship, centered around core painful feelings (chronic problematic emotion schemes). These chronic painful feelings become the focus of therapy through the therapist's following the pain compass (Greenberg & Goldman, 2007; Greenberg, 2015; 2016). The pain compass refers to sensitivity to primary emotions that are most painful for the client and are revealed in the client's narrative regarding what troubles him or her.

Usually, by the first few sessions, the therapist and the client are starting to get a sense of the chronic painful feelings that have come to define the client's sense of self (dominant self-organizations). They become the foci of therapeutic work. As we highlighted in Chapters 4 and 6, these core underlying feelings center around loneliness/sadness, shame, and fear-based feelings. Therapy will also focus on the self–other processes which trigger these painful, chronic feelings, as well as problematic, self–self processes (e.g., self-worrying, self-criticism, avoidance of emotions and triggers) that try to manage the self and the emotional experience in the context of upsetting or potentially upsetting triggers (see Chapters 7 and 8).

The exploratory nature of EFT distinguishes it significantly from CBT, which approaches working with GAD difficulties along the lines of a predetermined protocol dictating which tasks/techniques are used in which sessions and in which sequence. Obviously skilled application of CBT assumes a certain level of flexibility as the therapist adjusts, and tailors therapy to an individual client's presentation, and to the client's response to the therapy as it unfolds. However, there still is a more or less universal plan of what is roughly expected to occur, in what stage of therapy (cf. Dugas & Robichaud, 2007). For instance, it is planned that psychoeducation and self-monitoring precede relaxation techniques and these precede cognitive restructuring work and exposure work (cf. Hazlett-Stevens, 2008). In EFT, the approach is more flexible, as the therapeutic strategy responds to the client's in-session presentation, which unfolds in an associative manner. The client presents a narrative based on where their attention is focused, and the therapist attends to the most poignant aspects of this narrative and invites the client to explore the felt quality of what they are recounting. This, as we described in the part on focusing, leads to an unfolding of various aspects of ever-changing experience.

Obviously, how therapist and client interact is generally anchored in a broader social interaction, which unfolds between them as therapy progresses. For instance, each session therapist and client briefly check-in to see how the client is experiencing therapy. The therapist asks whether anything stayed with the client from the previous sessions, or how the client has been in-between sessions, or if the client has had any thoughts on what he or she would like to focus on in the session. As therapy progresses the therapist also starts to understand the client's more general way of interacting with others, and the self. At appropriate times (experientially salient) in the session, the therapist may suggest the focus, and see whether that focus is of immediate emotional relevance to the client, or at least, sufficiently salient for the client at that moment.

We are now going to focus on a typical course of therapy, regarding how it may unfold over time in a short-term and, briefly, in a more long-term therapy format. Given what we have said about the absence of a "protocol" in EFT, the reader is advised to see this as a probabilistic course for "typical" (if such a thing exists) EFT for people with GAD difficulties. This is to allow the reader to imagine how the course of therapy may appear over time.

Short-term therapy

As previously stated, we see short-term therapy as being conducted within 16 to 20 weeks. This may occasionally be extended for clinical reasons if, for example, the client has difficulty terminating therapy due to anxiety that they would be on their own without the support of their therapist. Alternatively, a client may experience an unanticipated event such as bereavement in the family, or may become distressed at losing a job, just as therapy was planning to end. Typically, therapy normally lasts for four to five months of weekly sessions, in some instances around six months. This is also a good timeframe for developing a sense of how the client's everyday life unfolds, as many things usually happen over such a period of time. This allows for interweaving what is happening in therapy with what happens in the client's everyday day life. As EFT tries to develop and strengthen adaptive self-organizations, it is important that the client has experience of consolidating new ways of being in everyday life.

Beginning (sessions one to three). The beginning of the course of EFT starts with the therapist providing a warm and caring presence, which should start to build the atmosphere of safety necessary for the client to be able to touch on, and express, painful feelings. Les Greenberg (2015) stresses that the therapist strives for "contact before the contract". The EFT therapist does not, therefore, start with inquisitive, detached, assessment questions, but rather with a warm interest in what it is that burdens the client. Information-gathering questions are present in early sessions, and to a lesser extent in those that follow. These questions not only facilitate the therapist's deeper understanding of the client, but are also used by the therapist in developing a caring empathic response, aimed at capturing the felt quality experienced by the client in relation to what they are expressing.

Given that there may be somewhat more information gathering in the initial sessions (Les Greenberg [2017] observes that in the first meeting, he spends one third of the session listening to the client, one third in trying to deepen the experience and, one third gathering information), the therapist generally explains that in the beginning of therapy, he or she may want to find out a bit more about the client, and may inquire about things which appear relevant to the difficulties the client describes. The therapist simply wants to know more about the client's circumstances, in so far as they are relevant to the client's experience.

In general, the therapist wants to know about interpersonal relationships, containing interactions that leave the client feeling uneasy or upset. The therapist may inquire about past relationships, for example, what it was like for the client growing up with their parents, siblings, and peers, or about current relationships, for example, whether there are emotionally salient relationships the client is in that serve as a support, or maybe are a source of upsetting feelings, or the combination of support and upset. The therapist may ask the client how he or she feels about him or herself in the context of the situations described as being relevant to their presenting issues. These information-seeking questions are, however, typically used in the context of what the client is revealing about their life situation. Accordingly, the therapist is constantly trying to meet the client close to where the client is, in his or her sharing, whether with empathic response or an information-seeking question. The use of information-seeking questions is quite rare when seen in comparison to diagnostic interviews or assessment questions asked in other approaches. The therapist does not want to give the impression that therapy is directed by the therapist's questions.

Depending on the context of the referral, the therapist normally also provides some information about the therapy in the initial session (see Chapter 4, the part discussing tasks and goals of therapy). After providing a rationale for therapy, the therapist makes a brief reference to how the therapy typically unfolds, for example, that it focuses on the client's painful experiences, and then tries to respond to those painful emotions, bringing experiences that can support the client in the hope that their lives might become more liveable, bearable, perhaps less limiting, and if appropriate, also more fulfilled or rich. The therapist typically also explains what the sessions may look like (e.g., that they focus on what is currently, emotionally salient for the client and, typically, also troubling, that they may use imaginary dialogues or other creative means to help the client to get in touch with their feelings). The content of the explanation depends on the client's presenting issues, is developed in collaboration with the client, and is articulated in a clear and jargon free manner. The therapist also offers the client an opportunity to ask any questions they may have about any aspect of the therapy.

From early on, the therapist subtly engages in various forms of perception-based assessment. The therapist will be taking note of how accessible the client's emotional experience is to him or her (or how avoidant of emotions the client is), how the client treats him or herself, or specifically in case of GAD difficulties, what the client worries about, to what extent, and how experientially distressing it is. The therapist may pay attention to secondary global distress, but immediately focuses on the underlying primary emotional experience through his or her empathic responses. Nevertheless, the therapist always follows the client's pace, confident that all relevant information will be unfolded later in therapy, particularly in the experiential tasks (see below).

Early on, in these very first sessions, the therapist helps the client to begin to get a sense of what would be useful to focus on in therapy. From session two, the therapist (early on in the session) may ask something like: *What would be good to focus on today?* The therapist follows the pain compass (see Chapter 6), which points towards the most painful aspects of the client's experience in session. These should help in formulating the focus of the overall therapy. Typically, this occurs early in therapy (the first three to eight sessions) as therapist and client are starting to get the sense of the contextually embedded, idiosyncratically articulated core painful feelings that will need to be focused on in therapy. Typically, these are idiosyncratic variations of not feeling loved, accepted, or protected, and the corresponding self–self process and self–other interactions that trigger or compound those painful feelings (see Chapters 4 and 6). The problematic processes and chronic painful emotions are particularly well articulated in tasks such as self–self two-chair dialogues for problematic self-treatment and self–other empty-chair tasks for emotional injury. The function of the worry may come to the surface here as well, but not necessarily (see the next section on middle, working, stages of therapy).

Middle, working, stages (session three to about three to five sessions before the end of therapy). The formulation of the therapy focus continues in the first half of therapy. Although it is good to have a clear focus early on (Les Greenberg [2017] suggests by session five), generally speaking, the focus gets reformulated and deepens as therapist and client repeatedly revisit the most painful aspects of the client's emotional experiencing. What also deepens is the therapist's understanding (conceptualization) of the client's pain and emotional processing difficulties, as well as the client's self-treatment and self–other interactions. Indeed, the early use of experiential tasks helps the therapist's assessment of the client's difficulties and informs the evolving, retweaked, conceptualization and thus also therapy focus and therapy strategy.

Although it may at first be necessary to use preparatory tasks (e.g., clearing a space, focusing), which help provide optimal access to emotional experience and inform the focus of therapy, in general, we start with evocative imaginary dialogue tasks early on. As early as session three, the therapist may offer a two-chair self–self dialogue for problematic self-treatment (self-criticism) or even the empty chair task for unfinished business (emotional injury) provided there is an appropriate marker, the client is not dysregulated, and there is agreement on the goals and tasks of therapy, i.e., alliance is forged. If the therapist is hesitant, because of the level of dysregulation, or because no clear agreement on the work was shared, then it is prudent to wait a session or two before introducing experiential chair tasks. It is, however, unusual to wait that long, particularly in a short-term therapy. Chair tasks are introduced at an early stage because we want the client to have some experience of how therapy will look from early on. We want to establish the focus of therapy, to acquire an experiential sense of the client's difficulties, but we also want to start to work on emotion transformation.

When imaginary dialogues are used early on in therapy, they are used flexibly and the therapist may fluidly track the client from worrying her or himself that something bad might happen (e.g., *my children may get hurt on the school trip*) to a critic (e.g., *I am a bad mother*) to an emotional injury and unfinished business (e.g., *I always got a message from my mother that I am a failure as a daughter and now as a parent*). The therapist may also observe the obstacles to the transformative processes, such as that the client is interrupting/preventing him or herself from standing-up for the self, or is so self-denigrating that he or she is not able to generate compassion or allow any compassion to get in (see below). This fluency and flexibility is characteristic of the whole working phase of therapy (see Chapters 7 and 8). After the first few dialogues, however, the therapist tries to ensure that all major processes, such as self-worrying, self-criticism, or unfinished business, are fully attended to and seen through, so that the client focusing on them in the tasks, can get to adaptive emotional experiences (e.g., standing-up to mistreatment and experiencing compassion towards the wound). We, therefore, want the client to have an experience of being able to stand-up to the worrier, the critic, or the other, not simply one of those processes.

Although it appears that when clients are able to stand up to the imagined other that hurt them, they are more likely to stand up to their own critic, it is still important that the client, in short-term therapy, has the experience of being able to stand up for the self in the context of all problematic processes, not just one of them. In long-term therapy, there is naturally enough space for this. In the context of short-term therapy, therapists must be aware of what has been attended to, so they do not omit some of the other major processes (e.g., the work on self-criticism at expense of working on self-worrying). For instance, worrying can easily turn into the critic dialogues (see Chapters 4, 6, 7, and 8). The therapist can therefore easily go with the critic, simply by following the client's flow. While it is okay to do this early on in therapy, as therapy progresses, the therapist needs to ensure that both processes are attended to. The therapist ensures that the self-worrying process is also attended to, even when the client tends to turn towards self-criticism. This may occur within the one session (in one dialogue that covers both self-critical and self-worrying processes) or in separate sessions.

It is our experience (as in the case of Tina, presented in previous chapters) that short-term therapy with clients with GAD difficulties may contain three to five worry dialogues, three to five critic dialogues, three to five primary unfinished business (emotional injury) dialogues and perhaps one or two other dialogues, such as emotional injuries (unfinished business) with other emotionally salient people (often similar injuries to the major one), and one or two other dialogues such as self-panicking, et cetera. As you may notice, the number of dialogues added up together is bigger than the number of sessions, suggesting there is more than one dialogue per session. This is due to fluency and flexibility in moving between the tasks, following the client's process.

What we have also observed is that the main processes, such as self-worrying, self-criticism, and primary emotional injury, need to be repeated so that the transformation progresses and becomes more solidified. We can, for instance, see that clients may be increasingly able to stand up to the worrier as the dialogues are repeated (e.g., Murphy *et al.*, 2017). We can see that clients access core pain more easily in the later dialogues with the same significant other, and that their self-compassion and protective anger are more easily accessible (cf. Crowley *et al.*, 2013; Hughes, Timulak, & McElvaney, 2014; Keogh *et al.*, 2014). This does not mean that the core pain disappears; it just means that when the core pain gets activated in the sessions the clients can more easily access adaptive self-organizations.

Use of homework. Any in-session progress achieved in the middle, working phase, of therapy is reflected on and the therapist, in collaboration with the client, plans how adaptive experiences and healthy self-treatment and self–other relating processes can be supported outside the therapy session. The reflection and homework exercises that were presented in Chapters 7 and 8 can serve as the basis for this process. Two key processes are being supported here. Awareness of one's own self–self and self–other functioning/experiencing, along with consolidation of adaptive self–self and self–other processes/experiences (cf. Greenberg & Warwar, 2006; Warwar, 2015). Therapists and clients may vary in their attitude towards the use of reflection exercises, so we are not prescriptive with regard to the use of homework. However, we do encourage therapists in the RCT we are currently conducting to check-in with clients regarding their attitude towards these types of activities, that is, whether they find them useful.

Ending. The ending of short-term therapy depends on the amount of time available. Optimally, when the therapist and the client are nearing the session limit, the client will have already had some transformative experiences, in which core chronic painful emotions and self–self and self–other relating processes were adaptively processed. In the context of short-term therapy, the fact that therapy will be coming to an end may be brought to the client's awareness, around five sessions before the actual end of therapy. Therapist and client focus on the consolidation of transformative experiences and their implementation in everyday life. Narrativization of the experience in therapy is important here (Grafanaki & McLeod, 1999). Clients are helped to make sense of their difficulties and of their experiences in therapy. Discussions also focus on the future, potential triggers of emotional pain, and recognition of one's own vulnerabilities and sensitivities. The therapist may encourage the client to reflect on what situations might lead to particular, difficult feelings and what compounding (e.g., self-criticism), problematically protective and avoiding strategies, the client would be likely using to complicate the experience. The client is thus being prepared for potential setbacks.

Some clients with GAD difficulties have difficulty ending therapy. Having settled into therapy, they experience it as soothing and reassuring. They may be reluctant to make any changes to something that appears to work for them. Therapy thus becomes a part of their avoidance. They do not want to be independent, facing the dangers and upsetting triggers, encountered in their everyday life, without the support provided by the therapist. Anxiety about ending therapy may manifest in the worsening of anxiety symptoms or global distress. Real life difficulties are responded to with greater distress than in the middle stages of therapy. Endings with such clients may be more gradual, perhaps a few extra sessions may be added (three to five sessions) and they may be spread out to fortnightly sessions (e.g., last three to five sessions), and there may be booster sessions offered (a month after the end of therapy or even later).

The ending may also focus on personal autonomy, independent living, and may reflect on how the ending brings anxiety. Clients may be encouraged to reframe current stressors as opportunities to test how they have changed with regard to their ability to live with painful emotion-triggering events. One of us worked with a client who had several current triggers that were anxiety provoking, towards the end of therapy. For instance, the client's 19-year-old daughter informed the client that she would like to move to another country for work experience for a year. While it initially created panic in the client, who was very protective of her daughter and unable to tolerate any perceived distress in her (this vulnerability was embedded in the client's personal history), she was eventually able to look at it as a test of her ability to let go, and trust that she would be able to bear such a difficult experience and mobilize inner emotional resources to get through the triggering situation.

Long-term therapy

While we studied EFT for GAD difficulties in the context of short-term therapy, we also have a lot of experience of conducting EFT for this type of difficulty in private practice, which offers a more long-term treatment (one to two years plus). This long-term therapy typically evolves out of an open-ended therapy that may or may not finish after the first four or five months. It is our experience that clients with GAD difficulties benefit from the longer-term therapy and if the resources are available, it can be a useful option for them (with the caveat of a possible dependence on therapy that would need to be monitored and reflected on). The beginnings of long-term therapy are very similar to those of short-term therapy with the exception that there is no time pressure necessitating focus on the main difficulties in a sustained manner. The long-term format may allow clients to experience more reflective sessions, or sessions that may focus on the everyday difficulties that interact with core painful emotions and problematic self–self and self–other processes.

Nevertheless, the emotion and experiential focus, together with the frequent use of experiential tasks such as two-chair and empty chair dialogues, is typical of the initial nine to 12 months of therapy. Provided that there is progression in the client's experiencing of his or her difficulties, after this time period, therapy starts to serve as an opportunity to reflect on one's own functioning with everyday stressors, bearing in mind one's own emotional vulnerabilities and characteristic self–self and self–other processes. Given the timeframe, many of the potentially anxiety-provoking triggers are actually encountered by the client in everyday life and thus create opportunities to try to apply new ways of being and experiencing, already generated in therapy. All of this is carried out with the support of the therapist. The focus of therapy may also move beyond the anxiety, to existential decisions, life plans, everyday close relationships, et cetera.

Difficulties in therapeutic process

Having discussed the course of therapy, we will now look at some difficulties that may be encountered in the therapy process. The first author's previous book (Timulak, 2015) dedicates an entire chapter to highlighting therapeutic strategies that the therapist may try to apply at various impasses encountered in the therapeutic process. Without wishing to appear repetitive, we feel it is important to briefly highlight some of the potential difficulties and potential therapeutic strategies that therapists may use when working with clients with GAD difficulties.

Alliance ruptures and interpersonal issues

Ruptures in the therapeutic relationship typically have an impact on the course of therapy. Many clients have a long history of difficulties with interpersonal relationships, and as they approach painful aspects of their experience in therapy, they may be particularly sensitive to the therapist's actions, which may potentially feel intrusive, misattuned, or failing to offer what the client may feel is needed. Work on therapeutic ruptures is standard EFT practice (see Chapters 3 and 5). The therapist must be sensitive to the client's deference (Rennie, 1994), which suggests that the client hides any potential difficulties that he or she may experience in the relationship. As the rupture is discovered, it is focused on, and the client is helped to reveal their experience of the difficulty. The therapist owns his or her own actions and apologizes if appropriate, helps the client to assert themselves, and empathizes with the client's underlying pain (cf. Elliott *et al.*, 2004; Safran & Muran, 2000). The therapist also encourages a frank discussion of the relationship and therapeutic work itself with the client. This may also pertain to instances when the therapist senses that the client is threatened by, and avoids, the therapeutic work. The therapist then initiates a frank and authentic, while deeply respectful, discussion about the issue.

In Chapter 5 we also emphasized that the therapeutic relationship is an important source of corrective emotional experiences (cf. Greenberg & Elliott, 2012). This requires the therapist to be brave, and authentically involved in the relationship, and not hiding behind a professional façade. The EFT therapist strives to build a caring relationship, which is used to help the client unfold chronic painful feelings, in order to heal them.

The way of the client's relating to others may be occasionally also a part of the focus of the client's exploration in therapy. Especially in a long-term therapy, the exploration of the client's relating to close ones can be a focus of a particular session or sessions. EFT conceptualizes several interpersonal cycles of relating in close relationships that may sensitize the therapist's empathy when conjecturing as to a client's possible experience (e.g., Greenberg & Goldman, 2008; Greenberg & Johnson, 1988). EFT has a differentiated understanding of how emotional injuries arise in close relationships, how they may lead to hurtful feelings and experiences of unmet needs, and what difficulties can arise when attempting to break the disruptive cycles that lead to pain.

Problems in clarifying the focus of therapy

While in our experience it does not, in general, pose a difficulty for therapists to develop a focus for therapy early in the therapeutic process, there are some clients with whom it may be more difficult. It may be particularly so with the clients who do not have a clear understanding of their difficulties. Some clients are particularly symptom-focused, that is, focused on their anxiety symptoms such as worrying, felt anxiety in their body, panicking, et cetera. It may be difficult for them to provide a textured narrative of their everyday life, or of their past, that would help to paint a picture of the triggers that bring underlying painful emotional experiences. In many cases this is a result of a socialization process, whereby clients were, from an early age, discouraged from reflecting on their experience.

In such cases, the therapist must remain patient and help the client to slowly become more able to focus on their interpersonal functioning, on their aspirations, on their past pivotal experiences, et cetera, without prematurely judging their emotional salience. This is done in the hope that the client's self-awareness and self-reflection (psychological mindedness) develops, and will allow them to differentiate the nuances of their perceptions and corresponding inner experiences. The use of experiential tasks such as chair dialogues may be particularly helpful here. Nevertheless, the impact of short-term therapy in such cases may be limited, as the necessary improvement in these forms of self-awareness and self-reflection develops gradually and may take months. The therapist therefore needs to tolerate ambiguity in the therapy focus.

Emotion dysregulation

Some clients with GAD difficulties may have issues with emotion regulation. In these cases, the therapist's first task is to help the client to regulate the affect. This may be achieved implicitly through offering an empathic presence that on its own has a regulatory function (see Chapter 5). Other means may also be used, such as the clearing a space task or a more coping-focused self-soothing task (for examples, see Chapter 8). In a more coping-focused (as opposed to transformative; cf. Elliott, 2016) self-soothing task the client is asked to nominate a person (current or past) who has a calming effect on them. The client then enacts that person, the soothing qualities of that person, and expresses the care towards the imagined self in the Experiencer chair. Once compassion and self-soothing have been enacted, the client is asked to switch chairs and let the caring presence in. Potential obstacles are overcome (see below on problems with self-compassion). This type of self-soothing differs from the transformative self-compassion experiences generated in the transformative self-soothing task. The transformative self-compassion enactment happens in the context of core painful feelings and unmet needs, while more regulatory self-soothing is facilitated in the case of global distress level dysregulation.

Overall, progress in therapy typically has an impact on the level of emotion regulation. For instance, as highlighted in previous work (Timulak, 2015), progress in generating protective anger in the course of therapy may also help the client to feel more emotionally resourceful, which may in turn have an impact on overall emotional resilience and regulation. A similar impact may derive from regular generation of self-compassion in various tasks, which may become internalized by the client.

Emotional avoidance

Clients, much like everybody else, often find it very difficult to touch on their painful emotions (see examples in Timulak, 2015). This appears to particularly affect clients struggling with anxiety. In Chapter 4 we described various emotional and behavioral avoidance strategies, engaged in by clients. In Chapter 7 we illustrated multiple ways of working with avoidance. Some clients may be particularly avoidant, and may have difficulty achieving optimal levels of emotional arousal (see Chapter 3 on emotional arousal). The therapist, therefore, has to be aware of clients' initial levels of emotional arousal, and benchmark any progress in accessibility of emotions with regard to that initial level. Work with clients who are emotionally overregulated requires the therapist to use a number of evocative empathic responses.

The therapist needs to pace experiential tasks, such as chair dialogues, in a way that keeps the client in contact with their experience, as they may have a tendency to wander off, change the topic, distract themselves, et cetera (see Chapter 4). Some clients may be even able to focus on their experience in a way that may appear productive in some tasks, such as focusing (e.g., using the focused vocal quality), however, this may actually be deployed as an interrupter against higher emotional arousal. Clients may lose contact with their own emotions, if they pause too long while focusing on the bodily felt sense. The therapist thus tries to avoid colluding with avoidance, and may try to overcome the avoidance by offering a somewhat faster pacing of his or her empathy and through the use of evocative interventions.

As EFT therapy progresses, the clients generally experience improved access to their emotions. However, for some clients, it may require long-term work to see progress and even here, results may be limited. The therapist, therefore, needs to be aware that the therapeutic processes may not always flow as easily, and with such emotional arousal as is commonly seen in EFT demonstration videos (which often depict an optimal process with emotionally accessible clients). Work with emotionally overregulated clients in general does not differ from work with more emotionally accessible clients. It may, however, be more focused, requiring a good deal of concentration and effort on the part of the therapist in his or her use of evocative empathy and tasks, with an optimal pacing to counterbalance inter-ruptions. The self-interruption task may also become an important part in therapy. Despite all this effort, the therapist needs to be realistic about how easily acces-sible emotions may be for some clients.

Difficulties in accessing and differentiating core pain

Some clients, who may not necessarily be emotionally overregulated, may be par-ticularly emotionally avoidant when touching on chronic painful feelings. Given that these chronic painful feelings are maladaptive and feel self-defining, clients may not have capacity to stay with them and differentiate them in symboliza-tion, language, or engage in further processing of them. Given that these feelings are so often chronically avoided, particularly by anxious clients, the clients may not have the vocabulary or capacity to recognize them and put them into words. Similar types of feelings might also have been difficult to process for caregivers, who provided emotional soothing, and facilitated emotional processing of experi-ence in the client's formative years. The therapist's empathy, and in particular conjecturing, may be decisive here as clients may genuinely lack the language and skill to differentiate those painful emotions. Consequently, the therapist's empa-thy may not only allow them to access the feelings, but it may also help to regulate them, through the use of narrative, and also soothe them through the therapist's relational, caring presence.

At times, in the empty chair dialogue with an imagined hurtful other, clients may have difficulty accessing painful vulnerable feelings, due to a fear of show-ing vulnerability in the presence of the imagined dangerous other. The therapist may need to bring an imagined caring figure to the dialogue, so that the client has somebody receptive to access and express the vulnerability to (see Chapter 8). Again, as therapy progresses, clients may develop their capacity to stay with the core chronic painful feelings and improve their ability to differentiate them in an emotionally productive way (Crowley *et al.*, 2013; Keogh *et al.*, 2014). More on working on accessing and differentiating core painful emotions can be found in Timulak (2015).

Difficulties in generating adaptive anger

Some clients with GAD difficulties may struggle with generating adaptive, protective anger in the face of mistreatment and in the context of core pain and unmet needs. Timulak (2015) describes several strategies that the therapist may use to access, generate, and harness adaptive anger. The simplest rule in trying to facilitate the adaptive anger is the highlighting of the mistreatment (from the other or the self) that triggers the core painful feelings (see Chapter 7 and 8). In the later stages of the chair dialogues, when the critic, worrier, interrupter, or injuring person does not soften, the therapist instructs the client to check-in to see how they wish to respond to the attacking stance. For many clients, this leads to spontaneous self-assertiveness.

However, some clients start to collapse when this happens, in which case, the therapist then needs to highlight the impact of the attack and encourage the client to see what he or she really wants. This may be also hypothetical, respecting that the client may not have capability to protect him or herself, but still may have a wish to do so, for example: *What would you want if you were able to do it?* At times when the client is collapsing, the therapist may use a paradoxical intervention, for instance: *Tell him/her you cannot face him/her and s/he can do whatever s/he wants with you.* And as the client expresses it, the therapist may check in and ask the client to see how it feels inside to express something like this. Typically, the clients dislike it. The therapist then harnesses it and asks the clients to express the dislike (which already comes in the form of a more assertive anger), for example: *I really resent saying those words (that I would comply with anything).* This can be quickly followed by an acknowledgment/validation and encouragement: *You don't want this, so what is it you really want?* Any expression of anger is then celebrated and the therapist may ask the client to express the anger again and again, and to observe how it feels inside when the anger is expressed. This is done to help the client see how inner confidence grows.

During the therapy process, clients may become more able to express adaptive anger in certain contexts. For instance, the client may be able to stand up to the imagined hurtful other, but may not be able to stand up to their own self-criticism. The therapist may then use the fact that the client is able to stand up for the self in the context of external attack, and facilitate the enactment of standing up for the self at a point, sequentially close to the already successful enactment. We provide an example of such an interaction in Chapter 8 (see also Timulak, 2015).

Protective anger can be also facilitated through the therapist's validation of the client's painful experiences and unmet needs. The therapist uses an authentic, interpersonal, validation to ensure that the client hears that the therapist believes that the client's unmet needs (e.g., for protection, connection, and acknowledgment) were violated and the client deserves a response to them. Availability of adaptive protective anger is important for building inner confidence, a sense of resilience, and inner resourcefulness. Particularly in case of anxiety difficulties, it is important that clients have the courage to face threat. This sense of personal power is important for it. Indeed, over the course of therapy, we observed that in successful cases, the clients built a sense of empowerment that followed on from experiences of adaptive, self-expanding anger. The reader can find more suggestions for working with the lack of healthy, boundary setting, protective anger in therapy in Timulak (2015).

Difficulties in generating compassion

Many clients with GAD difficulties are highly self-critical (e.g., self-contemptuous), which complicates the generation of self-compassion in them. The chair tasks described in Chapters 7 and 8 assume that in step five the therapist can check in with the client to see whether he or she can soften towards the expressed experience of core pain (or the toll of the worry/interruption) in the Experiencer chair. When the client struggles with softening, the therapist has several options (cf. Timulak, 2015). The therapist may simply acknowledge the difficulty, or may help the client to build protective anger that may be a particularly adaptive response to the mistreatment. As therapy progresses, it is, however, important that the clients also have experiences of self-compassion.

In Chapters 7 and 8 we suggested several possibilities that the therapist may attempt to facilitate. The client may internalize the therapist's caring, compassionate, empathic presence towards their experience. The accessibility of compassion is often a function of the level of hurt (core pain) expressed in the Experiencer chair. The more raw it is, the more likely the client will have a compassionate response towards it. Some clients are, however, very contemptuous towards their own vulnerability. The enactment of caring figures from their lives that they nominate in moments of vulnerability may be viable options to try. Similarly, work on their episodic memories from childhood may help to elicit compassion from the enacted adult self or other carer who may be potentially responsive to the vulnerable child. The therapist may also suggest working with the enactment of proxy figures such as a girl from the neighborhood (who was similar to the client in childhood) or an optimal, non-existing, carer (an ideal parent; see Elliott, 2016; see also Chapter 8).

The therapist's skillfulness plays a considerable role here. It is very important that the therapist validates the difficulty in generating compassion. Often clients are suspicious of compassion, as they may have a sense that it invalidates their suffering. At other times, they just feel so hopeless in relation to their chronic pain that the hopelessness needs to be validated. The therapist may then combine the acknowledgment of hopelessness with more hope promoting interventions, for example: *I hear that you feel helpless to care for that little girl. Tell her, "I feel hopeless. I am unable to be there for you"* ... (and as the client expresses it), *but if you were not helpless, what would you wish for the girl? See what comes from inside.*

The second common problem with self-compassion (see Chapters 7 and 8) is the difficulty of letting it in once it is expressed, e.g., from the Other/Critic/Worrier chair. Clients who are very self-critical, as well as clients who are not used to compassionate responses, may have a sense that they do not deserve the compassion expressed towards them, or they may not trust that it could be true. The therapist has to acknowledge this difficulty and still encourage the client to reflect inside on how it is to be on the receiving end of the expressed compassion, for example, *I hear you have a sense you do not deserve the care, it is too unrealistic to believe that it could be true ... but if you, for a moment, check inside, what happens as s/he says "I love you"? See how it feels inside.* The client's capability of letting compassion in, in successful cases, develops as therapy progresses (cf. Crowley *et al.*, 2013; Keogh *et al.*, 2014). Clients may be able to stay with the expression of compassion, and be able to increasingly receive and feel an experiential impact from it. For more on working with difficulties in generating compassion see Timulak (2015).

Life events and therapy

While clients are in therapy, it is safe to assume that many things are happening in their life outside the consulting room. The therapist must be aware that he or she needs to be flexible and must attend to whatever is happening in the client's life that may have an impact on their emotional well-being. For instance, the client may experience bereavement, work disputes, relationship issues, health issues, et cetera. The therapist, therefore, must naturally respond to those issues from a "common-sense" therapeutic perspective, and spend an appropriate time in therapy offering social and emotional support or even time to problem-solve. One can see this type of engagement would not be considered a mainstream EFT intervention, as the therapist in them is in "non-experiential mode" (see Elliott *et al.*, 2004).

Particularly in short-term therapy this common-sense approach is brief and corresponds with the requirements of the life-event it pertains to. The therapist must make an assessment regarding how much time is appropriate to devote to it, and not detract from the focus of therapy. The therapist must also ensure that such life-events are not being introduced to therapy as a form of avoidance, to distract from more emotionally painful topics. Again, the therapist uses all his or her professional knowledge for this assessment. In comparison, long-term therapy is much more naturally conducive to paying attention to various life events that are happening in the client's life. The therapist's response here may be more focused on how the client's vulnerabilities and the modes of self–self and self–other functioning interact with various client personal and professional life events.

Comorbidity and personality issues

The issue of comorbidity gets raised in the context of discussing psychotherapies for specific conditions. This was our experience when submitting various papers stemming from our EFT for GAD project. As Chapter 2 has shown, there are many issues with the current diagnostic criteria for mental health disorders including GAD. There is also a major issue regarding the absence of a clear etiology for GAD or other mental health disorders. Most of the etiological risk factors are shared with many other conditions, being particularly strong for anxiety disorders and depression, as currently conceptualized (see Chapter 2).

EFT is a generalist therapy. We do not assume that there are different procedures for various conditions. Our conceptualization is that the underlying core chronic painful emotions center around loneliness/sadness, shame, and primary fear, regardless of the more superficial, secondary symptoms of depression and anxiety. This is our experience when working with people who meet criteria for a variety of mood and anxiety disorders. In general, the knowledge that the client may meet criteria for other anxiety disorders or depression does not alter the way we work with the client. Obviously, there may be exceptions to this rule in the case of conditions such as psychosis, bipolar disorder, eating disorders, substance abuse, and other conditions, which may require other forms of treatment or multidisciplinary team (MDT) engagement.

Many clients with GAD difficulties meet criteria for comorbid personality disorders. In particular, clients who meet criteria for GAD may also meet criteria for cluster C personality disorders, such as avoidant, obsessive-compulsive, or dependent. If clients meet criteria for these types of personality disorders, it strongly indicates how complex their avoidance, or their need for control, is. This may also suggest that short-term therapy should be seen only as an important generator of new experiences that have to be transferred to everyday life and further supported, to have a more lasting effect.

Clients may also meet criteria for other personality disorders (such as borderline or paranoid), although these are rarer. If clients meet those criteria they may potentially evince greater sensitivity when forming the therapeutic alliance. Short-term therapy may not be ideal in such cases, as personality features may interact with the client's engagement in therapy and its optimal use. The GAD dynamic may only be a small part of other, particularly relational, issues. Short-term therapy may then be conceptualized as episodic. With, perhaps, further need for long-term work focused on transforming longstanding patterns of relating.

Use of medication

Many clients with GAD difficulties rely on medication; most typically antidepressant medication (see Chapter 2). Whether the client that attends EFT is on medication or not typically depends on the referral pathway, the client's preference, and their prescribing doctor's recommendation. Psychotherapy trials, including the ones we were involved in allow people on medication to enter the psychological therapy, provided the course of medication is stabilized (they have been on it for more than six weeks). Some clients object to the use of medication and prefer psychotherapy, for others it is the opposite, and for another group, a combination of psychotherapy and medication is preferred. In general, the use of antidepressant medication by clients with GAD difficulties who are in emotion-focused therapy is not an interfering issue.

Occasionally, the use of medication is discussed as the clients may contemplate discontinuing the medication, either because they are beginning to feel better or because they are wary of the medication's side effects. The therapist always recommends that this is something to be discussed with the prescribing physician. For some clients with anxiety difficulties, concurrent use of medication and psychological therapy may diminish trust in changes in emotional functioning the clients may have achieved in, and through, therapy. These clients may not fully trust that the experienced changes will last once they discontinue the use of medication. They are unsure as to what they ought to attribute to adaptive changes, and do not want to stop psychological therapy or medication out of the fear that the difficulties may return.

This is an important opportunity for the therapist to help the client to reflect on the changes in themselves, and to make sense of the role medication may have played (e.g., helping with physiological resilience). The focus is on the client's enhanced self-efficacy, new capacities to tolerate painful emotions, new capacity to generate adaptive emotion, new ways of self-treatment (e.g., self-compassion, self-affirmation), and new ways of relating to others (e.g., seeking support, setting appropriate boundaries). Time is spent preparing the client for when psychotherapy ends and on developing the resources the client will then have access to, and which the client can cultivate (see the part on ending the therapy).

Conclusion

This chapter addresses the challenges implicit in adapting therapeutic strategy to circumstances encountered in therapy. We consider the difference between long- and short-term treatment of clients with GAD difficulties, as well as implications for practice. We describe a typical course of EFT for GAD. We look at difficulties which may arise in the therapeutic process, including alliance ruptures and interpersonal issues, problems in clarifying the focus of therapy, emotion dysregulation, emotional avoidance, difficulties in accessing and differentiating core pain, difficulties in generating adaptive anger, difficulties in generating compassion, impact of life events, comorbidity and personality issues, and the impact of medication use on therapy.

Chapter 10

Incorporating EFT in therapist's repertoire

Learning emotion-focused therapy requires a lot of effort, as it is a very complex therapy. Therapists need to have both general mental health training and general psychotherapy training. They then have to learn complex skills such as relationship building and empathic attunement to the affect. Furthermore, therapists have to acquire complex conceptual understanding (necessary for understanding therapeutic process, the client's presentation, and therapeutic strategy), perceptual skills (e.g., emotion assessment, tasks markers assessment, etc.) and finally, sophisticated therapeutic skills (e.g., seeing the various tasks through). The training and subsequent supervision typically unfolds over several years, during which the therapists-in-training slowly incorporate EFT skills into their repertoire. Despite this, we have had experience of conducting intensive training over the course of a few months, as research requirements (e.g., deadlines in RCT) may demand to have a pool of rapidly trained therapists. This usually requires that the therapists are already very experienced, with a solid background in humanistic-experiential therapies. Despite this, therapists vary significantly in how quickly they acquire the skills necessary for conducting EFT.

Training standards of International Society for Emotion-focused Therapy

The International Society for Emotion-focused Therapy (ISEFT) was formed in 2011 to support the rapidly expanding, international EFT community. Its executive committee is composed of Les Greenberg, Robert Elliott, Rhonda Goldman, and Jeanne Watson, all of whom are prominent academics and clinicians who have been central to developing and promoting EFT. The society's stated aim is to inspire and guide further advances in EFT practice, theory, training, and research. The society's website is an important resource, providing information on up-coming EFT trainings from all around the world. It also, importantly, provides a list of the various international EFT training institutes, from Norway, Denmark, Hong Kong, Singapore, Australia, Belgium, Germany, Ireland, Portugal, Spain, Switzerland, The Netherlands, Turkey, and Israel.

To ensure that a high standard is achieved and maintained in both research and practice, clear guidelines have been established to ensure that general EFT training meets ISEFT standards. Six levels of accomplishment are described: Level A: Completion of basic EFT training, Level B: Completion of EFT supervised practice, Level C: Certified EFT therapist, Level D: Supervisor, Level E: Trainer. The criteria which need to be met for recognition at each level are laid out in detail on the website. Requirements for the first three levels are outlined below.

In Level A (for exact wording, see https://iseft.wildapricot.org/Standards), the completion of basic EFT training, candidates (who must already be accredited therapy practitioners and who optimally have either humanistic therapy background or an extensive training in empathy skills) must complete a didactic/experiential training (minimum eight days, often referred to as EFT Level 1 and EFT Level 2, each having at least four days) covering empathy/relational skills, emotion theory, emotion change principles, and emotional deepening, basic markers/tasks (e.g., focusing/clearing a space, systematic evocative unfolding, two and empty chair dialogues), and EFT case formulation. The training consists of a mixture of lectures, using a lot of videos of therapy and experiential work, where the trainees work on their own issues, using various EFT tasks. The experiential part of the training takes place in small groups, with one trainee being the client, another one the therapist, another one being the consultant therapist who is available if the assigned therapist requests the help. The rest of the group are observers. Trainees take turns in their engagement in small groups. The trainers, who go from group to group, normally model the experiential work by either providing feedback to the therapists, or taking over the therapist's role, and demonstrating how the therapeutic work might look.

Level A also requires initial experience of group supervision (e.g., also referred to as EFT Level 3, which should be over at least three days with active participation). In the case that the trainee cannot avail of the group supervision, an individual supervision equivalent is set. Level B of the training is focused on completion of EFT supervised practice. It normally takes place after Level A, and comprises direct supervision of recordings of the therapist's work (a minimum of 16 hours with at least two clients), and must be signed off by their approved EFT supervisor. Further supervised practice is recommended. Supervision focuses on the development of relational skills in the supervisee, the development of attitudinal qualities, perceptual, conceptual, and intervention (including tasks) skills, knowledge of self and others, as well as of emotional functioning (Greenberg & Tomescu, 2016). It is our experience that most of the focused learning happens in supervision. Individual therapists-in-training typically differ in their need for supervision. For some therapists, EFT comes more naturally, while others take significantly more time to learn it. It is, therefore, very important that the supervisor and the supervisee have frank discussions regarding progress in mastering this type of therapy.

The International Society for Emotion-Focused Therapy also recently developed guidelines for certification of EFT therapists, as in some jurisdictions there may be an explicit need to have more formal ways of recognizing one's competence. The international standards stipulate that to achieve Level C, that of a certified EFT therapist, candidates need to have completed Levels A and B of training and submit two recorded sessions (featuring two different clients) and a case description that demonstrates EFT case conceptualization skills. The evaluation of EFT skills, e.g., empathy, marker identification, emotional deepening, appropriate use of EFT tasks, ability to think about clients in EFT terms, et cetera is then assessed by a certified EFT supervisor.

In some European countries, training in EFT can be one of the primary trainings for somebody entering the profession of therapist. In these cases, the training often follows the standards of the European Association for Psychotherapy, which requires a four-year part-time post-graduate training. The EFT training is, in such cases, typically embedded in a comprehensive humanistic-experiential therapy training. It also relies on extensive experience of personal therapy and a broader theoretical input (e.g., including knowledge of psychopathology). All in all, the above described standards are just general guidelines and there may be local differences.

GAD specific training

EFT is a generalist approach to therapy, which means that it does not necessarily vary its work according to DSM or ICD diagnostic categories. Emotion-focused case conceptualization (see Chapters 4 and 6) focuses on the underlying chronic emotional pain, problematic emotion schemes that need to be accessed in therapy and transformed. The established diagnostic categories are, particularly in the case of depression and anxiety, seen as capturing secondary distress and are not seen as particularly informative for determining the course of therapy (see Chapter 2, and issues of non-specific etiology and high comorbidity in psychopathology and in depression, and anxiety in particular). This has implications for training. Professionals who are fully trained in EFT learn therapeutic skills that are broadly applicable to transformative work with human distress and core painful emotions. They are thus trained also in working with presentations currently conceptualized as GAD by the mainstream diagnostic frameworks. Therapists are trained in developing idiosyncratic case-specific case conceptualization that then guides their therapeutic strategy (cf. Timulak & Pascual-Leone, 2015).

If we are to offer GAD specific training focusing on any specific perceptual, conceptual, and intervention skills, we can then do it in a succinct manner sensitizing already trained EFT therapists to some of the things we learned when working with clients meeting the current criteria for GAD. Indeed, this book is an attempt to do so. For instance, we consider it useful if the therapist has some knowledge of GAD research and conceptualization (see Chapter 2 in this book). This helps the therapist to understand and communicate with clients, as well as with fellow professionals, about the difficulties captured by the GAD label. We believe that case conceptualization, as presented in Chapters 4 and 6, can help the therapist to be sensitive to a particular GAD dynamic, and the perception and conceptualization of GAD difficulties. The therapist can thus have a conceptualization of the presentation as well as a general guide for therapeutic strategy. It can be a useful resource when formulating "hot", experience-close, psychoeducational teaching, or when conceiving homework for the client between the sessions and once the therapy ends.

Corresponding modification of EFT tasks (such as self-interruption task, two-chair dialogue for problematic self-treatment and an empty chair task for an interpersonal injury) in a way that conceptually builds on our case conceptualization (e.g., that we want to transform chronic loneliness/sadness, shame, and fear, by generating compassion and protective anger responding to unmet emotional needs) is another goal of our specific trainings (se Chapters 7 and 8). We modified those tasks to emphasize the goals of transformation and building of emotional flexibility and resilience (cf. Pascual-Leone, 2009) rather than task/marker resolution as traditionally conceptualized in EFT (cf. Elliott *et al.*, 2004; Greenberg *et al.*, 1993). We want to stress by this that EFT is not a problem-solving but rather, an emotional capacity-building therapy. We also teach therapists the Worry task, the map of which we developed from our indigenous research (Murphy *et al.*, 2017), obviously building on the previous work of Greenberg and other authors (e.g., Elliott, 2013; Greenberg, 2015). We now also highlight clinically useful conceptualizations of working with self-panicking, self-scaring, et cetera. The training uses a mixture of teaching techniques, using both videos and the experiential part, similar to the work in small group in Level 1 and Level 2 training. The GAD specific training also focuses on discussing the issues pertaining to the course of therapy and therapy ending (see Chapter 9).

Incorporating aspects of EFT into other approaches

When we were working on the proposal for this book we received a suggestion from one of the reviewers to discuss the EFT approach for GAD in the context of other approaches and in the context of integrative therapy. Our first recommendation in this regard is that it is very important to learn EFT fully and to acquire full adherence to the model, before one would want to incorporate some aspects of it into other types of work. We believe that only full adherence and competence allows the therapist to appreciate the nuances of the approach as intended by the developers. Once this is achieved, we can see that the therapist could creatively incorporate aspects of the approach as described by us in other types of work (other approaches).

There are specific aspects of the approach that we described that could perhaps be highlighted and used as stand-alone features. The natural candidate is the experiential work with worry (see Chapter 7), and other anxiety processes such as self-panicking, self-scaring, et cetera. The two-chair dialogue for worry is a self-contained task that allows the client to get a greater awareness of their own agency in the worry and to experience the impact of the worry. The client also learns to let go of the worry, and to stop the worry by standing up to the worry process. We also provide a framework that can be used for psychoeducation and homework (see Chapter 7).

Similarly, other EFT tasks can be seen as self-contained and available to be used at the appropriate marker (e.g., clearing a space when the client is overwhelmed), which means that they are usable outside of the explicit EFT case conceptualization. Indeed, there are signs that experiential tasks, such as chair work, are starting to be used in varied formats, in recent CBT approaches (Pugh, 2017). They are, for instance, used in schema therapy (Young, Klosko, Weishaar, 2003), compassion-focused therapy (Gilbert, 2010), in CBT for psychosis, as described by Chadwick (2003), as imagery rescripting in cognitive therapy for social anxiety (Wild & Clark, 2011), et cetera. Again, given that the use of these experiential tasks differs in those approaches, we would strongly recommend mastery of them as postulated by EFT, before they would be incorporated in other approaches.

Finally, we believe that our conceptualization of GAD difficulties can offer useful insights to theoreticians and practitioners from other approaches. They may start to discover that the anxiety in clients meeting criteria for GAD is not totally indiscriminate, but rather highly idiosyncratic and embedded in the client's personal history. They may see worrying as a protective mechanism in which the client is very agentic. They may see that at the core of vulnerability are specific painful emotions that signal particular unmet needs that have to be responded to by generating adaptive emotional experiences. Again, this conceptualization may be also used in dialoguing with clients about their difficulties in experience-close psychoeducation.

Conclusion

This chapter acknowledges the complexity of EFT as a therapy and recognizes the demands it makes of EFT trainees. It describes the activities of the International Society for Emotion-focused Therapy (ISEFT), and delineates the thorough training standards set out by the (ISEFT). The chapter looks at general therapeutic advantages conferred upon the practitioner as a result of training in this modality, and it cautions against over-hasty attempts at integration or assimilation. It is vital that the various aspects and components, including tasks and theoretical considerations, of EFT are learned thoroughly before any attempt is made to fuse them with aspects of other approaches.

This is the final chapter in our book. In this book, we presented a coherent and comprehensive therapy manual for working with GAD that contains case conceptualization tools, relational pointers, and specific therapeutic skills (perceptual as well as intervention based). For the interested reader, we recommend other books, from the growing list, on EFT and its practice. We recommend further studying of EFT for GAD as provided in Watson and Greenberg (2017). The original outlines of EFT can be found in the early volume by Greenberg et al. (1993). Trainees may learn the basics of EFT in Elliott et al. (2004). A comprehensive theoretical exposure can be found in Greenberg (2011; 2016). A comprehensive account of practice can be found in Greenberg (2002; 2015), Goldman and Greenberg (2015), Greenberg and Goldman (in press), and Timulak (2015). The application of EFT for depression can be found in Greenberg and Watson (2006), for complex trauma, in Paivio and Pascual-Leone (2010), for couples, in Greenberg and Johnson (1988), Greenberg and Goldman (2008), and (Johnson, 2004).

References

American Psychiatric Association. (2013). *Diagnostic and statistical manual of mental disorders* (5th ed.). Washington, D.C.: Author.

Angus, L. E., & Greenberg, L. S. (2011). *Working with narrative in emotion-focused therapy: Changing stories, healing lives.* Washington, D.C.: American Psychological Association.

Angus, L., Watson, J. C., Elliott, R., Schneider, K., & Timulak, L. (2015). Humanistic psychotherapy research 1990–2015: From methodological innovation to evidence-supported treatment outcomes and beyond. *Psychotherapy Research, 25*(3), 330–347.

Auszra, L., & Greenberg, L. S. (2007). Client emotional productivity. *European Psychotherapy, 7*, 139–152.

Baldwin, D., Woods, R., Lawson, R., & Taylor, D. (2011). Efficacy of drug treatments for generalised anxiety disorder: systematic review and meta-analysis. *British Medical Journal, 342*, d1199.

Baldwin, D. S., & Brandish, E. K. (2014). Pharmacological treatment of anxiety disorders. In P. Emmelkamp, T. Ehring, P. Emmelkamp, T. Ehring (Eds.), *The Wiley handbook of anxiety disorders, Volume I: Theory and research; Volume II: Clinical assessment and treatment* (pp. 865–882). Hoboken, NJ: Wiley-Blackwell.

Barlow, D. H. (2002). *Anxiety and its disorders: The nature and treatment of anxiety and panic* (2nd ed.). New York, NY: Guilford Press.

Barrett, L. F., Wilson-Mendenhall, C. D., & Barsalou, L. W. (2014). A psychological construction account of emotion regulation and dysregulation: The role of situated conceptualizations. In J. J. Gross (Ed.), *The handbook of emotion regulation* (2nd ed., pp. 447–465). New York, NY: Guilford.

Behar, E., DiMarco, I., Hekler, E. B., Mohlman, J., & Staples, A. M. (2009). Current theoretical models of generalized anxiety disorder (GAD): Conceptual review and treatment implications. *Journal of Anxiety Disorders, 23*(8), 1011–1023. doi:10.1016/j.janxdis.2009.07.006

Berthoud, L., Kramer, U., Caspar, F., & Pascual-Leone, A. (2015). Emotional processing in a ten-session general psychiatric treatment for borderline personality disorder: A case study. *Personality and Mental Health, 9*, 73–78.

Beutler, L. E., & Malik, M. (Eds.). (2002). *Rethinking the DSM: A psychological perspective.* Washington, D.C.: American Psychological Association.

Blashfield, R. K., Keeley, J. W., Flanagan, E. H., & Miles, S. R. (2014). The cycle of classification: DSM-I through DSM-5. *Annual Review of Clinical Psychology, 10*, 25–51.

Blatt, S. J. (1995). The destructiveness of perfectionism: Implications for the treatment of depression. *American Psychologist, 50*(12), 1003.

Bordin, E. S. (1979). The generalizability of the psychoanalytic concept of the working alliance. *Psychotherapy: Theory, Research & Practice, 16*, 3, 252–260. http://dx.doi.org/10.1037/h0085885

Borkovec, T. D., Alcaine, O. M., & Behar, E. (2004). Avoidance theory of worry and generalized anxiety disorder. In R. G. Heimberg, C. L. Turk, & D. S. Mennin (Eds.), *Generalized anxiety disorder: Advances in research and practice* (pp. 77–108). New York, NY: Guilford Press.

Borkovec, T. D., & Costello, E., (1993). Efficacy of applied relaxation and cognitive-behavioural therapy in the treatment of generalized anxiety disorder. *Journal of Consulting and Clinical Psychology, 61*(4), 611–619.

Borkovec, T. D., & Inz, J. (1990). The nature of worry in generalized anxiety disorder: A predominance of thought activity. *Behaviour Research and Therapy, 28*, 153–158.

Borkovec, T. D., Mathews, A. M., Chambers, A., Ebrahimi, S., Lytle, R., & Nelson, R. (1987). The effects of relaxation training with cognitive or nondirective therapy and the role of relaxation-induced anxiety in the treatment of generalized anxiety. *Journal of Consulting and Clinical Psychology, 55*(6), 883–888. doi:10.1037/0022-006X.55.6.883

Borkovec, T. D., Newman, M. G., Pincus, A. L., & Lytle, R. (2002). A component analysis of cognitive-behavioural therapy for generalized anxiety disorder and the role of interpersonal problems. *Journal of Consulting and Clinical Psychology, 70*(2), 288–298.

Britton, J. C., & Rauch, S. L. (2009). Neuroanatomy and neuroimaging of anxiety disorders. In M. M. Antony, & M. B. Stein (Eds.), *Oxford handbook of anxiety and related disorders* (pp. 97–110). New York, NY: Oxford University Press.

Brown, T. A., Campbell, L. A., Lehman, C. L., Grisham, J. R., & Mancill, R. B. (2001). Current and lifetime comorbidity of the DSM-IV anxiety and mood disorders in a large clinical sample. *Journal of Abnormal Psychology, 110*(4), 585.

Brown, T. A., Moras, K., Zinbarg, R. E., & Barlow, D. H. (1993). Diagnostic and symptom distinguishability of generalized anxiety disorder and obsessive-compulsive disorder. *Behavior Therapy, 24*(2), 227–240.

Carter, R. M., Wittchen, H., Pfister, H., & Kessler, R. C. (2001). One-year prevalence of subthreshold and threshold DSM-IV generalized anxiety disorder in a nationally representative sample. *Depression and Anxiety, 13*, 78–88. doi:10.1002/da.1020

Cassidy, J., Lichtenstein-Phelps, J., Sibrava, N. J., Thomas, C. L., & Borkovec, T. D. (2009). Generalized anxiety disorder: Connections with self-reported attachment. *Behavior Therapy, 40*(1), 23–38.

Chadwick, P. (2003). Two chairs, self-schemata and a person based approach to psychosis. *Behavioural and Cognitive Psychotherapy, 31*, 439–449.

Clark, D.M. (2001). A cognitive perspective on social phobia. In R. Crozier & L.E. Alden (Eds.), *International Handbook of Social Anxiety*. Chichester: Wiley.

Craske, M. G., Rauch, S. L., Ursano, R., Prenoveau, J., Pine, D. S., & Zinbarg, R. E. (2009). What is anxiety disorder? *Depression and Anxiety, 26*(12), 1066–1085. doi:10.1002/da.20633

Crits-Christoph, P., Connolly Gibbons, M. B., & Crits-Christoph, K. (2004). Supportive-expressive psychodynamic therapy. In R. G. Heimberg, C. L. Turk, & D. S. Mennin (Eds.), *Generalized anxiety disorder: Advances in research and practice* (pp. 293–319). New York: Guilford Press.

Crits-Christoph, P., Connolly, M. B., Azarian, K., Crits-Christoph, K., & Shappell, S. (1996). An open trial of brief supportive-expressive psychotherapy in the treatment of generalized anxiety disorder. *Psychotherapy: Theory, Research, Practice, Training, 33*(3), 418–430. doi:10.1037/0033-3204.33.3.418

Crowley, N., Timulak, L., & McElvaney, J. (2013, November). *Emotion transformation in generalised anxiety disorder: A case study of emotion-focused therapy.* Annual conference of Psychological Society of Ireland, Sligo.

Cuijpers, P., Sijbrandij, M., Koole, S., Huibers, M., Berking, M., & Andersson, G. (2014). Psychological treatment of generalized anxiety disorder: A meta-analysis. *Clinical Psychology Review, 34*(2), 130–140. doi:10.1016/j.cpr.2014.01.002

Curtiss, J., & Klemanski, D. H. (2016). Taxonicity and network structure of generalized anxiety disorder and major depressive disorder: An admixture analysis and complex network analysis. *Journal of Affective Disorders, 199*, 99–105.

Diamond, G. S, Diamond, G. M., & Levy, S. A. (2014). *Attachment-based family for depressed adolescents.* Washington, D.C.: American Psychological Association.

Dillon, A., Timulak, L., & Greenberg, L. S. (2016). Transforming core emotional pain in a course of emotion-focused therapy for depression: A case study. *Psychotherapy Research*, ahead-of-press.

Dolhanty, J., & Greenberg, L. S. (2009). Emotion-focused therapy in a case of anorexia nervosa. *Clinical Psychology & Psychotherapy, 16*, 366–382. doi:10.1002/cpp.624

Dugas, M. J., Brillon, P., Savard, P., Turcotte, J., Gaudet, A., Ladouceur, R., Leblanc, R., & Gervais, N. J. (2010). A randomized clinical trial of cognitive-behavioral therapy and applied relaxation for adults with generalized anxiety disorder. *Behavior Therapy, 41*(1), 46–58.

Dugas, M. J., Buhr, K., & Ladouceur, R. (2004). The role of intolerance of uncertainty in etiology and maintenance. In R. G. Heimberg, C. L. Turk, & D. S. Mennin (Eds.), *Generalized anxiety disorder: Advances in research and practice* (pp. 143–163). New York, NY: Guilford Press.

Dugas, M. J., Ladouceur, R., Léger, E., Freeston, M. H., Langolis, F., Provencher, M. D., & Boisvert, J. M. (2003). Group cognitive-behavioral therapy for generalized anxiety disorder: Treatment outcome and long-term follow-up. *Journal of Consulting and Clinical Psychology, 71*(4), 821.

Dugas, M. J., & Robichaud, M. (2007). *Cognitive-behavioural treatment for generalized anxiety disorder.* New York, NY: Routledge.

Elliott, R. (2013). Person-centered/experiential psychotherapy for anxiety difficulties: Theory, research and practice. *Person-Centered/Experiential Psychotherapies, 12*, 16–32. doi:10.1080/14779757.2013.767750

Elliott, R. (2016, January). Emotion-focused therapy: Level 2. Training in emotion-focused therapy. Dublin, Ireland.

Elliott, R., Greenberg, L. S., & Lietaer, G. (2004). Research on experiential psychotherapies. In M. J. Lambert (Ed.), *Bergin & Garfield's handbook of psychotherapy and behaviour change* (5th ed., pp. 493–540). New York, NY: Wiley.

Elliott, R., Greenberg, L. S., Watson, J. C., Timulak, L., & Freire, E. (2013). Research on humanistic-experiential psychotherapies. In A. E. Bergin & S. L. Garfield (Eds.), *Handbook of psychotherapy and behavior change* (5th ed., pp. 495–538). New York: John Wiley & Sons.

Elliott, R., Watson, J. C., Goldman, R. N., & Greenberg, L. S. (2004). *Learning emotion-focused therapy: The process-experiential approach to change.* Washington, D.C.: American Psychological Association.

First, M. B., Gibbon, M., Spitzer, R. L., Williams, J. B., & Benjamin, L. (1997). *Structured clinical interview for DSM-IV personality disorders (SCID-II): Interview and questionnaire.* Washington, D.C.: American Psychiatric Press.

First, M. B., Spitzer, R. L., Gibbon M., & Williams, J. B.W. (1997). *Structured Clinical Interview for DSM-IV Axis I Disorders (SCID-I).* Washington, D.C.: American Psychiatric Press.

Gelernter, J., & Stein, M. B. (2009). Heritability and genetics of anxiety disorders. In M. M. Antony, M. B. Stein, M. M. Antony, M. B. Stein (Eds.), *Oxford handbook of anxiety and related disorders* (pp. 87–96). New York, NY: Oxford University Press.

Geller, S. M., & Greenberg, L. S. (2012). *Therapeutic presence: A mindful approach to effective therapy.* Washington, D.C.: American Psychological Association.

Gendlin, E.T. (1981). *Focusing* (2nd ed.). New York, NY: Bantam Books.

Gendlin, E.T. (1996). *Focusing-oriented psychotherapy. A manual of the experiential method.* New York, NY: Guilford Press.

Gilbert, P. (2010). *Compassion-focused therapy.* London: Routledge.

Gilbert, P., & Procter, S. (2006). Compassionate mind training for people with high shame and self-criticism: Overview and pilot study of a group therapy approach. *Clinical Psychology & Psychotherapy, 13*, 353–379.

Goldman, R., & Greenberg, L. S. (2015). *Case formulation in emotion-focused therapy: co-creating clinical maps for change.* Washington, D.C.: American Psychological Association.

Grafanaki, S., & McLeod, J. (1999). Narrative processes in the construction of helpful and hindering events in experiential psychotherapy. *Psychotherapy Research, 9*, 289–303.

Grant, B. F., Hasin, D. S., Stinson, F. S., Dawson, D. A., June Ruan, W., Goldstein, R. B., Smith, S. M., Saha, T. D., & Huang, B. (2005). Prevalence, correlates, co-morbidity, and comparative disability of DSM-IV generalized anxiety disorder in the USA: results from the National Epidemiologic Survey on Alcohol and Related Conditions. *Psychological Medicine, 35*, 1747–1759.

Greenberg, L. S. (1979). Resolving splits: Use of the two chair technique. *Psychotherapy: Theory, Research & Practice, 16*, 316–324. doi:10.1037/h0085895

Greenberg, L. S. (2002). *Emotion-focused therapy: Coaching clients to work through their feelings.* Washington, D.C.: American Psychological Association.

Greenberg, L. S. (2004). Emotion-focused therapy. *Clinical Psychology & Psychotherapy, 11*, 3–16. doi:10.1002/cpp.388

Greenberg, L. S (2006). Emotion-focused therapy: A synopsis. *Journal of Contemporary Psychotherapy, 36*, 87–93.

Greenberg, L. S. (2007). *Emotion-focused therapy over time.* DVD. Washington, D.C.: American Psychological Association.

Greenberg, L. S. (2011). *Emotion-focused therapy.* Washington, D.C.: American Psychological Association.

Greenberg, L. S. (2015). *Emotion-focused therapy: Coaching clients to work through their feelings* (2nd ed.). Washington, D.C.: American Psychological Association.

Greenberg, L. S. (2016). *Emotion-focused therapy* (2nd ed.). Washington, D.C.: American Psychological Association.

Greenberg, L. S. (2017, March). *Emotion-focused therapy: Level 1.* Training in emotion-focused therapy. Madrid, Spain.

Greenberg, L. S., Auszra, L. L., & Herrmann, I. R. (2007). The relationship among emotional productivity, emotional arousal and outcome in experiential therapy of depression. *Psychotherapy Research, 17*, 482–493. doi:10.1080/10503300600977800

Greenberg, L. S., & Dompierre, L. M. (1981). Specific effects of Gestalt two-chair dialogue on intrapsychic conflict in counseling. *Journal of Counseling Psychology, 28*, 288–294. doi:10.1037/0022-0167.28.4.288

Greenberg, L. S., & Elliott, R. (2012). Corrective experience from a humanistic–experiential perspective. In L. G. Castonguay, C. E. Hill, L. G. Castonguay, & C. E. Hill (Eds.), *Transformation in psychotherapy: Corrective experiences across cognitive behavioral, humanistic, and psychodynamic approaches* (pp. 85–101). Washington, D.C.: American Psychological Association. doi:10.1037/13747-006

Greenberg, L. S., & Goldman, R. (2007). Case formulation in emotion-focused therapy. In T. Eells (Ed.), *Handbook of psychotherapy case formulation* (pp. 379–411). Washington, D.C.: American Psychological Association.

Greenberg, L. S., & Goldman, R. N. (2008). *Emotion-focused couples therapy: The dynamics of emotion, love, and power.* Washington, D.C.: American Psychological Association.

Greenberg, L. S., & Goldman, R. N. (Eds.) (in press). *Clinical handbook of emotion-focused therapy.* Washington, D.C.: American Psychological Association.

Greenberg, L. S., & Higgins, H. M. (1980). Effects of two-chair dialogue and focusing on conflict resolution. *Journal of Counseling Psychology, 27*, 221–224. doi:10.1037/0022-0167.27.3.221

Greenberg, L. S., & Johnson, S. M. (1988). *Emotionally focused therapy for couples.* New York, NY: Guilford Press.

Greenberg, L. S., & Paivio, S. C. (1997). *Working with emotions in psychotherapy.* New York, NY: Guilford Press.

Greenberg, L. S., Rice, L. N., & Elliott, R. (1993). *Facilitating emotional change: The moment by moment process.* New York, NY: Guilford Press.

Greenberg, L. S., & Safran, J. D. (1987). *Emotion in psychotherapy: Affect, cognition, and the process of change.* New York, NY: Guilford Press.

Greenberg, L. S., & Tomescu, L. R. (2016). *Supervision essentials for emotion-focused therapy.* Washington, D.C.: American Psychological Association.

Greenberg, L. S., & Warwar, S. H. (2006). Homework in an emotion-focused approach to experiential therapy. *Journal of Psychotherapy Integration, 16*, 178–200.

Greenberg, L. S., & Watson, J. (2006). *Emotion-focused therapy for depression.* Washington, D.C.: American Psychological Association.

Hamilton, J. P., Farmer, M., Fogelman, P., & Gotlib, I. H. (2015). Depressive rumination, the default-mode network, and the dark matter of clinical neuroscience. *Biological Psychiatry, 78*, 224–230.

Hanrahan, F., Field, A. P., Jones, F. W., & Davey, G. L. (2013). A meta-analysis of cognitive therapy for worry in generalized anxiety disorder. *Clinical Psychology Review, 33*(1), 120–132. doi:10.1016/j.cpr.2012.10.008

Härter, M. C., Conway, K. P., & Merikangas, K. R. (2003). Associations between anxiety disorders and physical illness. *European Archives of Psychiatry and Clinical Neuroscience, 253*(6), 313–320. doi:10.1007/s00406-003-0449-y

Hayes-Skelton, S. A., Roemer, L., & Orsillo, S. M. (2013). A randomized clinical trial comparing an acceptance-based behavior therapy to applied relaxation for generalized anxiety disorder. *Journal of Consulting and Clinical Psychology, 81*(5), 761.

Hazlett-Stevens, H. (2008). *Psychological approaches to generalized anxiety disorder: A clinician's guide to assessment and treatment.* New York, NY: Springer

Hazlett-Stevens, H. (2009). Assessment and treatment of anxiety in primary care. In L. C. James, W. T. O'Donohue, L. C. James, W. T. O'Donohue (Eds.), *The primary care toolkit: Practical resources for the integrated behavioral care provider* (pp. 169–182). New York, NY: Springer Publishing Co.

Hazlett-Stevens, H., Pruitt, L. D., & Collins, A. (2009). Phenomenology of generalized anxiety disorder. In M. M. Antony, M. B. Stein, M. M. Antony, M. B. Stein (Eds.), *Oxford handbook of anxiety and related disorders* (pp. 47–55). New York, NY: Oxford University Press.

Hilbert, K., Pine, D. S., Muehlhan, M., Lueken, U., Steudte-Schmiedgen, S., & Beesdo-Baum, K. (2015). Gray and white matter volume abnormalities in generalized anxiety disorder by categorical and dimensional characterization. *Psychiatry Research: Neuroimaging, 234*(3), 314–320.

Hudson, J. L., & Rapee, R. M. (2004). From anxious temperament to disorder: An etiological model. In R. G. Heimberg, C. L. Turk, D. S. Mennin (Eds.), *Generalized anxiety disorder: Advances in research and practice* (pp. 51–74). New York, NY: Guilford Press.

Hughes, S., Timulak, L., & McElvaney, J. (2014, June). *Resolving Emotional Injury with a Significant Other through Empty Chair Dialogue in Clients with Generalised Anxiety Disorder (GAD).* Annual conference of the Society for Psychotherapy Research, Copenhagen, Denmark.

Hunot, V., Churchill, R., Teixeira, V., & Silva de Lima, M. (2007). Psychological therapies for generalised anxiety disorder. *Cochrane Database of Systematic Reviews, 1.* doi:10.1002/14651858.CD001848.pub4

Jenkins, R., Lewis, G., Bebbington, P., Brugha, T., Farrell, M., Gill, B., & Meltzer, H. (1997). The National Psychiatric Morbidity surveys of Great Britain – initial findings from the household survey. *Psychological Medicine, 27*, 775–789.

Johnson, S. M. (2004). *The practice of emotionally focused couple therapy: Creating connection.* New York: Routledge.

Kashdan, T.B., Barrett. L.F., & McKnight, P. E. (2015). Unpacking emotion differentiation: Transforming unpleasant experience by perceiving distinctions in negativity. *Current Directions in Psychological Science, 24*, 10–16.

Keogh, D., Timulak, L., & McElvaney, J. (2014, June). *Treating generalised anxiety disorder with emotion focused therapy: A case study investigation of emotional change processes.* Annual conference of the Society for Psychotherapy Research, Copenhagen, Denmark.

Kessler, R. C., Alonso, J., Chatterji, S., & He, Y. (2014). Disability and costs. In P. Emmelkamp, T. Ehring, P. Emmelkamp, T. Ehring (Eds.), *The Wiley handbook of anxiety disorders, Volume I: Theory and research; Volume II: Clinical assessment and treatment* (pp. 47–57). Chichester: Wiley-Blackwell

Kessler, R. C., Berglund, P., Demler, O., Jin, R., Merikangas, K. R., & Walters, E. E. (2005). Lifetime prevalence and age-of-onset distributions of DSM-IV disorders in the National Comorbidity Survey Replication. *Archives of General Psychiatry, 62*(6), 593–602. doi:10.1001/archpsyc.62.6.593

Kessler, R. C., Chiu, W., Demler, O., & Walters, E. E. (2005). Prevalence, severity, and comorbidity of 12-month DSM-IV disorders in the national comorbidity survey replication. *Archives of General Psychiatry, 62*(6), 617–627. doi:10.1001/archpsyc.62.6.617

Kessler, R. C., Walters, E. E., & Wittchen, H. (2004). Epidemiology. In R. G. Heimberg, C. L. Turk, D. S. Mennin, R. G. Heimberg, C. L. Turk, D. S. Mennin (Eds.), *Generalized anxiety disorder: Advances in research and practice* (pp. 29–50). New York, NY: Guilford Press.

King, M., Sibbald, B., Ward, E., Bower, P., Lloyd, M., Gabbay, M., & Byford, S. (2000). Randomised controlled trial of non-directive counselling, cognitive behaviour therapy and usual general practitioner care in the management of depression as well as mixed anxiety and depression in primary care. *Health Technology Assessment*, *4*(19), i+iii–iv+1–73.

Klein, M. H., Mathieu, P. L., Gendlin, E. T., & Kiesler, D. J. (1969). The experiencing scale (Vol. *1*). *A research and training manual.* Madison: Wisconsin Psychiatric Institute.

Kramer, U., Pascual-Leone, A., Berthoud, L., de Roten, Y., Marquet, P., Kolly, S., Despland, J.N, & Page, D. (2015). Assertive anger mediates effects of dialectical behavior-informed skills training for borderline personality disorder: A randomized controlled trial. *Clinical Psychology and Psychotherapy*. Ahead-of print. doi:10.1002/cpp.1956

Kramer, U., Pascual-Leone, A., Despland, J. N., & de Roten, Y. (2014). Emotion in an alliance rupture and resolution sequence: A theory-building case study. *Counselling and Psychotherapy Research*, *14*, 263–271. doi:10.1080/14733145.2013.819932

Kramer, U., Pascual-Leone, A., Despland, J.N., & de Roten, Y. (2015). One minute of grief: Emotional processing in short-term dynamic psychotherapy for adjustment disorder. *Journal of Consulting and Clinical Psychology*, *83*, 187–198. doi:10.1037/a0037979

Lane, R. D., Ryan, L., Nadel, L., & Greenberg, L. (2015). Memory reconsolidation, emotional arousal, and the process of change in psychotherapy: New insights from brain science. *Behavioral and Brain Sciences*, *38*, e1.

Le Doux, J. (2015). *Anxious: Using the brain to understand and treat fear and anxiety.* New York: Viking.

Leijssen, M. (1990). On focusing and the necessary conditions of therapeutic personality change. In G. Lietaer, J. Rombauts, & R. Van Balen (Eds.), *Client-centered and experiential psychotherapy in the nineties* (pp. 225–250). Leuven: Leuven University Press.

Leijssen, M. (1998). Focusing microprocesses. In L. S. Greenberg, G. Lietaer, & J. Watson (Eds.), *Handbook of experiential psychotherapy* (pp. 121–154). New York: Guilford.

Lenzenweger, M. F., Lane, M. C., Loranger, A. W., & Kessler, R. C. (2007). DSM-IV personality disorders in the national comorbidity survey replication. *Biological Psychiatry*, *62*(6), 553–564. doi:10.1016/j.biopsych.2006.09.019

Li, W., Cui, H., Zhu, Z., Kong, L., Guo, Q., Zhu, Y., Qiang, H., Zhang, L., Li, Q., Jiang, J., Meyers, J., Li, J., Wang, J., Yang, Z., & Li, C. (2016). Aberrant functional connectivity between the amygdala and the temporal pole in drug-free generalized anxiety disorder. *Frontiers in Human Neuroscience*, *10*, article 549.

Lietaer, G. (1993). Authenticity, congruence and transparency. In D. Brazier (Ed). *Beyond Carl Rogers* (pp. 17–46). London: Constable and Company.

Llera, S. J., & Newman, M. G. (2010). Effects of worry on physiological and subjective reactivity to emotional stimuli in generalized anxiety disorder and non-anxious control participants. *Emotion*, *10*(5), 640–650. doi:10.1037/a0019351

Loebach Wetherell, J., Thorp, S. R., Patterson, T. L., Golshan, S., Jeste, D. V., & Gatz, M. (2004). Quality of life in geriatric generalized anxiety disorder: a preliminary investigation. *Journal of Psychiatric Research*, *38*(3), 305–312.

Luborsky, L. (1984). *Principles of psychoanalytic psychotherapy: A manual for supportive-expressive treatment.* New York, NY: Basic Books

Luborsky, L., & Crits-Christoph, P. (1998). *Understanding transference: The Core Conflictual Relationship Theme method* (2nd ed.). Washington, D.C.: American Psychological Association. http://dx.doi.org/10.1037/10250-000

McNally, S., Timulak, L., & Greenberg, L. S. (2014). Transforming emotion schemes in emotion focused therapy: A case study investigation. *Person-Centered and Experiential Psychotherapies, 13*, 128–149. doi:10.1080/14779757.2013.871573

Mahoney, A. E., Hobbs, M. J., Newby, J. M., Williams, A. D., Sunderland, M., & Andrews, G. (2016). The Worry Behaviors Inventory: Assessing the behavioral avoidance associated with generalized anxiety disorder. *Journal of Affective Disorders, 203*, 256–264.

Mathew, S. J., & Hoffman, S. (2009). Pharmacotherapy for generalized anxiety disorder. In M. M. Antony, M. B. Stein, M. M. Antony, & M. B. Stein (Eds.), *Oxford handbook of anxiety and related disorders* (pp. 350–363). New York: Oxford University Press.

Mennin, D. S. (2004). Emotion regulation therapy for generalized anxiety disorder. *Clinical Psychology & Psychotherapy, 11*(1), 17–29. doi:10.1002/cpp.389

Mennin, D. S. (2006). Emotion regulation therapy: An integrative approach to treatment-resistant anxiety disorders. *Journal of Contemporary Psychotherapy, 36*(2), 95–105.

Mennin, D. S., Fresco, D. M., Ritter, M., & Heimberg, R. G. (2015). An open trial of emotion regulation therapy for generalized anxiety disorder and cooccurring depression. *Depression and Anxiety, 32*(8), 614–623.

Mennin, D. S., Heimberg, R. G., & Turk, C. L. (2004). Clinical presentation and diagnostic features. In D. S. Mennin, R. G. Heimberg, & C. L. Turk (Eds.). *Generalized anxiety disorder: Advances in research and practice* (pp. 3–28). New York, NY: Guilford Press.

Moffitt, T. E., Caspi, A., Harrington, H., Milne, B. J., Melchior, M., Goldberg, D., & Poulton, R. (2007). Generalized anxiety disorder and depression: Childhood risk factors in a birth cohort followed to age 32. *Psychological Medicine, 37*, 441–452.

Murphy, J., Rowell, L., McQuaid, A., Timulak, L., O'Flynn, R., & McElvaney, J. (2017). Developing a model of working with worry in emotion-focused therapy: A discovery–phase task analytic study. *Counselling and Psychotherapy Research, 17*, 56–70.

Newman, M. G., Castonguay, L. G., Borkovec, T. D., Fisher, A. J., Boswell, J. F., Szkodny, L. E., & Nordberg, S. S. (2011). A randomized controlled trial of cognitive-behavioral therapy for generalized anxiety disorder with integrated techniques from emotion-focused and interpersonal therapies. *Journal of Consulting and Clinical Psychology, 79*(2), 171–181. doi:10.1037/a0022489

Newman, M. G., & Llera, S. J. (2011). A novel theory of experiential avoidance in generalized anxiety disorder: A review and synthesis of research supporting a contrast avoidance model of worry. Clinical Psychology Review, *31*(3), 371–382. doi:10.1016/j.cpr.2011.01.008

Newman, M. G., Llera, S. J., Erickson, T. M., & Przeworski, A. (2014). Basic science and clinical application of the contrast avoidance model in Generalized Anxiety Disorder. *Journal of Psychotherapy Integration, 24*(3), 155–167. http://dx.doi.org/10.1037/a0037510155

Newman, M. G., Llera, S. J., Erickson, T. M., Przeworski, A., & Castonguay, L. G. (2013). Worry and generalized anxiety disorder: a review and theoretical synthesis of evidence on nature, etiology, mechanisms, and treatment. *Annual Review of Clinical Psychology, 9*, 275–297.

Newman, M. G., Shin, K. E., & Zuellig, A. R. (2016). Developmental risk factors in generalized anxiety disorder and panic disorder. *Journal of Affective Disorders, 206*, 94–102.

O'Brien, K., O'Keeffe, Cullen, H., Durcan, A., Timulak, L., & McElvaney, J. (2017). Emotion-focused perspective on generalised anxiety disorder: A qualitative analysis of the in-session presentations. Paper under review.

O'Flynn, R., & Timulak, L. (2016). *The Worry Resolution Scale.* Unpublished measure.

Paivio, S, C., & Pascual-Leone, A. (2010). *Emotion-focused therapy for complex trauma: An integrative approach.* Washington, D.C.: American Psychological Association.

Papageorgiou, C., & Wells, A. (2004). Nature, functions, and beliefs about depressive rumination. In C. Papageorgiou & A. Wells (Eds.), *Depressive Rumination: Nature, Theory and Treatment* (pp. 3–20). Chichester: Wiley.

Pascual-Leone, A. (2009). Dynamic emotional processing in experiential therapy: Two steps forward, one step back. *Journal of Consulting and Clinical Psychology, 77*(1), 113–126. doi:10.1037/a0014488

Pascual-Leone, A., & Greenberg, L. S. (2007). Emotional processing in experiential therapy: Why "the only way out is through". *Journal of Consulting and Clinical Psychology, 75*(6), 875–887. doi:10.1037/0022-006X.75.6.875

Pos, A. E., & Greenberg, L. S. (2012). Organizing awareness and increasing emotion regulation: Revising chair work in emotion-focused therapy for borderline personality disorder. *Journal of Personality Disorders, 26*, 84–107.

Pugh, M. (2017). Chairwork in cognitive-behavioural therapy: A narrative review. *Cognitive Therapy & Research, 41*, 16–30.

Rennie, D. L. (1994). Clients' deference in therapy. *Journal of Counseling Psychology, 41*, 427–437.

Rhodes, R. H., Hill, C. E., Thompson, B. J., & Elliott, R. (1994). Client retrospective recall of resolved and unresolved misunderstanding events. *Journal of Counseling Psychology, 41*, 473–483.

Rice, L. N., & Greenberg, L. S. (Eds.). (1984). *Patterns of change: An intensive analysis of psychotherapeutic process.* New York, NY: Guilford Press.

Rice, L. N., Koke, C. J., Greenberg, L. S., & Wagstaff, A. (1979). *Manual for client vocal quality.* Toronto: York University Counselling and Development Centre.

Rice, L. N., & Saperia, E. P. (1984). Task analysis of the resolution of problematic reactions. In L. N. Rice & L. S. Greenberg (Eds.), *Patterns of change* (pp. 29–66). New York: Guildford Press

Rickels, K., & Rynn, M. (2001). Overview and clinical presentation of generalized anxiety disorder. *Psychiatric Clinics of North America, 24*(1), 1–17. doi:10.1016/S0193-953X(05)70203-3

Roemer, L., & Orsillo, S. M. (2014). An acceptance-based behavioral therapy for generalized anxiety disorder. In D. H. Barlow (Ed.), *Clinical handbook of psychological disorders: A step-by-step treatment manual* (5th ed., pp. 206–236). New York: Guilford Press.

Roemer, L., Orsillo, S. M., & Barlow, D. (2002). Generalized anxiety disorder. In D. H. Barlow (Ed.), *Anxiety and its disorders* (2nd ed., pp. 477–515). New York, NY: Guilford Press.

Roemer, L., Orsillo, S. M., & Salters-Pedneault, K. (2008). Efficacy of an acceptance-based behavior therapy for generalized anxiety disorder: Evaluation in a randomized controlled trial. *Journal of Consulting and Clinical Psychology, 76*, 1083–1089. doi:10.1037/a0012720

Rogers, C. R. (1951). *Client-centered therapy.* Boston, MA: Houghton Mifflin.

Rogers, C. R. (1957). The necessary and sufficient conditions of therapeutic personality change. *Journal of Counselling Psychology, 21*, 95–103.

Rogers, C. R. (1959). A theory of therapy, personality and interpersonal relationships as developed in the client-centred framework. In S. Koch (Ed.), *Psychology; The study of a science* (Vol. *3*) (pp. 184–256). New York. NY: McGraw-Hill.

Rogers, C. R. (1961). *On becoming a person*. Boston, MA: Houghton Mifflin.

Ruscio, A. M., Gentes, E. L., Jones, J. D., Hallion, L. S., Coleman, E. S., & Swendsen, J. (2015). Rumination predicts heightened responding to stressful life events in major depressive disorder and generalized anxiety disorder. *Journal of Abnormal Psychology, 124*, 17–26.

Sadler, J. Z. (2005). *Values and psychiatric diagnosis* (Vol. 2). Oxford University Press.

Safran, J. D., & Muran, J. C. (2000). *Negotiating the therapeutic alliance: A relational treatment guide*. New York, NY: Guilford Press

Sanderson, W. C., Wetzler, S., Beck, A. T., & Betz, F. (1994). Prevalence of personality disorders among patients with anxiety disorders. *Psychiatry Research, 51*(2), 167–174. doi:10.1016/0165-1781(94)90036-1

Sareen, J., Cox, B. J., Afifi, T. O., de Graaf, R., Asmundson, G. J., ten Have, M., & Stein, M. B. (2005). Anxiety disorders and risk for suicidal ideation and suicide attempts: a population-based longitudinal study of adults. *Archives of General Psychiatry, 62*, 1249–1257.

Shahar, B. (2014). Emotion-focused therapy for the treatment of social anxiety: An overview of the model and a case description. *Clinical Psychology & Psychotherapy, 21*(6), 536–547.

Shahar, B., Bar-Kalifa, E., & Alon, E. (2017). Emotion-focused therapy for social anxiety disorder: Results from a multiple-baseline study. *Journal of Consulting and Clinical Psychology, 85*, 238–249.

Slade, T. T., & Andrews, G. G. (2001). DSM-IV and ICD-10 generalized anxiety disorder: Discrepant diagnoses and associated disability. *Social Psychiatry and Psychiatric Epidemiology, 36*(1), 45–51. doi:10.1007/s001270050289

Smoller, J. W., Cerrato, F. E., & Weatherall, S. L. (2015). The genetics of anxiety disorders. In K. J. Ressler, D. S. Pine, B. O. Rothbaum, K. J. Ressler, D. S. Pine, & B. O. Rothbaum (Eds.), *Anxiety disorders: Translational perspectives on diagnosis and treatment* (pp. 47–65). New York, NY: Oxford University Press. doi:10.1093/med/9780199395125.003.0004

Stein, D. J. (2014). Nosology and classification. In P. Emmelkamp & T. Ehring (Eds.), *The Wiley handbook of anxiety disorders* (pp. 13–25). Chichester: Wiley Blackwell.

Stein, M. B., & Heimberg, R. G. (2004). Well-being and life satisfaction in generalized anxiety disorder: Comparison to major depressive disorder in a community sample. *Journal of Affective Disorders, 79*(1), 161–166.

Stevens, E. S., Jendrusina, A. A., Sarapas, C., & Behar, E. (2014). Generalized anxiety disorder. In P. Emmelkamp, T. Ehring, P. Emmelkamp, & T. Ehring (Eds.), *The Wiley handbook of anxiety disorders, Volume I: Theory and research; Volume II: Clinical assessment and treatment* (pp. 376–423). Hoboken, NJ: Wiley-Blackwell.

Sutherland, O., Peräkylä, A., & Elliott, R. (2014). Conversation analysis of the two-chair self-soothing task in emotion-focused therapy. *Psychotherapy Research, 24*, 738–751.

Sutton, J. (2007). *Healing the hurt within, 3rd edition: Understand self-injury and self-harm, and heal the emotional wounds*. Oxford: How To Books.

Swift, J. K., Callahan, J. L., & Vollmer B. M. (2011). Preferences. *Journal of Clinical Psychology, 67*, 155–165.

Timulak, L. (1999). Humility as an important attitude in overcoming a rupture in the therapeutic relationship. *The Person-Centered Journal, 6*, 153–163.

Timulak, L. (2006a, July). *Contribution of person-centred and emotion-focused interventions to treatment of anxiety disorders: Case vignettes*. 7th World Person-Centred and Experiential Conference, Potsdam, Germany.

Timulak, L. (2006b, November). *Contribution of emotion-focused interventions to integrative treatment of anxiety disorders*. Annual conference of Psychological Society of Ireland, Galway, 8.–12.11.2006.

Timulak, L. (2008, July). *Experiential therapy of anxiety disorders*. 8th World Person-Centred and Experiential Conference, Norwich, UK.

Timulak, L. (2011). *Developing your counselling and psychotherapy skills and practice*. London: Sage.

Timulak, L. (2014). Witnessing clients' emotional transformation: An emotion-focused therapist's experience of providing therapy. *Journal of Clinical Psychology, 70*, 741–752.

Timulak, L. (2015). *Transforming emotional pain in psychotherapy: An emotion-focused approach*. London: Routledge.

Timulak, L. (2017). *Training in emotion-focused therapy for GAD: Training handouts*. Unpublished manuscript.

Timulak, L., & Iwakabe, S. (in press). Clinical implications of qualitative and case study research on emotion-focused therapy. In L. S. Greenberg & R. N. Goldman (Eds.), *Clinical handbook of emotion focused therapy*. Washington, D.C.: American Psychological Association.

Timulak, L., & McElvaney, J. (2016). Emotion-focused therapy for generalized anxiety disorder: An overview of the model. *Journal of Contemporary Psychotherapy, 46*(1), 41–52. doi:10.1007/s10879-015-9310-7

Timulak, L., McElvaney, J., Keogh, D., Martin, E., Clare, P., Chepukova, E., & Greenberg, L. S. (2017). Emotion-focused therapy for generalised anxiety disorder: An exploratory study. *Psychotherapy*, ahead-of-print.

Timulak, L., & Pascual-Leone, A. (2015). New developments for case conceptualization in emotion-focused therapy. *Clinical Psychology & Psychotherapy, 22*(6), 619–636.

Toolan, R. (2017). The relationship between self-worrying and self-criticism in clients with GAD. Trinity College Dublin, Ireland: Unpublished dissertation.

Van der Heiden, C., Muris, P., & van der Molen, H. T. (2012). Randomized controlled trial on the effectiveness of metacognitive therapy and intolerance of uncertainty therapy for generalized anxiety disorder. *Behaviour Research and Therapy, 50*, 100–109.

Veale, D., & Roberts, A. (2014). Obsessive-compulsive disorder. *British Medical Journal, 348*, g2183.

Wampold, B. E., & Imel, Z. E. (2015). *The great psychotherapy debate: The research evidence for what works in psychotherapy* (2nd ed.). New York: Routledge

Warwar, S. (2015, October). *Consolidating EFT chair work using in-session teaching and homework*. 1st Conference of the International Society for Emotion-Focused Therapy. Veldhoven, the Netherlands.

Warwar, S., & Greenberg, L.S. (1999). *Client Emotional Arousal Scale–III*. Toronto: York University. Unpublished manuscript.

Watson, J. C. (2002). Re-visioning empathy. In D. J. Cain & J. Seeman (Eds.), *Humanistic psychotherapies: Handbook of research and practice* (pp. 445–471). Washington, D.C.: American Psychological Association.

Watson, J. C. (2010). Case formulation in emotion-focused therapy. *Journal of Psychotherapy Integration, 20*, 89 –100.

Watson, J. C., Goldman, R., & Vanaerschot, G. (1998). Empathic: A postmodern way of being? In L. S. Greenberg, J. C. Watson, G. Lietaer, L. S. Greenberg, J. C. Watson, G. Lietaer (Eds.), *Handbook of experiential psychotherapy* (pp. 61–81). New York, NY: Guilford Press.

Watson, J. C., & Greenberg, L. S. (2017). *Emotion-focused therapy for generalized anxiety disorder*. Washington, D.C.: American Psychological Association.

Watson, J. C., Timulak, L., & Greenberg, L. S. (in press). Emotion-focused therapy for generalized anxiety disorder. In L. S. Greenberg & R. N. Goldman (Eds.), *Clinical handbook of emotion-focused therapy*. Washington, D.C.: American Psychological Association.

Weisberg, R. B. (2009). Overview of generalized anxiety disorder: Epidemiology, presentation, and course. *Journal of Clinical Psychiatry, 70* (Suppl 2), 4–9.

Wells, A. (1999). A metacognitive model and therapy for generalized anxiety disorder. *Clinical Psychology and Psychotherapy, 6*, 86–95.

Wells, A. (2004). A cognitive model of GAD: Metacognitions and pathological worry. In R. G. Heimberg, C. L. Turk & D. S. Mennin (Eds.), *Generalized anxiety disorder: Advances in research and practice* (pp. 164–186). New York, NY: Guilford Press.

Wells, A. (2005). The metacognitive model of GAD: Assessment of meta-worry and relationship with DSM-IV generalized anxiety disorder. *Cognitive Therapy and Research, 29*(1), 107–121. doi:10.1007/s10608-005-1652-0

Wells, A., Welford, M., King, P., Papageorgieu, C., Wisely, J., & Mendel, E. (2010). A pilot randomized trial of metacognitive therapy vs applied relaxation in the treatment of adults with generalized anxiety disorder. *Behaviour Research and Therapy. 48*, 5, 429–434. doi:10.1016/j.brat.2009.11.013

Whelton, W. J., & Greenberg, L. S. (2005). Emotion in self-criticism. *Personality and Individual Differences, 38*(7), 1583–1595.

Wiebe, S. A., & Johnson, S. M. (2016). A review of the research in emotionally focused therapy for couples. *Family Process, 55*(3), 390–407.

Wild, J., & Clark, D. M. (2011). Imagery rescripting of early traumatic memories in social phobia. *Cognitive and Behavioral Practice, 18*, 433–443.

Williams, R., Farquharson, L., Palmer, L., Bassett, P., Clarke, J., Clark, D. M., & Crawford, M. J. (2016). Patient preference in psychological treatment and associations with self-reported outcome: National cross-sectional survey in England and Wales. *BMC Psychiatry, 16*.

Wittchen, H. U. (2002). Generalized anxiety disorder: prevalence, burden, and cost to society. *Depression and Anxiety, 16*, 162–71. doi:10.1002/da.10065

Wittchen, H., Zhao, S., Kessler, R. C., & Eaton, W. W. (1994). DSM-III-R generalized anxiety disorder in the National Comorbidity Survey. *Archives of General Psychiatry, 51*(5), 355–364. doi:10.1001/archpsyc.1994.03950050015002

World Health Organization (1992). *The ICD-10 classification of mental and behavioural disorders: Clinical descriptions and diagnostic guidelines*. Geneva: World Health Organization.

Yang, M. J., Kim, B. N., Lee, E. H., Lee, D., Yu, B. H., Jeon, H. J., & Kim, J. H. (2014). Diagnostic utility of worry and rumination: a comparison between generalized anxiety disorder and major depressive disorder. *Psychiatry and Clinical Neurosciences, 68*(9), 712–720.

Young, J. E., Klosko, J. S., & Weishaar, M. E. (2003). *Schema therapy: A practitioner's guide*. New York: Guilford Press.

Index

For Product Safety Concerns and Information please contact our EU
representative GPSR@taylorandfrancis.com
Taylor & Francis Verlag GmbH, Kaufingerstraße 24, 80331 München, Germany